Elucidating the Intent

Treasury of the Buddhist Sciences series

Editor-in-Chief: Robert A.F. Thurman, Jey Tsong Khapa Professor Emeritus of Indo-Tibetan Buddhist Studies, Columbia University

Executive Editor: Thomas F. Yarnall, Columbia University

Associate Editor: Edward A. Arnold, Columbia University Center for Buddhist Studies

Series Committee: Daniel Aitken, David Kittelstrom, Tim McNeill, Robert A.F. Thurman, Christian K. Wedemeyer, Thomas F. Yarnall

Editorial Board: Ryuichi Abé, Jay Garfield, David Gray, Laura Harrington, Thubten Jinpa, Joseph Loizzo, Gary Tubb, Vesna Wallace, Christian Wedemeyer, Chun-fang Yu

The *Treasury of the Buddhist Sciences* series is copublished by the American Institute of Buddhist Studies and Wisdom Publications in association with the Columbia University Center for Buddhist Studies and Tibet House US.

The American Institute of Buddhist Studies (AIBS) established the *Treasury of the Buddhist Sciences* series to provide authoritative translations, studies, and editions of the texts of the Tibetan Tengyur (*bstan 'gyur*) and its associated literature. The Tibetan Tengyur is a vast collection of over 4,000 classical Indian Buddhist scientific treatises (*śāstra*) written in Sanskrit by over 700 authors from the first millennium CE, now preserved mainly in systematic 7th–12th century Tibetan translation. Its topics span all of India's "outer" arts and sciences, including linguistics, medicine, astronomy, socio-political theory, ethics, art, and so on, as well as all of her "inner" arts and sciences such as philosophy, psychology ("mind science"), meditation, and yoga.

Volumes in this series are numbered with catalogue numbers corresponding to both the "Comparative" (*dpe bsdur ma*) Kangyur and Tengyur ("CK" and "CT," respectively) and Derge (Tōhoku number) recensions of the Tibetan Tripiṭaka.

THE DALAI LAMA

Message

The foremost scholars of the holy land of India were based for many centuries at Nālandā Monastic University. Their deep and vast study and practice explored the creative potential of the human mind with the aim of eliminating suffering and making life truly joyful and worthwhile. They composed numerous excellent and meaningful texts. I regularly recollect the kindness of these immaculate scholars and aspire to follow them with unflinching faith. At the present time, when there is great emphasis on scientific and technological progress, it is extremely important that those of us who follow the Buddha should rely on a sound understanding of his teaching, for which the great works of the renowned Nālandā scholars provide an indispensable basis.

In their outward conduct the great scholars of Nālandā observed ethical discipline that followed the Pāli tradition, in their internal practice they emphasized the awakening mind of *bodhichitta*, enlightened altruism, and in secret they practised tantra. The Buddhist culture that flourished in Tibet can rightly be seen to derive from the pure tradition of Nālandā, which comprises the most complete presentation of the Buddhist teachings. As for me personally, I consider myself a practitioner of the Nālandā tradition of wisdom. Masters of Nālandā such as Nāgārjuna, Āryadeva, Āryāsaṅga, Dharmakīrti, Chandrakīrti, and Śāntideva wrote the scriptures that we Tibetan Buddhists study and practice. They are all my gurus. When I read their books and reflect upon their names, I feel a connection with them.

The works of these Nālandā masters are presently preserved in the collection of their writings that in Tibetan translation we call the Tengyur (*bstan 'gyur*). It took teams of Indian masters and great Tibetan translators over four centuries to accomplish the historic task of translating them into

Tibetan. Most of these books were later lost in their Sanskrit originals, and relatively few were translated into Chinese. Therefore, the Tengyur is truly one of Tibet's most precious treasures, a mine of understanding that we have preserved in Tibet for the benefit of the whole world.

Keeping all this in mind I am very happy to encourage a long-term project of the American Institute of Buddhist Studies, originally established by the late Venerable Mongolian Geshe Wangyal and now at the Columbia University Center for Buddhist Studies, and Tibet House US, in collaboration with Wisdom Publications, to translate the Tengyur into English and other modern languages, and to publish the many works in a collection called *The Treasury of the Buddhist Sciences*. When I recently visited Columbia University, I joked that it would take those currently working at the Institute at least three "reincarnations" to complete the task; it surely will require the intelligent and creative efforts of generations of translators from every tradition of Tibetan Buddhism, in the spirit of the scholars of Nālandā, although we may hope that using computers may help complete the work more quickly. As it grows, the *Treasury* series will serve as an invaluable reference library of the Buddhist Sciences and Arts. This collection of literature has been of immeasurable benefit to us Tibetans over the centuries, so we are very happy to share it with all the people of the world. As someone who has been personally inspired by the works it contains, I firmly believe that the methods for cultivating wisdom and compassion originally developed in India and described in these books preserved in Tibetan translation will be of great benefit to many scholars, philosophers, and scientists, as well as ordinary people.

I wish the American Institute of Buddhist Studies at the Columbia Center for Buddhist Studies, Tibet House US, and Wisdom Publications every success and pray that this ambitious and far-reaching project to create *The Treasury of the Buddhist Sciences* will be accomplished according to plan. I also request others, who may be interested, to extend whatever assistance they can, financial or otherwise, to help ensure the success of this historic project.

May 15, 2007

•TREASURY OF THE BUDDHIST SCIENCES•

Elucidating the Intent

A Noble Mahayana Sutra

(*Ārya Saṁdhinirmocana Sūtra*)

by Shākyamuni Buddha

Introduction and Translation
by Gregory Forgues

TREASURY OF THE BUDDHIST SCIENCES SERIES
TENGYUR TRANSLATION INITIATIVE
CK 124 (D 106)

COPUBLISHED BY
THE AMERICAN INSTITUTE OF BUDDHIST STUDIES AND WISDOM PUBLICATIONS
IN ASSOCIATION WITH THE COLUMBIA UNIVERSITY CENTER
FOR BUDDHIST STUDIES AND TIBET HOUSE US

Wisdom

Treasury of the Buddhist Sciences series
Tengyur Translation Initiative
A refereed series published by:

American Institute of Buddhist Studies
Columbia University
80 Claremont Avenue, Room 205
New York, NY 10027
www.aibs.columbia.edu

Wisdom Publications
132 Perry Street
New York, NY 10014 USA
wisdom.org

In association with Columbia University's Center for Buddhist Studies and Tibet House US.
Distributed by Wisdom Publications.

Library of Congress Cataloging-in-Publication Data
Names: Forgues, Gregory translator writer of introduction
Title: Elucidating the intent: a noble Mahayana sutra: Ārya saṁdhinirmocana sūtra / by Shākyamuni Buddha; introduction and translation by Gregory Forgues.
Other titles: Tripiṭaka. Sūtrapiṭaka. Saṃdhinirmocanasūtra. English
Description: New York, NY: American Institute of Buddhist Studies: Wisdom Publications, [2026] | Series: Treasury of the Buddhist sciences series | "Tengyur Translation Initiative. CK 124 (D 106)." | Includes bibliographical references and index.
Identifiers: LCCN 2025025146 |
ISBN 9781949163292 cloth | ISBN 9781949163353 ebook
Subjects: LCSH: Yogācāra (Buddhism)—Early works to 1800
Classification: LCC BQ2092.E5 F67 2026
LC record available at https://lccn.loc.gov/2025025146

ISBN 978-1-949163-29-2 (cloth) ISBN 978-1-949163-35-3 (ebook)
30 29 28 27 26 1 2 3 4 5

Cover and interior design by Gopa & Ted2, Inc. Set in Diacritical Garamond Pro 11/13.9.

Printed on acid-free paper and meets the guidelines for permanence and durability of the Production Guidelines for Book Longevity of the Council on Library Resources.

Printed in the United States of America.

This work is gratefully dedicated to
Dzongsar Khyentse Rinpoche

Contents

Acknowledgments . . . xi

Copublisher Preface . . . xiii

Abbreviations and Typographical Conventions . . . xvii

Part One: Introduction

Setting and Summary . . . 3

The Context . . . 3

Main Points of the Subject Matter . . . 5

Translation Issues and Academic Research . . . 15

Part Two: Annotated English Translation

Prologue . . . 35

Chapter 1 . . . 41

Chapter 2 . . . 47

Chapter 3 . . . 51

Chapter 4 . . . 59

Chapter 5 . . . 65

Chapter 6 . . . 71

Chapter 7 . . . 79

Chapter 8 97

Chapter 9 129

Chapter 10 151

Glossary

English-Tibetan-Sanskrit Glossary 171

Appendixes

Appendix I: The Translation Choice for *Nimitta* 193

Appendix II: Source Text and Various Versions 209

Bibliographies

Primary Sources 213

Modern Sources 215

Index 223

Acknowledgments

The initial editing of the text was conducted by Casey Forgues and Laura Goetz. With special thanks to Harunaga Isaacson, Matthew Kapstein, Klaus-Dieter Mathes, Jonathan Silk, Lambert Schmithausen, Robert A.F. Thurman, Tom Tillemans, and William Waldron for their helpful comments and advice.

I am deeply grateful to 84000: Translating the Words of the Buddha and to Andreas Doctor for their invaluable support and guidance during the initial translation phase. This translation was completed under their patronage and supervision, and through the generous sponsorship of Qiang Li (李强) and Ya Wen (文雅), which made this translation possible.

I would also like to thank the American Institute of Buddhist Studies (AIBS) editors of the *Treasury of the Buddhist Sciences* series, Robert A.F. Thurman and Thomas F. Yarnall, as well as Daniel Aitken at Wisdom Publications, for their support and guidance throughout the final stages of this project. My thanks also go to Edward Arnold of AIBS for finalizing the manuscript.

Copublisher Preface

Robert A.F. Thurman

The American Institute of Buddhist Studies and Wisdom Publications, with the Columbia Center for Buddhist Studies and Tibet House US, are honored to present this *Treasury of the Buddhist Sciences* series, which is dedicated to making available in English and other languages the entire Tengyur (*bsTan 'gyur*), the collection of Sanskrit scientific works preserved in Tibetan translations, and the originally Tibetan learned commentaries and treatises based upon them. Our main focus, as mentioned in the title of the series, is on the scientific works collected in the Tengyur, not on the purportedly recorded direct teachings of Shākyamuni Buddha that are counted as "scripture" and are collected in the set of Tibetan translations known as the Kangyur (*bKa' 'gyur*). This distinction between "scientific" and "scriptural" is of course quite arbitrary and almost self-contradictory both in modern scholarly terms and in traditional "Buddhist" understanding. Modern non-Tibetan scholars do not credit the traditional understanding of the Buddha's authorial role, nor do they consider any of the Buddhist writings as scientific, given their materialist narrowing of that term, and the traditional scholars consider the Buddha to be the Supreme Scientist of all time, knower of all that is important to know, and utterly empirical, non-dogmatic, and open minded, so they consider his statements to be based on his scientific discoveries of inner and outer realities of life and world. So, we have a disagreement to be so total it is almost an agreement! Perhaps this is only solvable by returning to the standard definition of "science" as the organized effort to understand accurately the reality of everything relevant to life in the universe. Then there can begin what my late sociological colleague Peter Berger called for: a real "contestation of truth claims!"

His Holiness the Dalai Lama has encouraged scholars to study and to make available translations and studies of the texts retrieved from the great library of Nālandā, sutric sciences and tantric technologies, with suitable commentaries, so people can see how firmly they are rooted in the enlightened principles of wisdom and compassion; how sophisticated and advanced are the yogic practices, presupposing prior achievement of a high degree of meditative ability, profound understanding of selflessness and emptiness, sincere motivation of the compassionate spirit of enlightenment, the vow to liberate all beings from suffering, and the courageous determination to accelerate the spiritual evolution of the human beings who can learn from them.

The scientific treatises (*śāstra*) of the great Indian Buddhist universities, accumulated during the fifteen-hundred-year flourishing of the Buddhist sciences from the Buddha's time until just after the end of the first millennium, are preserved mainly only in the Tibetan translation canon. Contrary to modern prejudices, these in matter of fact are scientific works (unless you insist on defining "science" as modern dogmatic materialism). Most are focused on the supreme science for human beings, the "inner science" of the psychology that investigates their inner experiences of birth and life and death, the causes of their suffering, and the pathways of their realization of their full potential through the humanly achievable transformation called "awakening" or "enlightenment."

Anticipating that glorious day, herein we are pleased to present Greg Forgues' very well researched and thoughtfully articulated study and translation of the extremely important Mahayana Sutra discourse, the *Elucidating the Intent*, which, as purporting to record the utterance of the Buddha in dialogue with various seekers of enlightenment, is counted as a sacred scripture. It is the very important one that introduces the Buddha's hermeneutical principles, putting forward a way to interpret the Buddha's various teachings that reconciles seeming contradictions between them. It is the locus classicus of the theory of the "three turnings of the Wheel of Dharma": the wheel that takes conventional reality as somewhat really existent, the wheel that seems to reject the existence of conventional reality; and the wheel that discriminates between realities that exist and those that do not exist. As such, it was the most important scripture for the noble

Asaṇga, the great founding philosopher-psychologist of the Mahayana Buddhist school of the Yogic Practitioners or Experientialists (*Yogāchāra* or *Vijñānavāda*). His predecessor, the noble Nāgārjuna, is considered the founder of the "profound worldview" tradition based on the Centrist (*Mādhyamika*) school, which comes to be coordinated with Asanga's "magnificent deeds" tradition based on the Experientialist school.

This deeply studied translation is based on wide ranging scholarship and thoughtful philosophical confrontation of the complexities of the Buddha's thought within it. Careful study of the text will reward the attentive reader with its illumination of the epistemological sophistication of the Experientialist way of understanding the Transcendent Wisdom sutras. Dr. Forgues is to be heartily congratulated for this great contribution.

It is my duty and pleasure to offer sincere acknowledgement and thanks to Columbia University's Department of Religion, faculty and administrators, and especially the current Jey Tsong Khapa Professor, Dr. Dominique Townsend, for their gracious hosting of the Center for Buddhist Studies and its formal affiliate, the American Institute of Buddhist Studies; to the Wang Foundation, whose generous grant enabled the always arduous editing process of this and other works, all eventually to be translated into Chinese as well as English; to the Conanima Foundation, the Infinity Foundation, the Sacharuna Foundation, the William T. Kistler Foundation, the National Endowment for the Humanities, the Omidyar Family Foundation, the Tsadra Foundation, and the Dzongsar Khyentse Foundation's 84000 Project, and the many other generous individual and institutional donors of the American Institute of Buddhist Studies, Wisdom Publications, and the Tibet House US, who have made our publications possible over the years and fortunately continue to do so.

I congratulate all the members of the AIBS Translation Team, especially Professors Thomas Yarnall and Edward Arnold, for their great work and continuous critical thought on how best to bring to life this literature of seminal importance to the Indian and Tibetan Buddhist inner science traditions, as preserved and further developed and refined in the monastic universities and retreat centers of Tibet. I also wish to express my gratitude to Wisdom Publications' Publisher (and this Treasury's co-publisher), Dr. Daniel Aitken, and his expert editorial, production, and management teams, especially Ben Gleason and Laura Cunningham, for their thoughtful, careful, and energetic collaboration in all that is involved in getting such complex works polished, finalized and sent out into the world.

Padma Shri Robert A.F. Thurman
Jey Tsong Khapa Professor Emeritus of Indo-Tibetan Buddhist Studies,
Department of Religion, Columbia University, New York;
Director, American Institute of Buddhist Studies;
President, Tibet House US.
October 3, 2025
Tibetan Royal Year 2145, Wood Snake Year

Abbreviations and Typographical Conventions

NOTE: See Bibliographies for full citations.

[...]	Material introduced by translators in translation to facilitate English readability
«...»	Paragraph numbering based on Lamotte's critical edition
Bd	Bardan (Zanskar) canonical collection
C	Chone xylograph Kangyur
CBETA	Chinese Electronic Buddhist Text Association (www.cbeta.org)
Cz	Chizhi Kangyur
D	Degé (*sde dge*) edition of the Tibetan Buddhist Canon
Dd	Dodedrak Kangyur
Dk	Dongkarla Kangyur
Do	Dolpo canonical collection
F	Phukdrak manuscript Kangyur
Go	Gondhla (Lahaul) canonical collection
Gt	Gangteng Kangyur
H	Lhasa xylograph Kangyur
He	Hemis I Kangyur
J	'Jang sa tham (Lithang xylograph Kangyur)
Kb	Berlin manuscript Kangyur
K0774	Peking 1737 xylograph Kangyur
L	London (Shelkar) manuscript Kangyur

Lg	Lang mdo Kangyur
Mvyut	Mahāvyutpatti
N	Narthang xylograph Kangyur
Ng	Namgyal Kangyur
Np	Neyphug Kangyur
O	Tawang Kangyur
Pj	Phajoding I Kangyur
Pz	Phajoding II Kangyur
R	Ragya Kangyur
S	Stok manuscript Kangyur
Saṁdh.	*Saṁdhinirmocanasūtra*
SaṁdhDh	Dunhuang manuscript: Stein Tib. n°194 (49 folios) and Stein Tib. n°683 (1 folio)
T	Tokyo manuscript Kangyur
Taishō 676	解深密經, translated by Xuanzang (596–664 CE)
TrBh	Sthiramati's *Triṁśikāvijñaptibhāṣyam*
U	Urga xylograph Kangyur
V	Ulaanbaatar manuscript Kangyur
VD	Degé xylograph of the *Viniścayasaṁgrahaṇī* of the *Yogācārabhūmi* from the Tengyur
VG	Golden xylograph of the *Viniścayasaṁgrahaṇī* of the *Yogācārabhūmi* from the Tengyur
VP	Peking xylograph of the *Viniścayasaṁgrahaṇī* of the *Yogācārabhūmi* from the Tengyur
VinSg	*Viniścayasaṁgrahaṇī* of the *Yogācārabhūmi*
X	Basgo manuscript Kangyur
YBhtP'i	Tibetan translation of *Yogācārabhūmi*, Peking Tengyur (n° 5540, sems tsam, 'i 143aI–382a5 (vol. III: 121–217)
Z	Shey Palace manuscript Kangyur

We have strived generally to present Tibetan and Sanskrit names and terms in a phonetic form to facilitate pronunciation. For most Sanskrit terms this has meant that—while we generally have kept conventional diacritics for vowels—we have added an *h* to convey certain sounds that the general reader will mispronounce without it (thus *ś*, *ṣ*, and *c* are rendered as *sh*, *ṣh*, and *ch* respectively). For Sanskrit terms that have entered the English lexicon (such as "nirvana"), we use no diacritical marks. In more technical contexts (notes, bibliographies, appendixes, and so on) we use full standard diacritical conventions for Sanskrit and Wylie transliterations for Tibetan.

Part One

Introduction

Introduction

Setting and Summary

In *Elucidating the Intent*, the Buddha gives a systematic overview of his three great cycles of teachings, which he refers to in this text as the "three Dharma wheels" (*tridharmacakra*). In the process of delineating the meaning of these doctrines, the Buddha elucidates several difficult points regarding the ultimate and relative truths, the nature of reality, and the contemplative methods conducive to the attainment of complete and perfect awakening, and he also explains what his intent was when he imparted teachings belonging to each of the three Dharma wheels. Through a series of dialogues with hearers (*śrāvakas*) and bodhisattvas, the Buddha thus offers a complete and systematic teaching on the Great Vehicle (Mahayana), to which he refers here as the "Single Vehicle."

The sutra is set in an unfathomable palace displayed by the Buddha's powers and attended by countless beings. The three gates of liberation (emptiness, absence of manifest characteristics, and absence of wish) are the entrance to this abode of the tathāgatas, the inconceivable nondual state of a buddha who, possessed of the gnosis (*jñāna*) of the Tathāgata's liberation, is dwelling in the domain of truth (*dharmadhātu*), together with an immeasurable retinue of hearers and a retinue of bodhisattvas including Gambhīrārthasaṁdhinirmochana, Vidhivatparipṛcchaka, Dharmodgata, Suvishuddhamati, Vishālamati, Guṇākara, Paramārthasamudgata, Avalokiteshvara, Maitreya, and Mañjushrī.

The Context

The sutra is structured in the form of a series of dialogues between the Buddha and advanced bodhisattvas or hearers, as well as between bodhisattvas (see chapter 1). These dialogues deal with both the theory and practice of the entire bodhisattva path. Narrative elements are extremely limited in this teaching. However, a narrative pattern can be found in chapters 2 and 3, which begin, respectively, with a story about a group of non-Buddhists (*tīrthikas*) and some followers of the Buddha who have gathered to discuss a difficult point regarding the nature of reality and cannot agree on anything. The main protagonists then beg the Buddha to provide an explanation for the quandary these assemblies cannot resolve, or alternatively to explain his underlying intent when he expounded the teachings that gave rise to conflicting interpretations.

Each chapter starts with a question on a topic requiring further elucidation: In the first chapter, the bodhisattva Vidhivatparipṛcchaka questions the bodhisattva Gambhīrārthasaṁdhinirmochana on the inexpressible (*anabhilāpya*) and nondual (*advaya*) ultimate. In the second chapter, the bodhisattva Dharmodgata questions the Buddha on the ultimate beyond speculation (*sarvatarkasamatikrānta*). In the third chapter, the bodhisattva Suvishuddhamati questions the Buddha on the ultimate that is beyond being distinct or indistinct (*bhedābhedasamatikrānta*) from conditioned phenomena. In the fourth chapter, Subhūti questions the Buddha on the ultimate that is of a single nature (*ekarasa*) within all phenomena. In the fifth chapter, the bodhisattva Vishālamati questions the Buddha on the secrets of mind (*citta*), thought (*manas*), and cognition (*vijñāna*). In the sixth chapter, the bodhisattva Guṇākara questions the Buddha on the three defining characteristics (*lakṣaṇa*) of phenomena. In the seventh chapter, the bodhisattva Paramārthasamudgata questions the Buddha on the three kinds of essencelessness (*niḥsvabhāvatā*) as well as on the Buddha's three turnings of the Dharma wheel. In the eighth chapter, the bodhisattva Maitreya questions the Buddha on the practice of mental stillness (*śamatha*) and insight (*vipaśyanā*). In the ninth chapter, the bodhisattva Avalokiteshvara questions the Buddha on the stages of the bodhisattva path and the Single Vehicle (*ekayāna*). In the tenth chapter, the bodhisattva Mañjushrī questions the Buddha on the bodies (*kāya*) and activity of the tathāgatas.[1]

From a broader perspective, it is possible to consider that the teaching imparted in this sutra is structured in terms of the basis (*āśraya*), the path

1. Editorial note: in chapter 10, in a few very lengthy passages of uninterrupted speech, we have inserted a gap to signal a change in speaker in order to facilitate ease of comprehension. These do not appear in the source texts.

(*mārga*), and the result (*phala*). The first four chapters on the five characteristics of the ultimate[2] as defined in the Prajñāpāramitā sutra represent a teaching on the abovementioned basis, namely, true reality (*tathatā*) as it is; chapters 5–9, a teaching on the path in terms of practices and stages to attain awakening; and chapter 10, a teaching on the result through the doctrine of the tathāgatas' bodies and activity to awaken beings. All major Tibetan traditions consider chapter 3, focusing on the relation between the two truths, and chapter 8, focusing on meditative practice, to be authoritative. These are among the scriptures most quoted on their respective topics by Tibetan authors regardless of lineage.

Main Points of the Subject Matter

The Basis

The first four chapters point out the nature of reality by distinguishing the unconditioned from the conditioned, the pure from the afflicted, the ultimate from the conventional, nondual gnosis from mind's elaborations, inexpressible reality from conventional expressions, and the actual from the imaginary. The first chapter thus starts with the distinction between conditioned and unconditioned phenomena, which became a prevalent theme in the various Abhidharmas. Through this distinction, the point is made that the ultimate is inexpressible and nondual. The realization of this inexpressible ultimate is achieved through gnosis alone. Conceptions in terms of conditioned and unconditioned merely exist in the way of a magical illusion. Yet, in order to lead beings to awakening, buddhas have to use such labels. The second chapter elaborates on this very point. Although the ultimate is beyond speculation, the Buddha teaches liberation by means of verbal expressions and conventions belonging to the domain of manifest characteristics (*nimitta*) and notions.

As a consequence, the first two chapters delineate two domains corresponding to the two truths (*satyadvaya*): (1) the pure domain of the ultimate, which, being inexpressible, nondual, and beyond speculation, is the realm of nonconceptual gnosis free from conventional appearance and notions, and (2) the afflicted domain of dualistic conventional expressions

2. See glossary entry "ultimate."

and notions, which is the realm of mental elaborations. These domains are respectively labeled by the buddhas as "the unconditioned" and "the conditioned" only for the sake of instructing beings, for the Buddha explains that this distinction between unconditioned and conditioned is only made on the level of the conditioned, namely, from the perspective of dualistic conventions. Within the realm of these conventional expressions, in the context of the path, it follows that these two domains are apparently mutually exclusive, although the Buddha hints at the fact that, from the perspective of the ultimate, the conditioned is not the conditioned and the unconditioned is not the unconditioned.

Chapter 3 explains how the relation between the ultimate and conditioned phenomena seen from this higher perspective should be communicated on the level of conventions. From this standpoint, one cannot say whether the ultimate is distinct or indistinct from conditioned phenomena. The Buddha shows that positing these two domains as distinct or indistinct is wrong. Since conditioned phenomena are characterized by the fact of being produced by causes and conditions, it is inappropriate to conceive (1) the conditioned and (2) the emptiness of an inherent nature as either identical or different. On the one hand, being conditioned (i.e., dependent on something other) is identical with being empty of an intrinsic nature; on the other hand, the domain of the conditioned is defined as the realm of afflictions, while the domain of the unconditioned is understood as the pure realm. Some might therefore think that phenomena and the nature of phenomena are distinct, but the Buddha teaches in the fourth chapter that the empty nature of conditioned phenomena, the ultimate, cannot be said to be distinct from those phenomena. As such, this subtle and profound ultimate is indeed of a single character within phenomena whose defining characteristic appears to be diverse. To realize this nature of phenomena, which is unconditioned selflessness, one should only rely on nondual gnosis, not mind.

The Path

Chapter 5 is a presentation of the "secrets of mind, thought, and cognition." Here the Buddha introduces the concept of "appropriating cognition" (*ādānavijñāna*), also called "subliminal cognition" (*ālayavijñāna*), "mind" (*citta*), or "mind containing all the seeds" (*sarvabījaṁ cittam*). This mind, in which mental events manifest, acts like a mirror in which reflections appear. It is the basis of previous mental imprints resulting from volitions and actions that create predispositions (i.e., latent dispositions) to experience reality in conventional terms. However, once bodhisattvas cognize in an intuitive and personal way the ultimate by means of gnosis, they no longer perceive this mind.[3] In the closing verses of this chapter, the Buddha explains that this mind is without a self, since it is conditioned by and composed of seeds. Through these definitions, the Buddha de facto delineates two realms: the domain of dualistic mind and the domain of nondual gnosis.

Chapter 6 is a teaching on the three defining characteristics (*lakṣaṇa*) of phenomena: the imaginary defining characteristic (*parikalpitalakṣaṇa*), the other-dependent defining characteristic (*paratantralakṣaṇa*), and the actual defining characteristic (*pariniṣpannalakṣaṇa*): (1) The imaginary defining characteristic is the superimposition onto phenomena of an essence or a defining characteristic existing from its own side by means of designations or conventional expressions. This imaginary characteristic is utterly false in the way of a visual aberration, since phenomena are ultimately devoid of any defining characteristic that makes them what they are. (2) The other-dependent defining characteristic corresponds to the dependent arising of phenomena. It refers to manifest characteristics upon which an imaginary defining characteristic is superimposed. This point is grasped once the imaginary defining characteristic of phenomena is understood to be a wrong conception. It is worth noting that the other-dependent defining characteristic delineates the domain of conditioned cognitions, namely, the mind as presented in chapter 5 (this point is made clear in 7.10[4] with regard to karma and rebirth), and, as such, represents the domain of affliction (see 6.11). (3) The actual defining characteristic is the permanent and immutable reality of phenomena. It is the ultimate unerring object that is manifest once the selflessness of phenomena, the nonexistence of any fictive defining characteristic in phenomena arising dependently, has been realized. Only the actual defining characteristic constitutes the domain of purification, since the other-dependent defines the domain of affliction,

3. See Brunnhölzl 2018, 1590n89, on this point.

4. The numbering of paragraphs of the *Saṁdhinirmocana Sūtra* (Saṁdh.) here follows Lamotte's critical edition.

namely, the realm of the conditioned. In the closing verses of this chapter, the Buddha gives a quintessential presentation of the path: one should first recognize that phenomena are devoid of imaginary defining characteristics by seeing them as mere designations superimposed on conditioned cognitions. At that time, one will abandon phenomena characterized by affliction, namely, conditioned phenomena in the form of conditioned cognitions, and turn toward phenomena characterized by purification that are in harmony with ultimate reality.

Chapter 7 begins with Paramārthasamudgata's question: why did the Buddha first teach the defining characteristic of phenomena, their arising, their cessation, and so forth through the notions of the five aggregates, the twelve sense domains, and so on, when he later explained that all phenomena are without an essence? The Buddha answers by teaching the three kinds of essencelessness, namely, essencelessness regarding defining characteristics, essencelessness regarding arising, and essencelessness regarding the ultimate. (1) Essencelessness regarding defining characteristics refers to the imaginary defining characteristic of phenomena. It is the essencelessness of what is utterly nonexistent (i.e., the defining characteristic), which is like a sky flower. (2) Essencelessness regarding arising refers to the other-dependent defining characteristic of phenomena arising from causes other than themselves. It is presented as the magic illusion of dependent arising, in the context of this teaching, as the magic illusion of mind. (3) Essencelessness regarding the ultimate has two aspects. The first is the essencelessness of all conditioned phenomena with regard to the ultimate. As a corollary of dependent arising, those phenomena are in fact not born as anything, being dependent on causes and conditions for their arising and therefore impermanent. The second aspect of essencelessness with regard to the ultimate refers to the only unconditioned object of purification, the actual defining characteristic of phenomena, the ultimate selflessness of phenomena, which is like space, itself also unconditioned. This permanent and immutable nature of phenomena is the primordial state of peace of that which, being without a defining characteristic, is unborn and unceasing, by nature in the state of nirvana.

In 7.10, the Buddha describes the entire process leading to confusion: beings reify the other-dependent and the actual defining characteristics in terms of the imaginary defining characteristic. Failing to understand that conventional expressions do not refer to actual things, they superimpose an essence on conditioned cognitions and imagine reality to be just as it is described by their linguistic conventions. Figments of imagination become causes and conditions for their mental activities, which will lead them to the afflictions of action and rebirth. The process described here is akin to a world of virtual reality where even the projector, the conditioned mind, is imaginary. As one takes the projected phenomena as real and reifies them, one acts, suffers, dies, and is endlessly "respawned" within this virtual reality. Although this pseudo-reality projected by mind is nonexistent, it will condition one's mind and one's future existence as one will act in accord with one's state of mind within this virtual reality. In 7.10, the other-dependent is therefore equated with the appropriating mind, the basis of the imaginary defining characteristic of phenomena, the object of dreamlike conceptualizations (see also 7.25).

Next, the Buddha explains how various beings relate to this process and how he has helped them with teachings corresponding to their circumstances and capacities. For example, some can understand on a dualistic level that defining characteristics (i.e., the virtual reality of phenomena) lack an essence, and thus slowly develop revulsion toward conditioned phenomena, even if they are not able to realize the ultimate nature of phenomena, their nondual primordial selflessness that is the domain of gnosis. In accord with this model of reality, the Buddha declares that there is only the path and journey toward liberation and thus a Single Vehicle for both hearers and bodhisattvas because there is only a single purification.

In 7.30, Paramārthasamudgata defines the three turnings of the wheel of Dharma. Because this doctrine is included in this specific chapter, it seems logical to interpret the three turnings of the wheel of Dharma in relation to the three kinds of essencelessness: (1) The first turning used the notion that phenomena have a defining characteristic to teach the essencelessness of these defining characteristics in a series of teachings such as the five aggregates, the twelve sense domains, and so on (see also 4.1–6). In our metaphor on virtual reality, one could see these teachings as being expounded on the basis of the very imaginary phenomena conceptualized as truly existing. When children experience a nightmare, their parents show that the monster does not exist by implicitly, i.e., provisionally, accepting its existence, saying, "Look! It is not there." (2) The second turning of the wheel teaches the first aspect of essencelessness with regard to the ultimate, stating that phenomena are unborn. From this perspective, the primordial selflessness of phenomena is still taught in relation to dualistic phenomena. As a consequence, Paramārthasamudgata considers this cycle of teachings as provisional. (3) The third turning of the wheel aims at teaching the second aspect of essencelessness with regard to the ultimate in a way that is not limited to the domain of dualistic phenomena. To pursue our metaphor, this third cycle of teachings gives a complete overview of the three defining characteristics of phenomena: the completely imaginary experience of a virtual reality, the magic illusion of the projecting mind, and the primordial domain of gnosis. Paramārthasamudgata declares the third turning to be of definitive meaning.

It is worth noting that the doctrine of the three defining characteristics can be seen as delineating three great categories of soteriological approaches found in Indo-Tibetan Buddhist traditions: (1) the deconstruction of putative notions of an individual self through mereological and relational strategies; (2) the deconstruction of notions of a self regarding conditioned phenomena through the impossibility of their ultimate arising, since these conditioned phenomena merely exist in dependence; and (3) the pointing out of the nondual ultimate nature of phenomena, which altogether bypasses imaginary mental constructions.

In the eighth chapter, the famous Maitreya chapter on meditation, the Buddha first gives a series of definitions followed by the description of a process, a pattern frequently used in this sutra. First, the objects of the practices of mental stillness (*śamatha*) and insight (*vipaśyanā*) are defined as, respectively, an image without and with conceptualization, while their objects, when both practices are combined, are the point where things end (*vastvanta*) and the accomplishment of the goal (*kṛtyānuṣṭhāna*, i.e., the attainment of the path). Mental stillness consists in directing one's attention (*manasikāra*) inward toward the mind that is directing attention (see 8.3). It follows a state of inner absorption produced by concentrating on a referential object. The practice of insight consists in analyzing, discerning, and differentiating the various cognitive aspects of the image (*pratibimba*) that is the object of concentration. These two practices are neither different nor identical. They are not different in that they take mind as a referential object, but they are not identical because insight takes a conceptual image as its referential object. The Buddha thus explains in an often-cited passage that this image taken as an object of concentration is not different from mind insofar as cognition is constituted by the mere representation (*vijñaptimātra*) that is the object of this cognition. The mind and the image, which is its object manifesting as a mental event, appear as different, although they are not. All mental images, whether in the context of practice or not, are mere representations. Once one has realized this, directing one's attention toward true reality is the one-pointedness of mind in which mental stillness and insight are unified. A superior way to practice this path is therefore to focus on that which is universal in all the various specific teachings imparted by the Buddha. This approach, which is based on a practice devoid of mental engagement (*vitarka*) and investigation (*vicāra*), directly focuses on the element that converges toward true reality. The ensuing shift in one's basis of existence (*āśrayaparivṛtti*) mentioned in this sutra does not here refer to a transformation of the subliminal cognition (*ālayavijñāna*). According to 10.2, this shift, once all corruption has been eliminated, consists in nothing other than the bodhisattva's attainment of the truth body (*dharmakāya*).

The Buddha then explains how one attends to manifest characteristics in an increasingly nonconceptual way. He also gives an elucidation of the analytical knowledge of designations (*dharmapratisaṁvid*) and their objects (*arthapratisaṁvid*) attained through the practice of mental stillness and insight. In this context, a few key definitions are given; for example, the true reality of representations is that all conditioned phenomena are mere representations (see 8.20.2.iii). When presented in four aspects, the analytical knowledge of designations and their objects encapsulate the entire path through the four stages of mental appropriation, experience, affliction, and purification. When asked about the nature of gnosis, the Buddha answers that it "consists in the mental stillness and insight that take a universal teaching as a referential object" while "perception consists in the mental stillness and insight that take a specific teaching as a referential object" (see 8.25). Practically, bodhisattvas direct their attention to true reality, discarding the manifest characteristics of designations and objects of designation. Without taking any essential characteristic as a referential object, they do not pay attention to manifest characteristics. Their attention is focused on that which is of a single character within all phenomena. The Buddha then gives a list of all the manifest characteristics eliminated by emptiness, from the emptiness of all phenomena up to the emptiness of emptiness. By letting go of their object of concentration, the manifest characteristic corresponding to a mental image, bodhisattvas free themselves from the bonds of conditioned manifest characteristics (*nimitta*). Connecting these instructions on meditative practice with his teaching on the three defining characteristics, the Buddha explains that he taught the defining characteristic of emptiness in the Great Vehicle as the nonexistence and nonperception of an imaginary defining characteristic with regard to both affliction and purification in the other-dependent and actual defining characteristics of phenomena.

Practical instructions are also given to overcome obstacles and distractions to the practice of mental stillness and insight. On the ultimate stage of the path, these practices eliminate extremely subtle obstructions resulting in the complete purification of the truth body. The gnosis and vision utterly free from attachment and hindrance are attained. Finally, the Buddha explains how bodhisattvas obtain their great powers by being skillful in the following six points: (1) the arising of the mind, (2) the underlying condition of the mind, (3) the emergence from the mind, (4) the increase of the mind, (5) the decrease of the mind, and (6) skillful means. In this section of the Maitreya chapter, an overview of the mere representation doctrine is given through the notion of cognition, which includes the appropriating cognition as well as the arising cognitions taking various manifest characteristics as their object. In this context, it is explained that the supramundane mind of the buddhas does not have any manifest characteristic as its object.

In chapter 9, the Buddha is questioned on the stages (*bhūmi*) of a bodhisattva and a buddha, the names of these stages, and their adverse factors and specific arising, as well as on the ten perfections (*pāramitā*). A final instruction is imparted regarding the Single Vehicle. As mentioned in previous chapters, the Buddha explains that he taught the essence of phenomena in the vehicle of hearers in terms of the aggregates, the sense domains, and so on, and that he presented these phenomena in the light of a single principle in the Great Vehicle, the domain of truth (*dharmadhātu*). Those who conceptualize these teachings by taking them literally do not understand his underlying intention, which is that both vehicles are in fact teachings based on a single principle.

The Result

In the tenth chapter, Mañjushrī questions the Buddha on the defining characteristic of the truth body of the tathāgatas. The Buddha explains the truth body in the sense of a result attained through the practice of the stages and perfections. This attainment consists in a shift in one's basis of existence. From the perspective of beings belonging to the domain of mental elaborations and conditioned phenomena, the truth body is therefore inconceivable, being utterly beyond mental elaborations. Here again the Buddha delineates two distinct realms. The tathāgatas, who appear as emanation bodies (*nirmāṇakāya*), are said to be like a manifestation, an apparition. Through their skillful means and sovereign power (*adhiṣṭhāna*), they liberate beings by imparting three kinds of teaching: the sutras, the Vinaya, and the *mātṛkās* (generally taken as more or less equivalent to the Abhidharma and related literature): (1) The sutras teach what was heard, how to take refuge, the training, and the awakening. (2) The Vinaya teaches the precepts and prātimokṣha vows to hearers and bodhisattvas. (3) The *mātṛkās* are systematic teachings on important doctrinal points, such as the defining characteristic of the conventional and the ultimate, the defining characteristic of referential objects consisting of the awakening factors and their features, and so forth. In the section of the *mātṛkā* pertaining to the ascertainment of the qualities of cognitive objects, the Buddha goes into a lengthy discussion on logical analysis according to the four principles of reason (*yukti*): (1) the principle of reason based on dependence (*apekṣāyukti*), (2) the principle of reason based on cause and effect (*kāryakāraṇayukti*), (3) the principle of reason based on logical proof (*upapattisādhanayukti*), and (4) the principle of reason based on the nature of phenomena itself (*dharmatāyukti*). The explanation given by the Buddha on the third reason of this list (cf. 10.7.4.vii.c) is very extensive and resembles a short treatise on epistemology in which the notion of means of knowledge or valid cognition (*pramāṇa*) is meticulously investigated. In this section, the Buddha explains the characteristics of valid and invalid reasonings. He concludes by stating that three types of valid cognition should be accepted: direct cognition (*pratyakṣa*), inference (*anumāna*), and authoritative scriptures (*āptāgama*).

The Buddha next elucidates "the meaning of the formula through which bodhisattvas comply with the underlying intention of the profound Dharma expounded by the tathāgatas, the complete meaning of the sutras, the Vinaya, and the *mātṛkās*." This quintessential teaching encapsulating the meaning of the entire Dharma states that beings are in truth beyond activity and beyond being afflicted or purified. It is only because of their reification of illusory phenomena in terms of identity and essence that they conceive their reality in the way they do, which leads them to suffering. Abandoning this "body afflicted by corruption" (*dauṣṭhulyakāya*),[5] they obtain the truth body that is inconceivable and unconditioned (i.e., *dharmakāya*). In this context, the Buddha concludes by explaining that the tathāgatas are not characterized by mind, thought, and cognition. Their mind arises without effort in the way of an emanation (*nirmāṇa*). In their case, one cannot say whether their mind exists or not, their domain consisting of pure realms. It follows that the tathāgatas are characterized by nonduality: "They are neither completely and perfectly awakened nor not completely and perfectly awakened; they neither turn the wheel of Dharma nor do not turn the wheel of Dharma; they neither attain the great parinirvana nor do not attain the great parinirvana. This is because the truth body is utterly pure and the emanation body constantly manifests." Once the truth body has been purified through the practice focusing on the domain of truth (*dharmadhātu*), "the great light of gnosis manifests in beings, and innumerable emanated reflections arise." One should keep in mind, though, the teachings imparted in chapter 3 on the conventional and ultimate truths. From the perspective of the ultimate, nothing has ever been purified by anybody, as the concluding verses of the formula in chapter 10 make clear:

> The possessors of qualities resulting from affliction and
>   purification
> Are all without movement and without a person;
> Therefore, I declare them to be without activity,
> As they are neither purified nor afflicted, be it in the past or the
>   future.
>
> Relying on views resulting from their latent dispositions,
> On account of which they wrongly conceive the body afflicted by
>   corruption,
> They reify [the ego through concepts such as] "I" and "mine."
> As a consequence, notions arise, such as "I see," "I eat," "I do," "I am
>   afflicted," and "I am purified."

5. See Radich 2007, 1257, on the relationship between *āśrayaparivṛtti* and *dauṣṭhulyakāya*. Saṁdh. is the only text in the entire Kangyur in which the term *dauṣṭhulyakāya* is found.

Thus, those who understand this fact as it really is
Abandon the body afflicted by corruption
and instead will obtain a body that is not a support for any
defilement,
Being free from mental elaborations and unconditioned.

Translation Issues and Academic Research

I have applied various methods and followed a series of six steps during the process of translating the *Saṁdhinirmocana Sūtra* from the Tibetan.

1. Identifying and organizing source texts

I first collated all the available Tibetan editions of the *Saṁdhinirmocana Sūtra*: Bd, C, D, Dunhuang (Hakayama 1984–87), Do, F, H, L, N, S, K0774, U, VD, X, and Z, as well as the various extant Sanskrit fragments found in Buescher (2007), Lévi (1925), Matsuda (1995, 2013), Nagao (1964), and Tucci (1971). For the Chinese, I used Xuanzang's translation.[6] I then produced a critical edition of the text's prologue (*nidāna*) to get a sense of the textual variations across major available editions of the Tshalpa (*tshal pa*), Thempangma (*them spangs ma*), mixed Kangyurs, and independent Kangyur groups. In addition, Dr. Kojirō Katō (Tokyo University), who has been editing the *Saṁdhinirmocana Sūtra*, kindly sent me his critical edition of the seventh chapter.[7] His work has proved invaluable to confirming the findings of my own work on the prologue. The editions belonging to the Thempangma differ significantly from those included in the Tshalpa line of transmission. As an independent Kangyur close to the Thempangma line, the Phukdrak (*phug brag*) edition offers very interesting readings on the level of syntax and lexicography compared to the editions of the Tshalpa group. It also diverges from the Thempangma witnesses in many locations. In the absence of colophons mentioning the translators' and editors' names across the available editions, it remains difficult to understand the history of these witnesses from the perspective of the underlying translation and

6. I would like to thank warmly Zhuoran Xie (Vienna University) for her assistance in reading this text.
7. See also Katō 2011 for textual variations.

editing process. As a consequence of its palatable variant readings compared to the Tshalpa and Thempangma editions, I used the Phukdrak witness quite extensively while translating the Degé edition, as well as the Stok edition and the Degé version of the *Viniścayasaṁgrahaṇī*, to examine more thoroughly the difficult passages. The available Sanskrit fragments were, on occasion, also useful to determine the Sanskrit equivalent of a Tibetan technical term. They, however, did not reveal major variations from the Tibetan texts. I referred to the Dunhuang recension sporadically, as Schmithausen warned us not to follow it blindly.[8] I also referred to Xuanzang's translation regarding a few difficult passages of the text. This translation is similar to those of the Tshalpa group and might have been carried out on the basis of a Sanskrit manuscript similar to the one (or those) used for the translation upon which the Tibetan Tshalpa editions are based.

2. Evaluating the available translations

The *Saṁdhinirmocana Sūtra* is a major text of Indian Buddhism that attracted the attention of Buddhist Studies scholars early on. It has been translated into French, English, and German (partially). Lamotte (1935) provided a critical edition and a translation from Tibetan (N) and Chinese (Taishō 676) into French. He also attempted to reconstruct or identify technical terms in Sanskrit, which have for the most part been confirmed by subsequent finds of Sanskrit fragments.[9] Lamotte's work is a major resource for the study of the sutra. It has been until now the standard edition and translation of this text on account of its accuracy and methodological academic approach. As a side note, I followed Lamotte's segmentation of the text into paragraphs. His French translation is generally reliable, although some technical passages can be significantly improved, particularly in the case of chapter 8 on meditation and chapter 10 on the result of the path. Frauwallner (1969) gives a partial translation (i.e., chapters 6 and 7) from Tibetan into German. As one would expect, Frauwallner's academic translation of these two chapters aims at accuracy over readability. Kawasaki (1976) is also a partial translation of chapter 8 into English (§6.1–9). This

8. See Schmithausen 2014, 425ff.

9. See Schmithausen 2014, 419–20n1852. On necessary adjustments to Lamotte's rendition of the original Sanskrit terms, see Hakayama 1984, 180, and Delhey 2013.

translation does not improve Lamotte's. Powers' (1995) translation from Tibetan (D) into English, in spite of its merit, could be widely improved upon in terms of methodology, accuracy, and readability.[10] Brunnhölzl (2018) offers a partial translation of chapter 7, as well as a few key passages from chapter 5.

Translations by Cleary (1999) and Keenan (2000) are from the Chinese into English. I used Keenan's work to get a sense of the Chinese text while translating the Degé edition but only referred to Cleary's occasionally. Keenan's work seems to me more accurate than Cleary's, although the latter was useful for unraveling difficult passages, since his style is more free and primarily intends to communicate the meaning of the text. Cornu (2005) has provided a translation of the text from Tibetan (D) into French that mainly follows Powers, a somewhat regrettable fact since Lamotte's is more accurate. Schmithausen's (2014) work contains numerous difficult passages of the *Saṁdhinirmocana Sūtra* translated from various Tibetan and Chinese editions into English. It is an invaluable resource for the study of the sutra. In addition, it offers useful Sanskrit reconstructions of important technical terms. Together with Lamotte's translation, it has been a constant companion while I translated the text.

3. Checking intertextual patterns and delineating the scope of primary sources

The *Saṁdhinirmocana Sūtra* is part of a larger network of texts, in both the Kangyur and the Tengyur:

The *nidāna* of the *Saṁdhinirmocana Sūtra* almost exactly matches those of the *Buddha-bhūmi-sūtra* (D275) and the *Tathāgataguṇajñānācintya-viṣayāvatāranirdeśa-sūtra* (D185). The *Buddha-bhūmi-sūtra* is a very short text that was also translated into Chinese by Xuanzang in 646 (see Keenan 1980, 336ff.). Textual parallelisms of this kind are useful for double checking some passages or gathering more background information about the source text.

As mentioned above, the *Saṁdhinirmocana Sūtra* is also found *in extenso* in the *Viniścayasaṁgrahaṇī* of the *Yogācārabhūmi* and is therefore

10. See Tillemans 1997 for a review of Powers 1995. From a general perspective, it seems that Powers chose to ignore the work and methodological approach of Lamotte and Frauwallner.

part of a tradition of texts sharing common ideas.[11] This point should be kept in mind while translating, particularly when one has to evaluate the potential impact of terminological choices from the perspective of a more philosophical approach to the text, which, in the case of the *Saṁdhinirmocana Sūtra*, should be a major concern. For example, one should pay attention to the fact that interpreting "representation-only" (*vijñaptimātra*) as a strong form of idealism essentializing mind could be misleading from the perspective of a cultural translation of the worldview propounded in the sutra, since mind, just as much as the external object, is explicitly declared to be empty of any own-being, essence, or intrinsic nature in this text.[12]

Another important point is the presence of the aforementioned five commentaries on the *Saṁdhinirmocana Sūtra* found in the Tengyur (D).[13] I occasionally referred to these works while finalizing the final draft of the translation. However, I first focused on the available editions of the sutra itself as I did not want to be influenced by the interpretations of later authors. Instead, I attempted to go through all possible logically meaningful readings according to the Tibetan and Sanskrit sources without any preconceptions resulting from my reading of later commentarial traditions.

In the same vein, one should note that the *Saṁdhinirmocana Sūtra* has played a major role in Tibetan hermeneutical debates. For centuries, it has been considered a central scripture referred to extensively in the writings of Tibet's great luminaries, such as Jey Tsongkhapa (*rje tsong kha pa*, 1357–1419) and Jamgön Mipham Gyatso (*'jam mgon mi pham rgya mtsho*, 1846–1912). While it would certainly be fascinating to study the impact of the *Saṁdhinirmocana Sūtra* in the context of Tibetan Madhyamaka,[14] I have chosen not to take into account Indian or Tibetan commentaries or exegeses of the sutra in order to focus on the source text itself.

11. See Schmithausen 1987 and 2014, Delhey 2013, and Skilling 2013 on the simile of the illusionist (*māyākāra*), which is also included *inter alia* in the *Māyājāla*, a sutra also quoted in the *Yogācārabhūmi*.

12. On this issue, see Brunnhölzl 2018, 414–18n5.

13. See Steinkellner 1989 and Powers 1992a, 1992b, and 1998. For a review of Powers 1998, refer to Wedemeyer 2003.

14. See for instance Hopkins 1999, 2002, and 2006.

4. Collating academic research

I proceeded to search all articles and monographs referring to the *Saṁdhinirmocana Sūtra* I could find at the very beginning of this translation project. In this quest for relevant academic research, I benefited from the excellent bibliography found in Delhey (2013) regarding research done on the *Viniścayasaṁgrahaṇī* of the *Yogācārabhūmi*, which I expanded with a list of complementary reference works (see the bibliography). Among the existing academic literature on the *Saṁdhinirmocana Sūtra*, Schmithausen (2014) stands out and, unsurprisingly, proved to be a major resource for this translation project.

5. Organizing academic resources according to the text structure and specific translation issues

The translation of the title of the text became the object of several discussions among scholars regarding the meaning of the Sanskrit words "*saṁdhi*" and "*nirmocana*" as a consequence of Lamotte's first complete translation of the text.[15] Among the various available options, I opted for simplicity and initially translated the Sanskrit *Saṁdhinirmocana Sūtra* with "The Sutra Unraveling the Intent," which I believe renders accurately the meaning and structure of the text. However, I later chose to translate the title of the text as "The Sutra Elucidating the Intent" to avoid any negative semantic prosody associated with the verb *to unravel*. Both translations make sense since, in this sutra, various interlocutors ask the Buddha repeatedly to explain difficult points in order to clarify the purpose of his seemingly contradictory or complex doctrines on the nature of reality.

Regarding the content of the sutra itself, I proceeded to organize secondary sources by chapter and referenced this research in the notes accompanying my translation.[16] The last chapter of the *Saṁdhinirmocana Sūtra*

15. See Lamotte 1935, 12ff.; Ware 1937; Edgerton 1937; Edgerton 1953, 558; and later Keenan 1980, 126; Powers 1991a; and Powers 1993b, 28ff.

16. Research relevant to terminological choices, syntactic reading of complex passages, and interpretation of the meaning includes Powers 1991b, 1991c, 1993b, 41–77 (chapters 1 to 4); Tillemans 1997 (chapter 1); Matsuda 2013 on Sanskrit terms (chapter 2); Mathes 2007, Matsuda 2013, Tillemans 1997, Wayman 1974 (chapter 3); Brunnhölzl 2018, Buescher 2007, 2008, Katō 2002, Lusthaus 2002, Muller 2011, Schmithausen 1987 and 2014, Waldron 2003

includes a very technical passage on valid cognition (*pramāṇa*) whose definitions predate Dignāga's system of logic. Translating Trisong Detsen's **Samyagvāk-pramāṇoddhṛta-sūtra*, which is a commentary on the teaching on the four principles of reason (*rigs pa bzhi*), would help us better understand pre-Dignāgean Buddhist logic.[17]

6. Translating the text

In this stage of the overall process, I followed Jean-François Billeter's pragmatic approach to the translation of classical Chinese texts. This approach consists in five operations: explanation, or analysis; understanding, or synthesis; target-language formulation; target-language verification; and polishing, or final editing.[18]

The first stage of the translation process is purely analytical. A passage is translated on the basis of lexicographical resources (e.g., dictionaries) and syntactic rules (e.g., grammars). During this operation, it is important to distinguish what is understood and what still remains problematic. All options should be kept open. Interpretations or eisegetical readings should be rejected. From a practical perspective, I systematically used the Mahāvyutpatti to find the Sanskrit terms behind general Tibetan expressions. For technical terms, I relied on Schmithausen (2014) and the academic research mentioned above.

Our Tibetan text is itself a translation. This somewhat complicates our task since we have to decipher the Sanskrit behind the Tibetan in order to make sense of some difficult sentences or passages. However, this approach is necessary on a lexicographical and syntactic level as can be seen in the following examples: One should read the Tibetan *brtsams pa* as *ārabhya*, a Buddhist Hybrid Sanskrit expression that has the meaning of "referring

(chapter 5); Frauwallner 1969, Schmithausen 2014, Takahashi 2006 (chapter 6); Brunnhölzl 2018, Frauwallner 1969, Mathes 2007, Schmithausen 2014, Tillemans 1997, Tucci 1971 (chapter 7); Lamotte 1970, Lin 2010, Matsuda 2013, Schmithausen 1984, 1987, 2005, and 2014, Takasaki 1966 (chapter 8); Obermiller 1933, Matsuda 1995 (chapter 9); Braarvig 1985, Kapstein 1988, Lin 2010, Sakuma 1990, Steinkellner 1989, Xing 2005, Yoshimizu 1996, 2010, and 2022 (chapter 10).

17. For a detailed introduction to this text, see Steinkellner 1989.

18. See Billeter 2014. I would like to thank Professor Tom Tillemans for having drawn my attention to Billeter's principles of translation.

to / having to do with" and not "beginning with."[19] Likewise, *rab tu phye ba* stands for the Sanskrit *prabhāvita*, which in the *Saṁdhinirmocana Sūtra* means "consisting in / characterized as / characterized by" and not "distinguished."[20] The problem is even more acute in the case of Sanskrit compounds that have been translated into Tibetan according to the way they were formulated in Sanskrit. As an illustration of this, compounds ending with *-lakṣaṇa* (Tib. *mtshan nyid*) often make more sense as *bahuvrīhis* than *karmadhārayas* or *tatpuruṣas*, not to mention *dvandvas* in the sutra.[21] Lamotte thus reads *rtog ge kun las 'das mtshan nyid* (*sarvatarkasamatikrāntalakṣaṇa*) as a *bahuvrīhi*,[22] which I believe is appropriate in the context of the passage in question.

Once a "technically correct" translation of the source text has been produced, Billeter advises us to bring together the various elements of a sentence or a passage until we obtain a clear picture of what is said in the source text. This step therefore consists in understanding the meaning of the translated passage by literally seeing (or visualizing) its meaning. In a way, the first operation is about explanation ("das Erklären"), while the second concerns understanding ("das Verstehen"). In this sense, the latter uses the resources of one's imagination and metalinguistic knowledge to establish connections with a web of meaning that is not restricted to the translated sentence or passage alone.

The second operation is therefore a synthesis, a recognition of relations between meaning units of various orders (one would think here of the idea conveyed by the Sanskrit *saṁjñā* and similar terms in which the *upasarga sam-* plays a central role), whereas the first phase is analytical (in the sense of *vicara*, *vicārana*, and *vijñāna*, in which the *upasarga vi-* expresses the notion of taking apart). In fact, translators translate into the target language their comprehension of the source text. They actually never translate the text itself but their understanding or representation of ideas, situations, and emotions conveyed by a text. To illustrate this point, one could mention the problem, encountered by scholars, of translating terms related to meditative practice. The Maitreya chapter of the *Saṁdhinirmocana Sūtra*

19. See Edgerton 1953, 102.
20. See Schmithausen 2014, 400n1770.
21. On Sanskrit nominal compounds, see Tubb and Boose 2007, 85–146.
22. See Lamotte 1935, 174.

is probably the most difficult to understand if one is not familiar with Buddhist practice. Lamotte translates *manasikāra* with "réflection," while Frauwallner uses the literal "observation" ("Beobachtung"). Both of these translation choices obfuscate the meaning of what the term "directing one's attention" actually denotes. This is not in itself a major issue, but if such inaccuracies proliferate in the same passage or chapter, the meaning of the translation becomes unclear, although it may well be technically correct on a syntactic level and lexicographical perspective (at least when it comes to correctly identifying Tibetan technical terms on the basis of the Sanskrit).

In the context of pre-Dignāgean Buddhist logic, chapter 10 represents another case in point. This chapter is indeed replete with abstruse concepts not belonging to the well-researched and documented later systems of Buddhist logic. In this case, translating the many occurrences of the Tibetan connective particle *kyi* in long compounds with the English preposition "of" will not help the reader much, though it will certainly give the translators the peace of mind of having produced a "technically correct" translation. However, I believe that translators have only two options here: (1) take a risk and, for example, tell us if they actually understand the connective *kyi* in the sense of "belonging to," "resulting from," "consisting of," and so on; or (2) admit that they do not understand the source text. In the case of the technical compounds found in chapter 10, I therefore have tried to ask myself: to what these terms actually refer, what could have been the system of logic presented in these pages? For example, I read the Tibetan *gzhan gyi rigs kyi dpe nye bar sbyar ba'i mtshan nyid* (*anyajātīyadṛṣṭāntopasaṁhāralakṣaṇa*)[23] as rendering a Sanskrit *bahuvrīhi*. As a consequence, I translated this long compound with "[The logical proof] characterized by a demonstration through an instance belonging to a different class [of phenomena]."

It goes without saying that these translations are at this stage provisional, as further research on the subject matter is necessary. But in order to translate these technical terms, we cannot just give a technically correct translation of a succession of words. Beyond the first phase of the work, which is purely analytical, we still need to develop a mental representation of the situation presented in the text by establishing relations with a context that might go beyond the text.

In the third operation, Billeter insists on the necessity for translators to

23. See Mvyut 4414.

become writers. They should formulate in the target language their understanding of the source text as accurately and naturally as possible. At this stage, translators should focus on literary elements of the translation, such as idioms, voice, and figures of speech. According to Billeter, difficulties in writing accurately and naturally in the target language are often the direct consequence of not having performed the second operation. The translation might well be technically correct, but it still does not make sense, an experience all translators go through when they fail to understand the meaning (or visualize the situation) referred to by the source text.

In the fourth operation, translators should reflect on the role played by linguistic constraints and conventions in the formulation of the source text as well as those imposed by the target language. What options did the author of the text have in terms of expression? How would someone express the same ideas in the target language? As a consequence, the notion of form and pragmatics in the target language becomes central.

To detail the various operations leading to an actual translation, Vinay and Darbelnet's model is useful.[24] Translators should first identify the units of translation in relation to the translation process: the lexicon (e.g., semantic values, objective and affective aspects, lexical associations and modulations), the syntactic structure (e.g., transpositions between word classes, supplementation of pronouns or conjunctions, modifications in terms of gender, number, characterization, tenses, voice, modality, and verbal aspects), and the message (e.g., meaning, stylistics, pragmatics, topicalization, figures of speech, metalinguistic aspects, specific segmentation of reality). Then translators should examine the descriptive, affective, and intellectual content of the units of translation in the source text to reconstitute the situation at the origin of the message. These two first steps correspond to Billeter's two first operations. Finally, they propose, translators still have to formulate the message in the target language without omitting any relevant element from the source language.

To achieve this, Vinay and Darbelnet argue that translators have only two methods: direct and oblique translation. *Direct translation* includes three strategies:

Borrowing: here, the term in the source language is used in the target

24. See Vinay and Darbelnet 1958.

language to overcome an insuperable metalinguistic lacuna, or it is used because the term is also commonly used in the target language. For instance, I use the Sanskrit terms "bodhisattva" and "nirvana" in my English translation.

Calque: I translated *bodhicitta* with "awakening mind," which is both a lexical and structural calque, i.e., loan translation, a literal word-for-word translation borrowed from another language.

Literal translation: most lists and simple sentences are, for instance, relatively unproblematic direct translations of the source language.

When a literal translation fails to render the message, is structurally impossible, or misleads the reader due to the lack of a corresponding expression belonging to the same register, one should turn to an *oblique translation* method among the following several strategies:

Transposition: here the translator replaces a word class by another. For example, the frequent nominalizations of Sanskrit and Tibetan are turned into verb clauses. The highly technical nature of some terms makes it necessary to reflect the Sanskrit as much as possible while "unpacking" what is a condensed compound. As an illustration, I translated the Sanskrit phrase *tadanyavairūpyopalabdhi* with the English "a perception that does not conform with anything other than the [thing to establish]," in which *vairūpya* is translated as a verb.

The sutra is mostly written in the same way as a treatise (*śāstra*), reflecting what is referred to as the nominal style in Sanskrit, or scholastic Sanskrit, in which the nominalization of verbal clauses by means of compounds or suffixes is common. As is often the case in technical or highly specialized environments, processes or conceptual frameworks are encapsulated as technical terms (often nouns) implying a complex or recurring pattern. As an analogy, think of a medical term such as "hemiglossectomy" standing for the removal of a part of the tongue. The passive impersonal phrase "a hemiglossectomy was performed on the patient at 11 pm" includes the nominalization of an action through a compound (hemiglossectomy). It could be rewritten as "[the surgeon] removed a portion of the patient's tongue at 11 pm." As can be seen from the translations by Lamotte and Frauwallner, nominalization seems to be less of a problem in French and German than it is in modern (American) English in which readability is more of a concern. When translating the *Saṁdhinirmocana Sūtra*, I therefore tried to turn nominal compounds common in scholastic Sanskrit into English verbal sentences by transposing these compounds into verbal sentences. However, since the text is very technical (particularly from chapter 7 onward), I decided in some cases to keep nominal compounds that were indicative of a technical term and not just a nontechnical action or state of affairs. For example, the text mentions throughout a "concept" being referred to a "X" (see, for instance, 7.3–6). Just like the surgical term above, such complex nominal compounds stand for a specific action or concept and are part of a specialist's jargon. Turning these compounds into verbal sentences might have the counterproductive effect of erasing an essential feature of this kind of literature consisting in endless lists of often technical terms. Therefore, in this particular case, it would probably be best to avoid transposition.

Modulation: this strategy implies a change of perspective or standpoint made in order to avoid an awkward rendering of the source language. In its simplest form, translating the Tibetan *sla ba ma yin* (D, folio 25.b, 7.32) with "it is difficult" is an illustration of an optional modulation. Any change of syntactic subject for the sake of clarifying a sentence would be a modulation. Whether this decision is appropriate or not on the part of the translator is something that one should evaluate on a case-by-case basis.

I would like to illustrate this point with issues related to the *nidāna* of the sutra, in which topicalization plays an important role. The first paragraph of the prologue is a presentation of the place where the Buddha is dwelling. The topicalization of the temple (*khang*) is achieved through a succession of compounds, mainly *bahuvrīhis*. Lamotte's translation reflects this thematization to perfection. In contrast, Powers fails to topicalize the palace to the same degree. In his translation, the logical subject of the several clauses describing this palace is sometimes ambiguous. In this case, one should consider the fact that the Sanskrit structure of this paragraph is built on a process of topicalization that we can easily render in English. In a word, we have no reason to alter this literary device by inducing a modulation of the translation through a change of perspective induced, for example, by a modification of the grammatical or logical subject in the target language.

Equivalence: the same situation can be expressed both in the source language and the target language in completely different stylistic and structural ways due to the necessity to resort to idioms in order to convey the message of the source text. For example, I translated the Sanskrit *evam etat* (Tib. *de de bzhin te/no*) literally with "so it is" in English, which is a slightly pompous and old-fashioned expression that no one would probably use today. Instead, one would probably say in an actual dialogue something like "You are right, Dharmodgata" or "This is true, Dharmodgata."[25]

Adaptation: This method aims at replacing altogether a reference to a situation in the source language if it is completely unknown in the target language. I generally try to avoid adaptations while translating, for the simple reason that one has to be certain that, for instance, two different metaphors or examples refer to the same situation or object.

To conclude on this point, it seems to me that a number of fixed or technical expressions in the Kangyur could be translated in a systematic way following Vinay and Darbelnet's approach. This research would establish a set of solid conventions that would improve accuracy and readability.

Returning to Billeter's schema: in his fourth operation—reflecting on linguistic constraints and conventions in the source texts and target language—the translator should verify that what has been translated into the target language corresponds to the meaning of the source text. Do the two texts express the same idea? Do they produce the same effect on the reader? To answer these questions, Billeter recommends reading one's text aloud. During this operation, translators should also check whether the translation fits within a specific cultural register in the target language. Discourses take place within a corpus of existing literature that is culturally determined by centuries of textual production. Some statements from a different cultural background resonate through a web of meaning, discursive practices, or literary figures of speech once expressed in the target language. In fact, the web of meaning of the target language within which the translation is received finds its parallel in the web of meaning within which the source text was produced. Within the source text and culture, concepts, ideas, and references resonate throughout sentences, paragraphs, chapters, works, and genres. For example, some philosophical definitions can represent intratextual and extratextual variations on a theme for which there is no metalinguistic context in the target language. Translators therefore need to understand the text not only as a whole and in relation to its various components, but also in connection with both the source and the target cultures. This is of course particularly true of more "philosophical" texts for

25. Or even "Yep," "I'm with you," "So true," etc.

which it is essential to evaluate how the translation interacts with the webs of meaning of the source and target cultures. Practically, it is important to cross check the consistency (or lack thereof) of meaning units across the text while keeping in mind that the translation is also obviously culturally situated. This process is fundamental because it facilitates the validation (or invalidation) of translation hypotheses resulting from the two first steps of the translation process.

In the context of the *Saṁdhinirmocana Sūtra*, these concerns are compounded by the fact that the sutra can be read as a collection of independent texts that would have been put together during the third or fourth century CE. The academic community considers the sutra to be a highly composite compilation lacking coherence from a philological perspective.[26] Lamotte contends that the first four chapters represent a Prajñāpāramitā perspective for the reasons mentioned above. He sees chapters 5 through 7 as forming a second group of ideas found in the Prajñāpāramitā literature that influenced the Yogāchāra school. Finally, he considers chapters 8 through 10 to be later additions.

It is undeniable that the various recensions in Tibetan and Chinese refer to texts that are quite different in structure. For instance, Paramārtha's translation includes only the first four chapters, which, according to Lamotte, might have originally formed an independent sutra. In addition, it is obvious that the ten chapters of the *Saṁdhinirmocana Sūtra* do not follow a consistent textual pattern. The first six have no title. They are concluded by a few summarizing *gāthās* and a standard formula indicating the name of the person who questioned the Buddha and the number of the chapter (e.g., "This was the chapter of Guṇākara—the sixth chapter"). Chapter 7 has a whole summary of the chapter in the form of a supplement right after the concluding *gāthās*, while in chapter 10 the Buddha is questioned on complementary topics once the concluded *gāthās* have been proclaimed. Chapters 7, 8, 9, and 10 each come to an end with a *nītārthanirdeśa* (instruction of definitive meaning) on the chapter topic. This *nītārthanirdeśa* is referred to as a *saṁdhinirmocana* and used as the chapter title. On account of this, Lamotte surmises that there might have originally been several independent

26. "Une compilation assez maladroite"; see Lamotte 1935, 17. For an extensive discussion on the date and composition of Saṁdh., see Lamotte 1935, 14–25. See also Schmithausen 2014, 354ff. regarding the relation between the various chapters of Saṁdh.

Saṁdhinirmocana sutras that came to be grouped together as the text we know today.

One should also note that the dialogue structure of chapters 1 through 7 differs from that of chapters 8 through 10. In the first group, the Buddha elaborates on a topic in the form of a monologue once his interlocutor has questioned him on a specific topic, whereas in the second group a dialogue takes place through short questions and answers. As a consequence of all these philological divergences, one has to conclude that the text is rather composite in nature and probably the result of a succession of additions and adjustments. In a word, I agree with Schmithausen that the *Saṁdhinirmocana Sūtra* is not an organic whole that would have been composed from the outset in its present form and that its chapters are not mutually dependent.[27] However, this hypothesis should ideally be the object of further research following an approach similar to that of Jonathan Silk's European Research Council project "Open Philology—The Composition of Buddhist Scriptures," in which I have had the good fortune to take part. For this research program, focusing on the Ratnakūṭa collection of sutras, we developed digital and philological tools to identify, analyze, and map the fluidity and modularity of Great Vehicle texts. The multiformity and intertextuality of Great Vehicle sutras are not the result of a linear development from an Ur-text but the expression of oral-formulaic processes of composition and transmission. By applying corpus-based methods, we could better understand the historical development of the complex textual environment of the *Saṁdhinirmocana Sūtra*, which includes several translations and many witnesses of this work.[28]

From the perspective of the narrative and doctrinal content of the Tibetan translation, a somewhat different picture emerges. Even if each chapter does not depend on all others in terms of meaning, there is definitely a progression with regard to the flow of thought in the *Saṁdhinirmocana Sūtra* insofar as later chapters do depend on the definitions and lines of thinking posited in the earlier chapters, a central fact for translators of this complex text. We can perceive this continuity in the intratextual cross-references that create a terminological resonance echoing throughout

27. See Schmithausen 2014, 354–55.

28. On corpus-linguistic methods applied to a large corpus of texts, see Forgues 2024. On digital aligners to produce critical editions of Tibetan canonical texts, see Forgues n.d.

the text. Unraveling these cross-references is as important during the translation process as noting the textual variations indicating a deviation from a specific literary pattern. While translating I thus tried to evaluate the text in terms of regularities and discontinuities in the use of definitions and the flow of meaning unfolding throughout the text. One should therefore temper the impression that the text has been "patched" together on the basis of loosely related texts on the basis of philological arguments whose significance is difficult to assess. For example, the fact that chapter 1 is the only chapter in which a dialogue occurs between two bodhisattvas has never been mentioned by any researcher as a textual inconsistency preventing them from considering the first four chapters as a coherent whole. Minor divergences, therefore, should not deter us from asking ourselves why these chapters were taught or put together in the first place.

I would like to illustrate with a few concrete examples the doctrinal coherence of the text. The term *ādānavijñāna* in 5.3 is also found in 8.37.1.i; the model of the three kinds of essencelessness (*niḥsvabhāvatā*) of chapter 7 corresponds to the model of the three defining characteristics (*lakṣaṇa*) of chapter 6, of which two are foreshadowed in 1.2 through the terms *parikalpa* (*kun tu rtog pa*) and **aparinispanna* (*yongs su ma grub pa*); the other-dependent defining characteristic (*paratantralakṣaṇa*) introduced in chapter 6 is mentioned in 7.10; chapter 8 presupposes chapters 5 and 6;[29] the concluding paragraphs of 7.33 and 8.41 are almost identical; as noted by Schmithausen, *saṁskāranimitta* is referred to in similar ways in both 1.5 and 7.25–27;[30] **viśuddhyālambana* is mentioned with the same function in 4.8, 7.6, 7.25–27, and 8.20; 10.7.2 refers to the seven aspects of true reality (*tathatā*) defined in 8.20.2; 8.21 and 10.7.4.ii contain the same formulation; the famous quote "Whether tathāgatas . . ." is found in 4.10, 7.9, and 10.7.4.vii.d; 10.9 mentions the enumeration *citta*, *manas*, and *vijñāna* exactly in the way it is expressed in 5.1–6; 10.9 enumerates the domains as in 8.23.

On account of the elements adduced above, and with Davidson's principle of charity in mind, I would like to formulate the hypothesis that there is a good reason why these chapters are found in this order: the structure of the text as we know it today is necessary to provide Great Vehicle

29. See Schmithausen 2014, 365.
30. See Schmithausen 2014, 359.

practitioners with a systematic teaching on (1) ultimate reality *qua* basis, which is the nondual inexpressible domain of gnosis (chapters 1 through 4), (2) the path to awakening from the domain of mind to the domain of gnosis (chapters 5 through 9), and (3) ultimate reality *qua* result of the path, which represents a shift in one's basis of existence as one attains the domain of gnosis (chapter 10).[31]

Indeed, it seems impossible to deny that—when considered as a single text and not as a succession of independent texts—the *Saṁdhinirmocana Sūtra* aims at providing a systematic teaching on the Single Vehicle through the three aspects of basis, path, and result in order to solve seeming contradictions and quandaries in doctrines that were of primary importance for followers of the Great Vehicle (e.g., the two truths in chapter 3 and meditative practice in chapter 8). Now, if we read the *Saṁdhinirmocana Sūtra* as a single text, we have to confront the web of meaning found in this text in its entirety with the web of meaning of the target culture in order to avoid potential misunderstandings.

This operation has a major impact on the translation of some key terms, such as *vijñaptimātra*. Since idealism (in the sense that mind is an unchanging essence) is not an option given the teaching imparted in this sutra, I have tried to avoid any potential confusion resulting from an unfortunate choice of terminology. In a word, I would rather stay on the safe side than insert in my translation a potentially misleading term. As a consequence, I decided to translate *vijñaptimātra* as "a mere representation" instead of using nominalizations such as "cognition-only." The first expression is relatively unambiguous in the target culture as it minimizes the risk of misunderstanding the message of the text. Another option would be "just a representation." These formulations mitigate the risk of superimposing an essence on what is meant by *vijñapti*.[32] The formulation "cognition-only" in the sense of "pure cognition" is, in contrast, ambivalent. It could also (but not necessarily) signify that only cognition truly exists and, by extension, that only mind exists as an essence.

In the last step of the translation process, Billeter recommends that translators perform various operations aiming at polishing the translation,

31. In his recent publication, Waldron explains in detail the cognitive reframing of emptiness expounded in the *Saṁdhinirmocana Sūtra* (see Waldron 2023, 147–96).
32. On the usage and various shades of meaning of *vijñapti*, see Hall 1986.

such as replicating the possible effects of semantic resonance throughout the text, improving the connection between sentences and paragraphs, modifying the order of clauses, solving problems of euphony, or editing the translation to make it clearer and simpler by chunking long sentences or eliminating repetitions. To illustrate one of these various tasks in the context of the present project, I decided to review all the terminology pertaining to the semantic field of insight (*vipaśyanā*) after I had finished translating the entire text. I took as a starting point 8.4, in which *vipaśyanā* is defined by means of a series of technical terms, such as *pratyavekṣaṇa*, *vibhājanā*, *pravicaya*, *paritarka*, *parimīmāṁsā*, *nitīraṇa*, and *vitarka*. I first tried to find the best translation for each term in the context of this chapter. Next, I checked the usage of all these terms and other related concepts (e.g., *pratisaṁkhyā*) throughout the text to standardize the corresponding English terminology. I also tried to minimize the use of square brackets indicating additions to the text when these additions were logically implied by the source text. A typology of such situations would include various operations, such as breaking down a compound, clarifying an abbreviated form corresponding to a well-attested collocation, stating a logical subject, object, or verb that is elided in the source text, mentioning the number of a technical term that usually comes as a list of individual items.

Through all these operations, my aim has been to maximize both accuracy and readability while maintaining the consistency of the very systematic presentation of the Great Vehicle developed in the *Saṁdhinirmocana Sūtra*. This text is important in this spiritual tradition, since it condenses all aspects of the Great Vehicle. I hope that this translation will contribute to the improvement of our understanding of the interplay between liberation as a path and primordial freedom as the ground of being.

Part Two

Annotated English Translation

Prologue

Homage to all buddhas and bodhisattvas!

Thus have I heard at one time. The Blessed One was dwelling in an unfathomable palace, built with the blazing seven precious substances,[33] that emitted[34] great light rays suffusing countless universes.[35] Each of its rooms was well arranged, and its design was infinite. It was the undivided mandala, the domain transcending the three worlds. Arising from the supreme roots of virtue of the one who transcends the world,[36] it was

33. *rin po che sna bdun* does not refer only to "jewels," as found in Lamotte (1935) and Keenan (2000). I follow here Powers (1995), Cornu (2005), and Cleary (1999).

34. The logical subject of *'jig rten gyi khams dpag tu med pa rgyas par 'gengs pa'i 'od zer chen po shin tu mnga' ba* is the palace (*khang*). Cornu (2005) and Keenan (2000) seem to read this phrase as a qualifier for the seven precious substances.

35. The first paragraph of the *nidāna* is a presentation of the place where the Buddha is dwelling. As already mentioned in the introduction, a succession of compounds, mainly *bahuvrīhi*s, enables the topicalization of the temple (*khang*). Lamotte's translation reflects this literary device, contrary to Powers who does not topicalize the palace to the same degree on account of some ambiguities regarding the logical subject of a few clauses describing this palace. To illustrate this point, it seems unclear whether the adjectives "steadfast," "enduring," or "free" in Powers' translation qualify the temple or the beings attending it. Cornu mainly follows Powers here, but the grammatical necessity to indicate the gender and number of qualifiers in French limits the risk of confusion, which is obviously not the case in English. Regarding the usage of tenses, Lamotte is the only translator who uses both narrative past and present in this first paragraph. He thus switches from the past tense to the present tense in order to describe the characteristics of the temple, a decision I chose not to follow in the present translation.

36. Lamotte, Cornu, and Powers do not translate the anaphoric pronoun *de* in *'jig rten las 'das pa de'i bla ma'i dge ba'i rtsa ba las byung ba*. Powers explains in a footnote (see Powers 1995, 313, n. 3) that this pronoun refers to gnosis according to Wonch'uk, although his translation does not reflect this interpretation. Since wisdom has not been mentioned earlier in the text and since the pronoun *de* is anaphoric, I read *de* as referring to the Buddha.

characterized by the perfectly pure cognition of the one who has achieved complete mastery.[37] The Abode of the Tathāgata, where the assembly of innumerable bodhisattvas gathered, was attended by countless gods, nāgas, yakṣhas, gandharvas, demigods, garuḍas, kinnaras, mahoragas, humans, and nonhumans. Supported by the great joy and bliss of savoring the Dharma and designed to accomplish the complete welfare of all beings, it was free of any harm caused by the stains of afflictions and clear of any demon. Surpassing all manifestations, this unfathomable palace was displayed by the sovereign power of the Tathāgata. Mindfulness, intelligence, and realization were its pathway;[38] mental stillness and insight were the vehicle leading to it; the great gates of liberation—emptiness, wishlessness, and absence of manifest characteristics—were its entrance. It was set on foundations adorned with an infinite accumulation of excellent qualities, which were like great kings of jeweled lotuses.[39]

Moreover, the concept of "root of virtue" is usually associated with persons, and we have a reference to *dbang sgyur ba* in the next qualifying phrase.

37. The clause *dbang sgyur ba'i rnam par rig pa shin tu rnam par rig pa'i mtshan nyid* is problematic. Lamotte translates it in the following way: "très pur, il se caractérise par une pensée maîtresse de soi." Cornu and Powers follow the reading found in D, folio 2.a; S, folio 4.a; K0774, folio 1.a; L, folio 3.a; and H, folio 3.a (*dbang sgyur ba'i rnam par rig pa shin tu rnam par rig pa'i mtshan nyid*) and render the two occurrences of *rnam par rig pa* by an apposition: "It was characterized by perfect knowledge, the knowledge of one who has mastery" (Powers 1995, 5). However, in F, folio 4.b, we find a variant reading that, I believe, makes more sense: *dbang byed pa'i rnam par rig pa shin tu rnam par dag pa'i mtshan nyid.* The Tibetan verbal prefix *shin tu rnam pa* is used to render the Sanskrit *upasarga* "*su-*" as in *suviśuddha.* In Mvyut 351, *blo shin tu rnam par dag pa* thus translates the Sanskrit *suviśuddhabuddhiḥ.*

38. *nges par 'byung ba.* In Skt. *niḥsaraṇa* or *niryāṇa*, which have the meaning of "setting forth, issue, exit, departure, escape, a road out of town." The analogy here is not about emancipation or renunciation, as Powers and Cornu translated it, but rather with the metaphor of the journey. In that sense, what is meant here is the departure to reach the palace. Lamotte (1935), Keenan (2000), and Cleary (1999) follow Xuanzang's translation: 大念慧行以為游路 (CBETA, Taishō 676). Interestingly enough, F does not have *nges par 'byung ba* but just *'byung ba.*

39. *rin po che'i pad ma'i rgyal po chen po yon tan gyi tshogs mtha' yas pas brgyan pa'i bkod pa la rten pa na bzhugs te.* This clause has been translated in various ways depending on how one understands the compound *rin po che'i pad ma'i rgyal po chen po yon tan gyi tshogs mtha' yas pas.* Lamotte (1935), Powers (1995), and Cornu (2005) read it as a *dvandva*: "Il est orné de qualités infinies, de joyaux, de lotus et de grands rois" (Lamotte 1935, 167); "this palace was adorned with boundless masses of excellent qualities, and with great kingly jeweled lotuses" (Powers 1995, 5–6); "paré d'infinies qualités et de grands lotus royaux incrustés de pierreries" (Cornu 2005, 26). However, it seems to me that it would be better to read this compound as a *karmadhāraya.* Folio 5.a offers a variant reading that could support this interpretation: *yon*

The Blessed One had a perfectly realized mind and was free from dualistic behavior. Absorbed in the Dharma of the nonexistence of defining characteristics, he was residing in the domain of the buddhas. He had attained equality with all buddhas. His realization was unobstructed and his qualities[40] were irreversible. He could not be overcome by objects of experience.[41] His abode was inconceivable.[42] Perfectly skilled in the sameness of the three times,[43] his five bodies were present in all worlds. His knowledge of all phenomena was free from doubt. He understood all practices. His knowledge of phenomena was without uncertainty. His body was unimaginable. He possessed the gnosis that bodhisattvas vow to accomplish.[44] He had attained the nondual abode of the buddhas, the sublime perfection, the supreme indivisible gnosis of the Tathāgata's liberation.[45] He had realized

---

tan gyi tshogs mtha' yas pas / brgyan pa'i rin po che chen po pad mo'i rgyal po'i bkod pa'i gnas na nyan thos kyi dge 'dun tshad med pa dang / thabs gcig tu bzhugs te. In addition to this problem, one should note that Lamotte's translation of the compound *rin po che'i pad ma'i rgyal po chen po* as a *dvandva* is inaccurate here. Powers' reading of this term is correct.

40. *chos* in the sense of qualities as understood by Lamotte (1935), Powers (1995), and Cleary (1999).

41. *spyod yul*; *gocara*. This term refers here to an object perceived by the six senses, so its semantic field pertains to perception as opposed to meditative practice, in which case it would be close in meaning to *ālambana* ("referential object"). Translating all these terms with "object" would conflate these various semantic fields in the context of the present text.

42. *bsam gyis mi khyab pa rnam par 'jog pa* (cf. *rnam par gzhag pa bsam gyis mi khyab pa*; *acintyavyavasthānaḥ*, see Mvyut 359). Compare with Lamotte: "ses attributs sont inconcevables" (Lamotte 1935, 168); Powers: "positing [doctrines] inconceivably" (Powers 1995, 7); Cornu: "il était entré dans l'indicible" (Cornu 2005, 26).

43. *dus gsum mnyam pa nyid tshar phyin pa*; *tryadhvasamatāniryātaḥ* (Mvyut 360). The term *niryāta* means here "adept, perfected, perfectly skilled" (see Edgerton 1953, 303).

44. *byang chub sems dpa' thams cad kyis ye shes yang dag par blangs pa*. See Mvyut 366: *ye shes byang chub sems dpa' thams cad kyis yang dag par mnos pa*; *sarvabodhisattvasampratīcchitajñānaḥ*. One should follow here the translations of Lamotte (1935), Keenan (2000), and Cleary (1999).

45. *de bzhin gshegs pa ma 'dres pa'i rnam par thar par mdzad pa'i ye shes kyi mthar phyin pa*. See Mvyut 368: *de bzhin gshegs pa ma 'dres pa'i rnam par thar pa'i mdzad pa'i ye shes kyi mthar phin pa / de bzhin gshegs pa ma 'dres pa'i rnam par thar par mdzad pa'i ye shes kyi mthar phin pa*; *asaṁbhinnatathāgata-vimokṣajñānaniṣṭhāgataḥ*. See also Mvyut 5192: *dbyer med pa*; *ma 'dres pa*; *ma 'dres pa'm dbyer med pa*; *asaṁbhedaḥ*. If we understand *ma 'dres pa* in the sense of *dbyer med pa*, or even *zung 'jug* (*yuganaddha*), the meaning of the term is "indivisible / in unity," conveying the notion of nonduality of the sameness mentioned several times in this introduction. Lamotte translates *ma 'dres pa* with "non diversifié," Cornu with "distinctement," Powers with "uniquely," Keenan with "unified." I don't think one should understand *ma 'dres pa* with the meaning of *kevala* in the present case since it is associated with *ye shes*

the sameness [of all phenomena], the state of a buddha in which there is neither a center nor a periphery,[46] and reached the ultimate within the domain of truth, the point where the sphere of space ends.[47]

The Blessed One was accompanied by the entire immeasurable assembly of hearers. Children of noble family, they were the heirs of the Buddha. Their minds were liberated, their wisdom was emancipated, and their discipline was completely pure. They happily gathered with those who longed for the Dharma. They had heard much, kept in mind what they had heard, and accumulated [merit from] what they had heard. They excelled in thought, speech, and deeds. Their wisdom was swift, quick, sharp, emancipating,[48] discerning,[49] vast, extensive, profound, and unequaled. They possessed the jewel of wisdom and the three forms of knowledge. They had attained the supreme state of happiness in this life. The purity of their merit,[50] the excellence of their peaceful conduct, their patience, and their gentleness were vast.[51] They were fully engaged in the teaching of the Tathāgata.

The Blessed One was also accompanied by all the innumerable bodhisattvas assembled from various buddha realms. Firmly settled and engaged

---

in other contexts where the idea of being exclusive to a particular person (e.g., buddhas) is negated (see Keenan 1980, 782ff.).

46. *mtha' dang dpung med pa'i sangs rgyas kyis mnyam pa nyid thugs su chud pa*. One should read here instead: *mtha' dang dbus med pa'i sangs rgyas kyi sa mnyam pa nyid bu thugs su chud pa*; *anantamadhyabuddhabhūmisamatādhigataḥ* (see Mvyut 369).

47. D, folio 2.b: *nam mkha'i khams kyi mthas gtugs pa*, which stands in apposition to *chos kyi dbyings kyis klas pa* ("the ultimate within the domain of truth"). See Mvyut 6430: *nam mkha'i dbyings kyi mtha' gtugs pa*, *nam mkha'i khams kyi mthar gtugs* for the Sanskrit *ākāśadhātuparyavasānaḥ*. Compare with Mvyut 371: *nam mkha'i khams kyi mtha' klas pa*, *nam mkha'i khams kyi mthas klas pa* as Tibetan equivalents of *ākāśadhātuparyavasānaḥ*. In Mvyut 431, *don gyi mthar gtugs pa* and *don gyi mthar thug pa* are Tibetan translations of *paryavasitārthaḥ*.

48. *nges par 'byung ba* was used to translate several Sanskrit terms such as *niryāṇika* or naiṣkramya. Powers (1995) and Cornu (2005) translate it as "renunciation."

49. See Mvyut 7450: *nges par rtog pa*/*nges par rtogs pa*; *nirūpaṇā*. Translated by Lamotte with "pénétrante" and by Keenan with "penetrating," while Powers and Cornu opted respectively for "certain realization" and "réalisation certaine."

50. See Mvyut 1113: *yon yongs su sbyong ba chen po*; *mahādakṣiṇāpariṣodhakaḥ*. D, K0774, and H omit *yon*, while F reads *sbyin pa*.

51. Powers (1995) and Cornu (2005) read *nges pa*, but one should read here instead the graphically very similar *des pa* ("gentleness") as in Mvyut 1115 where this expression is also found extensively: *bzod pa dang des pa chen po dang ldan pa*; *mahākṣāntisauratyasamanvāgataḥ*.

in a vast state, they had gone forth through the Dharma of the Great Vehicle. Impartial toward all beings, they were free from all conceptions, conceptualizations, and fabrications. Victorious over all demons and opposition, they were not involved with the considerations of the hearers and solitary realizers. Steadfast through the great joy and happiness of savoring the Dharma, they were free from the five great fears. Solely progressing toward the stages from which there is no regression, they had perfectly actualized the stage in which one pacifies the torment of beings. Among them were thus the bodhisattva-mahāsattvas Gambhīrārthasaṁdhinirmochana, Vidhivatparipṛcchaka, Dharmodgata, Suvishuddhamati, Vishālamati, Guṇākara, Paramārthasamudgata, noble Avalokiteshvara, Maitreya, and Mañjushrī.

Chapter 1

«1.1»At that time, the bodhisattva Vidhivatparipṛcchaka questioned the bodhisattva Gambhīrārthasaṁdhinirmochana on the ultimate whose defining characteristic is inexpressible and nondual:[52] "O son of the Victorious One, when it is said that all phenomena are nondual, what are these phenomena? In what way are they nondual?"

Gambhīrārthasaṁdhinirmochana replied, "Noble son, all phenomena, what we refer to as all phenomena, are of just two kinds: conditioned and unconditioned. With respect to these, the conditioned is neither conditioned nor unconditioned. The unconditioned is neither unconditioned nor conditioned."

«1.2»Vidhivatparipṛcchaka inquired, "O son of the Victorious One, why is the conditioned neither conditioned nor unconditioned and the unconditioned neither unconditioned nor conditioned?"

Gambhīrārthasaṁdhinirmochana answered, "Noble son, the term *conditioned* is a word, a label used by the Teacher. Words that are labels used by the Teacher are conventional expressions arising from imagination. These conventional expressions arising from imagination are always unreal[53] conventional expressions arising from imagination in its diversity. Therefore, the term *conditioned* is not the conditioned. Noble son, the term

52. *brjod du med pa dang / gnyis su med pa'i mtshan nyid.* I read this compound as a *bahuvrihi.* The full clause [*brjod du med pa dang / gnyis su med pa'i mtshan nyid*] + [*don dam pa*] is a *karmadhāraya* meaning literally "the ultimate that is that whose defining characteristic is inexpressible and absolute." Powers' suggestion is also possible here ("the ultimate whose defining characteristic is inexpressible and non-dual"). Lamotte leaves out *mtshan nyid.* Cornu somewhat mixes qualifiers and qualified terms in his rendering of this clause.

53. *yongs su ma grub pa*; probably for *aparinispanna.* This paragraph establishes the opposition between the imaginary (*parikalpita*) and the actual (*parinispanna*). These two aspects are found in the teaching on the three kinds of essencelessness: see chapters 6–8.

unconditioned is also included within conventions, just as expressions other than conditioned and unconditioned are and will [always] be. One might object that there is, however, no expression in the absence of the object [to which it refers]. What then is this object? It is the complete and perfect awakening to inexpressible [reality] through the sublime gnosis and vision[54] of the noble ones.[55] But in order[56] to lead [others] to the perfect realization of this very inexpressible nature of phenomena, the Teacher labels this object with the term *conditioned*.

«1.3» "Noble son, the term *unconditioned* is also a word, a label used by the Teacher. Words that are labels used by the Teacher are conventional expressions arising from imagination.[57] These conventional expressions arising from imagination are always conventional expressions deprived of any actuality that arise from imagination in its diversity. Therefore, the term *unconditioned* is not the unconditioned. Noble son, the term *conditioned* is also included within conventions, just as expressions other than conditioned and unconditioned are and will [always] be. One might object that there is, however, no expression in the absence of the object [to which it refers]. What then is this object? It is the complete and perfect awakening to inexpressible [reality] through the sublime gnosis and vision of the noble ones. But in order to lead [others] to the perfect realization of this very inexpressible nature of phenomena, the Teacher labels this object with the term *unconditioned*."

«1.4» Vidhivatparipṛcchaka asked, "O son of the Victorious One, as the noble ones completely and perfectly awaken to inexpressible [reality] through their sublime gnosis and perception, why do they label this object with the terms *conditioned* and *unconditioned* in order to lead [others] to the perfect realization of this very inexpressible nature of phenomena?"

Gambhīrārthasaṁdhinirmochana replied, "Noble son, it is like the fol-

54. *shes pa dang mthong ba*; *jñānadarśana*. D, folio 3.b: *shes pa* but F, folio 6.b; S, folio 5.a; VD, folio 44.b: *ye shes*. I emended the text in this way throughout the sutra since this expression is repeated several times.

55. Xuanzang's translation reads 謂諸聖者以聖智聖見離名言故現等正覺 (CBETA, Taishō 676).

56. As noted by Tillemans (1997), Powers reads *phyir* in the sense of "because" here. Keenan and Cleary's readings of Xuanzang's translation (為慾令他現等覺故, CBETA, Taishō 676) agree with Lamotte's and Tillemans' understanding of this passage.

57. *ston pas btags pa'i tshig yin te*. VD, folio 44.b: om.

lowing example: A magician or his skillful apprentice, finding himself at the juncture of four great roads, assembles grass, leaves, twigs, pebbles, or stones and produces all kinds of magical illusions, such as regiments of elephants, horses, chariots, and soldiers or collections of jewels, pearls, beryl, seashells, crystal, and coral, as well as an abundance of wealth and grain in treasuries and granaries. At that time, in the presence of these illusions, those who are naive, slow-witted, or confused, not perceiving the grass, leaves, twigs, pebbles, or stones, see and hear those magic tricks and think that whatever appears exists—that these regiments of elephants, horses, chariots, and soldiers or collections of jewels, pearls, beryl, seashells, crystal, and coral, as well as this abundance of wealth and grain, treasuries and granaries, exist. Clinging to these magical illusions according to the way they see and hear things and strongly believing in them, they express themselves through conventions, such as 'This one is true but the other is false.' They still need to examine these illusions.

"Those who are not naive or confused but have wisdom perceive the grass, leaves, twigs, pebbles, or stones. They see and hear those magic tricks and understand that whatever appears does not exist—that these regiments of elephants, horses, chariots, and soldiers or collections of jewels, pearls, beryl, seashells, crystal, and coral, as well as this abundance of wealth and grain, treasuries and granaries, do not exist. Yet they understand that the conception of an elephant regiment exists since its manifestation as a conception through an expedient[58] exists, as do the manifestations as conceptions of regiments of horses, chariots, and soldiers or collections of jewels, pearls, beryl, seashells, crystal, and coral, as well as this abundance of wealth and grain, treasuries and granaries, together with other similar manifestations. So they understand that all those magical illusions, these magical illusions deceiving the eye, exist [in the way magical illusions do].[59] Thinking in this way, [these wise beings] do not express themselves through conventions, such as 'This one is true but the other is false,' on account of clinging to these magical illusions in the way they see and hear things and thus strongly believing in them.[60] However, they do express themselves through

58. *rnam grangs*; *paryāya*. The Dunhuang manuscript of the sutra instead has *gzhung du 'du shes* (n°194 folio 62.a; see Hakayama 1984, 187).

59. See section 1.5.

60. VD, folio 45.b, reads the demonstrative pronoun as a plural (i.e., *de dag*) throughout this paragraph.

conventions in order to convey the true nature[61] [of these illusions to others], although they do not need to examine further these illusions.[62]

«1.5»"Likewise, some childish or ordinary beings have not attained the transcendent sublime wisdom. They have not understood that the nature of all phenomena is inexpressible. When those beings perceive conditioned and unconditioned phenomena, they believe that whatever appears as a conditioned or unconditioned phenomenon exists, and they express themselves through conventions, such as 'This one is true but the other is false,' on account of clinging to these appearances according to the way they see and hear things and thus strongly believing in them. They still need to examine these appearances.

"With regard to this, some beings who are not childish and have seen the truth have attained the transcendent sublime wisdom. They have understood that the nature of all phenomena is inexpressible. When they perceive conditioned and unconditioned phenomena, they believe that whatever appears as a conditioned or unconditioned phenomenon does not exist. However, with respect to these appearances, they think that the conceptions in terms of conditioned and unconditioned, the manifestation of conceptions through an expedient in terms of conditioned and unconditioned, the occurrence of conceptualization, and the manifest characteristic of conditioned phenomena exist in the way magical illusions do. That which deludes the mind exists [in the way magical illusions do].[63] Thinking in that

61. *'di ltar don* in the sense of *yathārtha*.

62. Powers' and Cornu's translations are inaccurate here: "Subsequently they do not make the conventional designations: 'This is true, the other is false.' They make conventional designations because they completely understand the object in this way." (Powers 1995, 17). "Comme ils connaissent parfaitement le sens réel de ces phénomènes . . ." (Cornu 2005, 32). Lamotte seems to have translated 1.4 on the basis of the Chinese. In addition, *rjes su* should be read as *rjes su tha snyad* for *anuvyavahāra*.

63. Lamotte's rather free translation of 1.5 fails to render the opposition between what does not exist and what does, according to the sutra: *'di snyam du sems te / 'dus byas dang / 'dus ma byas snang ba gang yin pa 'di ni med kyi / gang la 'dus byas dang 'dus ma byas kyi 'du shes dang / 'dus byas dang / 'dus ma byas kyi rnam grangs kyi [F.5.a] 'du shes 'byung ba / rnam par rtog pa las byung ba / 'du byed kyi mtshan ma sgyu ma lta bu 'di ni yod / blo rnam par rmongs par byed pa 'di ni yod do.* The first chapter gives an introduction to central concepts, such as conditioned/unconditioned, existent/nonexistent, imaginary/actual. It prefigures the treatment of the two truths (*bden pa gnyis*; *satyadvaya*) in chapter 3 as well as that of the three natures/essences and three kinds of nonexistence of nature/essence (*ngo bo nyid [med pa] nyid*; *[niḥ] svabhāvatā*) expounded in Saṁdh. (cf. chapters 6–8).

way, they do not express themselves through conventions, such as 'This one is true but the other is false,' on account of clinging to these appearances according to the way they see and hear things and thus strongly believing in them. However, they do express themselves through conventions in order to convey the true nature [of these appearances to others], although they do not need to further examine these appearances.

"Noble son, the noble ones are thus completely and perfectly awakened to inexpressible [reality] through their sublime gnosis and vision of this object, but in order to lead [others] to the perfect realization of this very inexpressible nature of phenomena, they label this object with the terms *conditioned* and *unconditioned*."

«1.6» At that time, the bodhisattva Gambhīrārthasaṁdhinirmochana recited these verses:

> "The profound, which is inaccessible to foolish beings,
> Inexpressible and nondual, has been taught by the Victorious One.
> Yet fools deluded by ignorance
> Take delight in mental elaborations and dwell on duality.
>
> "Deprived of understanding, afflicted by misunderstanding,
> They will be reborn as sheep or oxen.
> Casting aside the words of the wise,
> They will wander in samsara for a great length of time."

This was the chapter of the bodhisattva Gambhīrārthasaṁdhinirmochana—the first chapter.

Chapter 2

«2.1» Then the bodhisattva Dharmodgata spoke these words: "Blessed One, very long ago in ancient times, beyond as many universes as there are grains of sand in seventy-seven Ganges rivers, I was residing in the world Kīrtimat of the tathāgata Vishālakīrti. There I saw 7,700,000 non-Buddhists, together with their teachers, who had gathered in one place to consider the ultimate defining characteristic of phenomena.[64] Although they had examined, analyzed, investigated, and considered in detail the ultimate defining characteristic of phenomena, they did not understand it. They had changing opinions, lacked certainty, and were slow-witted as well as argumentative. Insulting one another with harsh words, they became abusive, agitated, unprincipled, and violent. Then, Blessed One, I thought to myself, 'This is so sad, and yet how marvelous, how wonderful are the manifestations of the tathāgatas in the world and, through their manifestations, the realization and actualization of the ultimate whose defining characteristic is beyond all speculation!'"[65]

«2.2» The Blessed One answered the bodhisattva Dharmodgata: "So it is, Dharmodgata. So it is. I have completely and perfectly awakened to the ultimate characterized as being beyond all speculation. Yet,[66] after I

64. *brtsams pa*; *ārabhya* with the meaning of "referring to / having to do with," a frequent occurrence in Saṁdh. See Edgerton 1953, 102.

65. *rtog ge thams cad las yang dag par 'das pa*; *sarvatarkasamatikrānta*. Regarding the translation of the term *rtog ge* (*tarka*), Powers 1995, 25, suggests "argumentation," but the emphasis in the present context is not on logical reasoning. The term *tarka* denotes here any kind of assumption, presupposition, representation, or conjecture regarding the absolute that is the product of the intellect (*manas*).

66. The English translation of this passage should convey the paradox of the situation. Although the ultimate is inexpressible, the Buddha gave countless teachings. Syntactic connective particles between clauses about the inexpressible ultimate and the domain of expression and reasoning have therefore an adversative meaning in the present paragraph: *ngas ni*

attained complete and perfect awakening, I communicated through words, gave explanations, established distinctions, expressed myself through conventions, and imparted teachings. One might ask why I did this. I have explained that the ultimate is what is cognized by noble beings in a personal and intuitive way,[67] whereas ordinary beings' knowledge [resulting from interacting] with one another belongs to the domain of speculation.[68] Therefore, Dharmodgata, you should know in this way through this approach that the ultimate is what is characterized as transcending all speculation. Moreover, Dharmodgata, I have explained that the ultimate represents the domain in which there is no manifest characteristic,[69] whereas speculation is the domain of manifest characteristic. Therefore, Dharmodgata, you should know in this way through this approach that the ultimate is what is characterized as transcending all speculation. Moreover, Dharmodgata, I have explained that the ultimate is inexpressible, whereas speculation is the domain of verbalization. Therefore, Dharmodgata, you should know in this way through this approach that the ultimate is what is characterized as transcending all speculation. Moreover, Dharmodgata, I have explained that the ultimate is free from all conventions, whereas speculation is the domain of conventions. Therefore, Dharmodgata, you should know in this way through this approach that the ultimate is what is characterized as tran-

---

don dam pa rtog ge thams cad las yang dag par 'das pa'i mtshan nyid mngon par rdzogs par sangs rgyas te / mngon par rdzogs par sangs rgyas nas kyang bsnyad cing gsal bar byas / rnam par phye / gdags par byas / rab tu bstan to / de ci'i phyir zhe na. Lamotte's and Powers' translations do not make this point clear.

67. *so so(r) rang rig pa*; *pratyātmavedya/pratyātmavedanīya/pratyātmajñāna/prātyatmam* (see Schmithausen 2014, 346), in the sense of realizing or understanding for oneself in an intuitive way, as personal experience. Powers' translation does not reflect the meaning of this term: "I have explained that the ultimate is realized individually by the Aryas, while objects collectively known by ordinary beings [belong to] the realm of argumentation." In the sutra, *so so(r) rang rig pa* is a synonym or a qualifier of *ye shes* (*jñāna*).

68. Lamotte translates *rtog ge'i spyod yul* by "affaire de tradition"; see Lamotte 1935, 173. Beyond the fact that this is wrong, it is worth noting that the opposition here is between the intuitive and personal knowledge of the noble beings and the intellectual and transactional knowledge of ordinary beings, namely, between gnosis and mind. Powers 1995, 27, reflects the personal aspect of *so sor rang gi rig* but not its intuitive quality.

69. *mtshan ma*; *nimitta*. Although "notion" would fit well here, one should keep in mind that *nimitta* as a polysemic term denotes manifest characteristic throughout the sutra. However, it is clear that "manifest characteristic" and "notion" are two terms that are joined at the hip from the perspective of the doctrine expounded in Saṁdh. Please see appendix I on this choice of translation.

scending all speculation. Moreover, Dharmodgata, I have explained that the ultimate is devoid of argumentative disputation, whereas speculation is the domain of argumentative disputation. Therefore, Dharmodgata, you should know in this way through this approach that the ultimate is what is characterized as transcending all speculation.[70]

«2.3»"Dharmodgata, it is like this: beings who have only tasted pungent or bitter flavors their entire lives cannot imagine, infer, or appreciate the taste of honey and sugar. Those who have indulged in desire and have been burnt by the torment of desire for a long time cannot imagine, infer, or appreciate the inner happiness of the recluse, which is independent from all manifest characteristics related to form, sound, smell, taste, and contact. Those who have indulged and taken delight in conversations for a long time cannot imagine, infer, or appreciate the inner happiness of the noble beings who remain silent. Those who have indulged and taken delight in conventions for a long time through seeing, hearing, discriminating, and cognizing cannot imagine, infer, or appreciate the cessation of all conventions, the nirvana that is the extinction of transitory aggregates. Dharmodgata, it is like this: Those who have indulged and taken delight in argumentative disputations for a long time on account of their attachment to the self cannot imagine, infer, or appreciate that there is no attachment to the self and no argumentative disputations in Uttarakuru.

"Dharmodgata, likewise, those who [have indulged for a long time in] speculation cannot imagine, infer, or appreciate the ultimate whose defining characteristic transcends all speculation."

«2.4»Then, at that moment, the Blessed One spoke these verses:

"It is the domain whose characteristic must be intuitively cognized,
Beyond all expressions, apart from all conventions,

70. In 2.2, the Buddha mentions a paradox. He gives explanations about the ultimate in speculative terms, although the ultimate is inexpressible. This paradox is best rendered in English or French by reading the particle *la* in the statements in question as having an adversative meaning. For example: *chos 'phags gzhan yang don dam pa ni tha snyad thams cad yang dag par chad pa yin par ngas bshad la / rtog ge ni tha snyad kyi spyod yul yin te.*

And free from argumentative disputations—[71]
Such is the ultimate whose characteristic transcends all speculation."[72]

This was the chapter of the bodhisattva Dharmodgata—the second chapter.

71. The Turfan Sanskrit fragment found by Matsuda reads *paramārtha*[*dhar*]*mā vigatābhilāpaḥ* at the end of chapter 2's closing *gāthā* (cf. Sanskrit text in Matsuda 2013, 940 *ad* Lamotte 1935 VIII.41). In D, folio 6.b, and F, folio 10.b, I have instead the Tibetan term *rtsod dang bral ba*. It is possible that *brjod med* in line 2 and *rtsod dang bral ba* were inverted *metri causae*.

72. Powers reads *don dam pa* and *mtshan nyid* as being in apposition in the sentence *de* [i.e., *don dam pa*] *ni rtog ge kun las 'das mtshan nyid*. Lamotte reads *rtog ge kun las 'das mtshan nyid* (*sarvatarkasamatikrāntalakṣaṇa*) as a *bahuvrīhi*, which is much better. See Powers 1995, 31, and Lamotte 1935, 174.

Chapter 3

«3.1» Then the bodhisattva Suvishuddhamati addressed the Blessed One, "Blessed One, at an earlier time, you spoke these words: 'The ultimate is subtle and profound. Characterized as transcending what is distinct or indistinct[73] [from conditioned phenomena], it is difficult to understand.' How wonderful indeed are these words of yours! Blessed One, regarding this point, I once saw many bodhisattvas who, having attained the stage of engagement through aspiration,[74] assembled in one place to discuss in the following way whether conditioned phenomena and the ultimate are distinct or indistinct. Among them, some declared, 'The defining characteristic of conditioned phenomena and the defining characteristic of the ultimate are indistinct.'[75] Others replied, 'It is not the case that the defining characteristic of conditioned phenomena and the defining characteristic of the ultimate are indistinct, for they are distinct indeed.' Some others, who were perplexed and lacked certainty, said, 'Some pretend that the defining characteristic of conditioned phenomena and the defining characteristic

73. I am using the adjective "indistinct" here in the sense of the first definition given in the Oxford English Dictionary: "1. Not distinct or distinguished from each other, or from something else; not kept separate or apart in the mind or perception; not clearly defined or marked off." *Oxford English Dictionary Online*, s.v. "indistinct," accessed July 20, 2020, https://www-oed-com.ezproxy.leidenuniv.nl:2443/view/Entry/94602.

74. *mos pa*; *praṇidhāna*. See *mos pa spyod pa'i sa*. See Mvyut 897: *mos pa spyod pa'i sa*; *adhimukticaryābhūmiḥ*.

75. Schmithausen reads *don dam pa'i mtshan nyid* (*paramārthalakṣaṇa*) as "the defining characteristic that is the ultimate" in 3.5 (see Schmithausen 2014, 558, §512.3). However, Saṁdh. chapter 3 is about conditioned phenomena in relation to the ultimate when their respective defining characteristics are examined. The question here is not to determine whether the ultimate is the defining characteristic of conditioned phenomena. Rather, it is to determine whether the conditioned and the ultimate are different by examining their defining characteristics. Therefore, I read *don dam pa'i mtshan nyid* as "the defining characteristic of the ultimate," namely, as a genitive *tatpuruṣa* and not as a *karmadhāraya*.

of the ultimate are distinct. Some pretend that they are indistinct. Which bodhisattvas speak the truth? Which speak falsity? Which are mistaken? Which are not?' Blessed One, I thought to myself, 'So none of these noble sons understands the ultimate whose subtle defining characteristic transcends whether it is distinct or indistinct from conditioned phenomena. These bodhisattvas are truly[76] naive, confused, dull, unskilled, and mistaken.' "

«3.2» The Blessed One replied to the bodhisattva Suvishuddhamati, "So it is, Suvishuddhamati. So it is. Indeed, none of these noble sons understands the ultimate whose subtle defining characteristic transcends whether it is distinct or indistinct from conditioned phenomena. These [bodhisattvas] are truly naive, confused, dull, unskilled, and mistaken. Why is this so? Suvishuddhamati, it is because those who analyze conditioned phenomena in this way neither realize nor actualize the ultimate.

«3.3» "Why? Suvishuddhamati, if the defining characteristic of conditioned phenomena and the defining characteristic of the ultimate were indistinct, [even] spiritually immature people—all ordinary beings—would, as a consequence, realize the truth. As mere ordinary beings,[77] not only would they attain nirvana, the unsurpassable good,[78] but they would also fully and completely awaken to unsurpassable, complete, and perfect awakening.

"If the defining characteristic of conditioned phenomena and the defining characteristic of the ultimate were distinct, even those who realize the truth would, as a consequence, not be detached from the manifest characteristics of conditioned phenomena. Since they would not be detached from the manifest characteristics of conditioned phenomena, they would also not be liberated from the bondage of manifest characteristics. If they were not liberated from the bondage of manifest characteristics, they would

76. To render *sha stag*.

77. I did not translate the phrase *so so'i skye bo kho nar gyur bzhin du* in an adversative mode (e.g., "though merely ordinary") because the same phrase is found in the next paragraph in a parallel construction where the syntax in relation to the meaning cannot be interpreted to express contrast. Here *bzhin du* stands for *yathā* in the sense of "as" (i.e., "en tant que" in French).

78. *grub pa dang bde ba*; *yogakṣema* (see Edgerton 1953, 448a,b). Refer to Tillemans 1997, 157ff for a discussion of Powers' rendering of the term in his translation (Powers 1995). Lamotte translates this term with "de sécurité suprême." See Lamotte 1935, 175.

not be liberated from the bondage of corruption. If they were not liberated from these two kinds of bondage, those who realize the truth would neither attain nirvana, the unsurpassable good, nor fully and completely awaken to the unsurpassable, complete, and perfect awakening.

"Suvishuddhamati, ordinary beings do not realize the truth and,[79] as mere ordinary beings, neither do they attain nirvana, the unsurpassable good, nor do they fully and completely awaken to the unsurpassable, complete, and perfect awakening. For these reasons, it is not correct to say that the defining characteristic of conditioned phenomena and the defining characteristic of the ultimate are indistinct. Regarding this point, you should know through this approach that those who consider the defining characteristic of conditioned phenomena and the defining characteristic of the ultimate to be indistinct are not right but wrong.

"Suvishuddhamati, it is not the case that those who realize the truth are not detached from the manifest characteristic of conditioned phenomena, for they are indeed detached from it.[80] Neither are they not liberated from

79. I linked the two clauses with "and" because these two clauses are part of the logical argument on being "not different." We have here a relative-correlative syntactic structure: *gang gi phyir . . . de'i phyir* (i.e., *yasmāt . . . tasmāt*). The first two clauses linked by "and" represent the *hetu* ("premise" or "reason") posited by *yasmāt*. The logical structure of the paragraph is "since (1), (2), and (3), therefore (4)" [the conclusion that is stated in the very next sentence "For this reason . . ."]: "Suvishuddhamati, ordinary beings (1) do not realize the truth and, as mere ordinary beings, (2) neither do they attain nirvana, the unsurpassable good, (3) nor do they fully and completely awaken to the unsurpassable, complete, and perfect awakening. For these reasons [*de'i phyir*, referring to (1), (2), and (3)], it is not correct to say that the defining characteristic of conditioned phenomena and the defining characteristic of the ultimate are indistinct." D, folio 7.b: *blo gros shin tu rnam dag gang gi phyir so so'i skye bo bden pa mthong ba ma yin / so so'i skye bo kho nar gyur bzhin du grub pa dang / bde ba bla na med pa'i mya ngan las 'das pa 'thob par yang mi 'gyur / bla na med pa yang dag par rdzogs pa'i byang chub mngon par rdzogs par 'tshang rgya bar mi 'gyur ba de'i phyir 'du byed kyi mtshan nyid dang / don dam pa'i mtshan nyid tha dad pa ma yin zhes bya bar mi rung ste.*

80. This entire paragraph is problematic in D: *blo gros shin tu rnam dag gang gi phyir bden pa mthong ba rnams 'du byed kyi mtshan ma* ***dang bral ba ma yin gyi*** */ bral ba kho na yin pa dang / bden pa mthong ba mtshan ma'i 'ching ba las rnam par* ***grol ba ma yin gyi*** */ rnam par grol ba yin pa dang / bden pa mthong ba gnas ngan len gyi 'ching ba las rnam par* ***grol ba ma yin gyi*** */ rnam par grol ba dang / 'ching ba de gnyi ga las rnam par grol na grub pa dang / bde pa bla na [F.8.a] med pa'i phyir mya ngan las 'das pa 'thob par 'gyur ba dang / bla na med pa yang dag par rdzogs pa'i byang chub mngon par rdzogs par 'tshang rgya bar yang 'gyur ba.* However, Lamotte, Keenan, and Cleary translate the phrases in bold with a double negation. If we look at the same paragraph in F, folio 10.a, we find an interesting textual variant in which the expected double negation is found: *ma bral ba'ang ma yin te* and *ma grol ba'ang ma yin te*, just

the bondage of manifest characteristic, for they are indeed liberated from it. Nor are they not liberated from the bondage of corruption, for they are indeed liberated from it. Since they are liberated from these two kinds of bondage, not only do they attain nirvana, the unsurpassable good, but they will also fully and completely awaken to the unsurpassable, complete, and perfect awakening.[81] For all these reasons, it is not correct to say that the defining characteristic of conditioned phenomena and the defining characteristic of the ultimate are distinct. Regarding this point, you should know through this approach that those who consider the defining characteristic of conditioned phenomena and the defining characteristic of the ultimate to be distinct are not right but wrong.

«3.4» "Moreover, Suvishuddhamati, if the defining characteristic of con-

---

like in Xuanzang's translation (由此道理當知一切非如理行 不如正理善清淨慧。由於今時非見諦者。於諸行相不能除遣。然能除遣非見諦者。CBETA, Taishō 676). Powers chose to translate this passage without proceeding to any emendation, which makes little sense from the perspective of the argument expounded in this section of the text: "Suvishuddhamati, it is not the case that seers of truth are free from the signs of the compounded; they are simply free. Moreover, seers of truth are not liberated from the bondage of signs, but they are liberated. Seers of truth are not liberated from the bondage of errant tendencies, but they are liberated." (Powers 1995, 41).

81. We have here again a complex relative-correlative syntactic structure: *gang gi phyir . . . de'i phyir* (i.e., *yasmāt . . . tasmāt*). All the clauses between *gang gi phyir* and *de'i phyir* represent the *hetu* ("premise" or "reason") posited by *yasmāt*. The logical structure of the paragraph is "since (1), (2), (3), (4), therefore (5)" [the conclusion that is stated in the very next sentence, "For all these reasons, . . ."]: "Suvishuddhamati, it is not the case that (1) those who realize the truth are not detached from the manifest characteristic of conditioned phenomena, for they are indeed detached from it. (2) Neither are they not liberated from the bondage of manifest characteristics, for they are indeed liberated from it. (3) Nor are they not liberated from the bondage of corruption, for they are indeed liberated from it. (4) Since they are liberated from these two kinds of bondage, [F.8.a] not only do they attain nirvana, the unsurpassable good, but they will also fully and completely awaken to the unsurpassable, complete, and perfect awakening. (5) For all these reasons [*de'i phyir* referring to (1), (2), (3), and (4)], it is not correct to say that the defining characteristic of conditioned phenomena and the defining characteristic of the ultimate are distinct." D, folios 7.b–8.a: *blo gros shin tu rnam dag gang gi phyir bden pa mthong ba rnams 'du byed kyi mtshan ma dang bral ba ma yin gyi / bral ba kho na yin pa dang / bden pa mthong ba mtshan ma'i 'ching ba las rnam par grol ba ma yin gyi / rnam par grol ba yin pa dang / bden pa mthong ba gnas ngan len gyi 'ching ba las rnam par grol ba ma yin gyi / rnam par grol ba dang / 'ching ba de gnyi ga las rnam par grol na grub pa dang / bde ba bla na med pa'i phyir mya ngan las 'das pa 'thob par 'gyur ba dang / bla na med pa yang dag par rdzogs pa'i byang chub mngon par rdzogs par 'tshang rgya bar yang 'gyur ba de'i phyir 'du byed kyi mtshan nyid dang / don dam pa'i mtshan nyid tha dad pa zhes byar mi rung ste.*

ditioned phenomena and the defining characteristic of the ultimate were indistinct, then, just as the defining characteristic of conditioned phenomena is encompassed by the defining characteristic of affliction, so too would the defining characteristic of the ultimate be included in the defining characteristic of affliction.

"However, Suvishuddhamati, if the defining characteristic of conditioned phenomena and the defining characteristic of the ultimate were distinct, then the defining characteristic of the ultimate could not be the universal defining characteristic within all the defining characteristics of conditioned phenomena.

"Suvishuddhamati, the defining characteristic of the ultimate is not encompassed by the defining characteristic of affliction, and the defining characteristic of the ultimate is the universal defining characteristic within all the defining characteristics of conditioned phenomena. For these reasons, it is not correct to say that the defining characteristic of conditioned phenomena and the defining characteristic of the ultimate are either indistinct or distinct. Regarding this point, you should know through this approach that those pretending that the defining characteristic of conditioned phenomena and the defining characteristic of the ultimate are indistinct or distinct are not right but wrong.

«3.5» "Moreover, Suvishuddhamati, if the defining characteristic of conditioned phenomena and the defining characteristic of the ultimate were not distinct, then, just as the defining characteristic of the ultimate is not specific to any defining characteristic of conditioned phenomena, so too would all defining characteristics of conditioned phenomena not be specific to any conditioned phenomenon, and yogis would also not look for the ultimate beyond whatever they see, hear, distinguish, or know with regard to conditioned phenomena.[82]

"However, Suvishuddhamati, if the defining characteristic of conditioned phenomena and the defining characteristic of the ultimate were distinct, then the mere selflessness and essencelessness of conditioned phenomena would not be the defining characteristic of the ultimate. The defining characteristic of affliction and the defining characteristic of purity themselves would be simultaneously established as distinct defining characteristics of conditioned phenomena.

82. On a similar line of thought, see 4.10.

"Suvishuddhamati, the defining characteristics of conditioned phenomena are specific and not unspecific to conditioned phenomena; yogis do look for the ultimate beyond whatever they see, hear, distinguish, or know with regard to conditioned phenomena; the ultimate is indeed characterized by the mere selflessness and essencelessness of conditioned phenomena; and the defining characteristic of affliction and the defining characteristic of purity also are not simultaneously established as distinct defining characteristics of conditioned phenomena. For all these reasons, it is not correct to say that the defining characteristic of conditioned phenomena and the defining characteristic of the ultimate are neither indistinct nor distinct. Regarding this point, you should know through these approaches that those pretending that the defining characteristic of conditioned phenomena and the defining characteristic of the ultimate are indistinct or distinct are not right but wrong.

«3.6» "Suvishuddhamati, it is like this: It is not easy to decide[83] whether the whiteness of the conch is distinct or indistinct from the defining characteristic of the conch, likewise with the yellowness of gold. It is not easy to decide whether the quality of the sound produced by a vīṇā is distinct or indistinct from the defining characteristic of sound, likewise with aloe and its fragrance, pepper and its heat, myrobalan and its astringency, cotton and its softness, and clarified butter and butter. Thus it is not easy to decide whether the impermanence of all conditioned phenomena is distinct or indistinct from the defining characteristic of conditioned phenomena, likewise with the suffering of all beings with outflows and the defining characteristic of beings with outflows, as well as the selflessness of all phenomena and the defining characteristic of phenomena.

"Suvishuddhamati, it is like this: It is not easy to decide whether the defining characteristic of restless desire and the defining characteristic of afflictions are distinct or indistinct from the defining characteristic of desire. You should know it is just like this with anger and delusion, too. Likewise, Suvishuddhamati, you should not see anything good[84] in deciding whether the defining characteristic of conditioned phenomena and the

83. *gdags pa*; *prajñapti*. Lamotte translates this term with "dire." This does not convey the meaning of *gdags pa*, which implies the idea of imputation, intimation, conceptualization, or representation. Here, in the sense of "decide," see Edgerton 1953, 359.

84. *mi bzod*; *na kṣamate*, *na kṣamati* (see Edgerton 1953, 199). Pāli: *khamati* (see *The Pali–English Dictionary* [Rhys-Davids and Stede 1921], 234).

defining characteristic of the ultimate are distinct or indistinct. In this way, Suvishuddhamati, I have completely and fully awakened to the ultimate that is subtle, extremely subtle, [profound], extremely profound, difficult to understand, extremely difficult to understand, and characterized as transcending being distinct or indistinct from conditioned phenomena.[85] Yet, after I attained complete and perfect awakening, I communicated through words, gave explanations, established distinctions, expressed myself through conventions, and imparted teachings."[86]

«3.7» Then, at that moment, the Blessed One spoke these verses:

> "The defining characteristics of the domains of conditioned
> phenomena and of the ultimate
> Are free from being distinct or indistinct.[87]
> Those who imagine them to be distinct or indistinct are mistaken.
>
> "As beings practice mental stillness and insight,
> They will be liberated from the bonds of corruption
> And the bonds of manifest characteristic."[88]

This was the chapter of the bodhisattva Suvishuddhamati—the third chapter.

85. D: *blo gros shin tu rnam dag ngas ni de ltar don dam pa phra ba mchog tu phrag mchog tu zab pa / rtogs par dka' ba / mchog tu dka' ba / tha dad pa dang / tha dad pa ma yin pa nyid las yang dag par 'das pa'i mtshan nyid mngon par rdzogs par sangs rgyas te.* I read *tha dad pa ma yin pa nyid las yang dag par 'das pa'i mtshan nyid* as a *bahuvrīhi*, not a *tatpuruṣa*. The terms *don dam pa* and *mtshan nyid* are not in apposition in chapter 3, since the two terms are repeatedly connected through a genitive particle: *don dam pa'i mtshan nyid* (which occurs 32 times in folios 5.a, 5.b, 6.b, 7.a, 7.b, 8.a, 8.b, and 9.a). I also understand similar constructions with *don dam pa* and *tshan nyid* in the following chapter as *bahuvrīhis*.

86. This phrase is also found in 2.2, 3.6, and 4.7 (see also folios 5.b, 9.a–b, and 10.b–11.a): *mngon par rdzogs par sangs rgyas nas kyang bsnyad cing gsal bar byas / rnam par phye / gdags pa byas / rab tu bstan to.*

87. Powers translates *mtshan nyid* as singular (see Powers 1995, 49). But the question of the identity or difference in this chapter is evaluated from the perspective of two defining characteristics, namely, the defining characteristic of the conditioned and the defining characteristic of the unconditioned.

88. The last two lines are quoted in the *Bhāvanākrama*; see Tucci 1971, 1: *nimittabandhanāj jantur atho dauṣṭhulabandhanāt / vipaśyanāṁ bhāvayitvā śamathañ ca vimucyata iti.*

Chapter 4

«4.1» Then the Blessed One spoke these words to Subhūti: "Subhūti, do you know how many beings in the world[89] display their knowledge[90] under the influence of conceit? Do you know how many beings in the world display their knowledge without conceit?"

Subhūti answered, "Blessed One, according to my knowledge, there are only a few in the world of beings who present their knowledge without conceit, but countless, innumerable, and inexpressible in number are those who do so under its influence. Blessed One, at one time I was staying in a hermitage set in a great forest. There were many monks living in the vicinity who had also established themselves there. At sunrise, I saw them gather together. They showed their knowledge and revealed their understanding by taking various aspects of phenomena as referential objects.[91]

«4.2» "Some showed their knowledge by taking the five aggregates as referential objects: their manifest characteristic, their arising, their disintegration, their cessation, and the acknowledgment of their cessation. In the same way, some showed their knowledge by taking the twelve sense domains as referential objects, some by taking dependent arising as a referential object. Some showed their knowledge by taking the four kinds of

89. Lit. "in the world of beings."

90. F reads here *shes pa* in agreement with D. See F, folio 14.bff.

91. *dmigs pa*; *ālambana*. I think it is important here to read *dmigs pa* as meaning "object" because in folio 11.a the Buddha contrasts these various objects (aggregates, sense sources, constituents, truths, etc.) with the "object conducive to purification" (*rnam par dag pa'i dmigs pa*, **viśuddhyālambana*; see Schmithausen 2014, 362, §306.5 and n. 1644). Translating *dmigs pa* here as "observing" would weaken the central opposition between (1) the objects taken as a reference point for their practice by those who have not realized the defining characteristic of the ultimate and (2) the object conducive to purification, which is present within all phenomena. The purpose of this chapter is to introduce this fundamental point.

sustenance as referential objects: their manifest characteristic, their arising, their disintegration, their cessation, and the acknowledgment of their cessation.

«4.3»"Some showed their knowledge by taking the four noble truths as referential objects: their defining characteristic, the comprehension of suffering, the abandoning of the cause of suffering, the actualization of the cessation of suffering, and the practice of the path.

«4.4»"Some showed their knowledge by taking the eighteen constituents as referential objects: their manifest characteristic, their varieties, their manifoldness, their cessation, and the actualization of their cessation.

«4.5»"Some showed their knowledge by taking the four applications of mindfulness as referential objects: their manifest characteristic, their adverse factors, their antidotes, their practice, their arising from having been non-arisen, their remaining after they arose, and their maintaining, resuming, or increasing. In the same way, some showed their knowledge by taking as referential objects the four correct self-restraints, as well as the four bases of supernatural powers, the five faculties, the five forces, and the seven branches of awakening. Some showed their knowledge by taking as referential objects the eight branches of the noble path: their manifest characteristic, the antidotes to their adverse factors, their practice, their arising from having been non-arisen, their remaining after they arose, and their maintaining, resuming, or increasing.[92]

«4.6»"Then I thought to myself, 'These venerable monks displayed their knowledge by revealing their understanding by taking various aspects of phenomena as referential objects, but they have not perceived the ultimate, whose defining characteristic is of a single nature[93] everywhere.' These venerable persons have conceit and, without doubt, display their knowledge under the influence of conceit. Blessed One, at an earlier time, you spoke

92. This paragraph deals with the thirty-seven branches of awakening (*byang chub kyi yan lag*; *bodhyaṅgāni*).

93. *ro gcig pa*; *ekarasa*. I read the compound *thams cad du ro gcig pa'i mtshan nyid*; *sarvatraikarasalakṣaṇa (?) as a *bahuvrīhi*; see D, folio 12.a: *rab 'byor de bzhin du don dam pa yang mtshan nyid tha dad pa'i chos rnams la thams cad du ro gcig pa'i mtshan nyid yin par blta bar bya'o*. I understand *thams cad du ro gcig pa'i mtshan nyid* to refer here to the defining characteristic of the ultimate since this definition presents *dharma* as having various *lakṣaṇa*. As a consequence, I read this sentence as stating that the ultimate is that whose defining characteristic is always of a single nature in all phenomena that have diverse defining characteristics. See also 4.8, which supports this interpretation.

these words: 'The ultimate is subtle, profound, difficult to understand, extremely difficult to understand, and characterized as being of a single nature everywhere.' How wonderful indeed are these very words of yours! Blessed One, if even those who practice your teaching, such as these beings who became monks, find it difficult to understand in this way the ultimate whose defining characteristic is of a single nature everywhere, what need is there to mention how difficult it is for those outsiders who do not follow your teaching?"

«4.7» The Blessed One replied, "So it is, Subhūti. So it is. I have completely and fully awakened to the ultimate that, being characterized as being of a single nature everywhere, is subtle, extremely subtle, profound, extremely profound, difficult to understand, and extremely difficult to understand. Yet, after I attained complete and perfect awakening, I communicated through words, gave explanations, established distinctions, expressed myself through conventions, and imparted teachings. One might ask why I did this.

«4.8» "Subhūti, it is because I teach that the ultimate is the referential object conducive to purification[94] within the aggregates, as well as within the sense domains, dependent arising, the sustenances, the truths, the constituents, the applications of mindfulness, the self-restraints, the bases of supernatural powers, the faculties, the forces, the branches of awakening, and, Subhūti, the eightfold path. This referential object conducive to purification within the aggregates is of a single nature everywhere and its defining characteristic is not different from theirs. It is just the same from the sense domains up to the eightfold path: the referential object conducive to purification within these various referential objects is of a single nature everywhere and its defining characteristic is not different from theirs. Subhūti,

94. *rnam par dag pa'i dmigs pa*; **viśuddhyālambana*. Lamotte reads here *rnam par dag pa'i dmigs pa* with the meaning of *viśuddhālambana* ("objet pur"), but Schmithausen gives **viśuddhyālambana* as the Sanskrit equivalent for the Tibetan (see Schmithausen 2014, 362, §306.5 and n. 1644). It is worth noting that this term is also found in chapter 7, where it is again equated with the ultimate (*don dam pa*). In this context, it is said that *paratantra* is not an object conducive to purification whereas the actual (*pariniṣpanna*) is. In this sense, one should make the distinction here between *vastu* and *ālambana*. The ultimate is conceived here as the referential object, or support object, of a purification that leads to awakening. The usage of *ālambana* in reference to the ultimate clearly refers to practice in the present chapter.

through this approach, you should thus know that what is characterized as being of a single nature everywhere is the ultimate.[95]

«4.9» "Moreover, Subhūti, once renunciants who practice yoga have realized in reference to a single aggregate the selflessness of phenomena, which is the ultimate reality,[96] they do not look for this ultimate reality, this selflessness, individually within the other aggregates or in the sense domains, dependent arising, the sustenances, the truths, the constituents, the applications of mindfulness, the self-restraints, the bases of supernatural powers, the faculties, the forces, the branches of awakening, and the eightfold path. Instead, they rely upon the nondual gnosis[97] that is in accord with true reality. Through this alone,[98] they infallibly ascertain and realize the ultimate, characterized as being of a single nature everywhere. Subhūti, through this approach, you should thus know that what is characterized as being of a single nature everywhere is the ultimate.

«4.10» "Moreover, Subhūti, if ultimate reality itself, the selflessness of phenomena, had a defining characteristic distinct [from the defining characteristics of phenomena] in the way the aggregates, the sense domains, dependent arising, the sustenances, the truths, the constituents, the applications of mindfulness, the self-restraints, the bases of supernatural powers, the faculties, the forces, the branches of awakening, and the eightfold path have defining characteristics distinct from one another, then, on account of this, ultimate reality itself, the selflessness of phenomena, would have causes and arise from causes. If it arose from causes, it would be conditioned. If it were the conditioned, it would not be the ultimate. If it were not the ultimate, one would need to look for some other ultimate. Subhūti, this ultimate, the selflessness of phenomena, does not arise from causes. It is not conditioned. Neither is it the case that it is not the ultimate. One must

95. Compare D, folio 11.a: *rab 'byor rnam grangs des na khyod kyis 'di ltar thams cad du ro gcig pa'i mtshan nyid gang yin pa de ni don dam pa yin par rig par bya'o* with D, folio 12.a: *rab 'byor de bzhin du don dam pa yang mtshan nyid tha dad pa'i chos rnams la thams cad du ro gcig pa'i mtshan nyid yin par blta bar bya'o* (passim).

96. *de bzhin nyid*; *tathatā*. I translate *tathatā* with "true reality" (in the sense of the true state or nature of things) instead of the more usual "suchness" or "thusness." However, when *de bzhin nyid* is qualified by an adjective such as *don dam pa*, I simply translate it with "reality" to improve readability. See Schmithausen 2014, 356, §303.1 (passim), in which *tathatā* is translated with "True Reality" or "Suchness."

97. D reads *gnyis med pa'i shes pa*, while F, folio 16.b, reads *gnyis su med pa'i ye shes*.

98. *kho na*; *eva*. For a comparison between Buescher's and Schmithausen's translations of this sentence, see Schmithausen 2014, 380, §324.

[therefore] not look for an ultimate other than that ultimate. Thus, whether tathāgatas manifest or not, because it is the case that it permanently and immutably abides within phenomena, only this nature of phenomena, this constituent abiding in phenomena, is constant.[99] Subhūti, for all these reasons, you should know through this approach that the ultimate is characterized as being of a single nature everywhere.

«4.11» "Subhūti, it is like this: although there are many varieties of forms with distinct defining characteristics within space, since space itself is free from manifest characteristics, devoid of conceptions, and without change, its defining characteristic is of a single nature everywhere. Likewise, Subhūti, you should know that the ultimate is characterized as being of a single nature everywhere, within all phenomena whose defining characteristics are distinct from one another."

«4.12» Then, at that moment, the Blessed One spoke these verses:

"As proclaimed by the buddhas,
This ultimate is not distinct from phenomena,
And its defining characteristic is everywhere of a single nature.
Those who imagine it to be distinct from phenomena
Are conceited and deluded."

This was the chapter of Subhūti—the fourth chapter.

99. D: *de bzhin gshegs pa rnams byung yang rung ma byung yang rung ste / rtag pa rtag pa'i dus dang / ther zug ther zug gi dus su chos gnas par bya ba'i phyir chos rnams kyi chos nyid dbyings de ni rnam par gnas pa kho na yin pa*. Lamotte translates *chos gnas par bya ba'i phyir* with "pour le maintien des choses," but *phyir* does not have a dative function here. Powers' translation reads, "because phenomena abide in permanent, permanent time and in everlasting, everlasting time, the domain of reality of phenomena alone abides." This does not make sense either. Conditioned phenomena are impermanent as explained at length in the first four chapters. The argument simply runs as follows: since it is present in all things, this alone is permanent. As for the expression *chos nyid dbyings*, D, folio 11.b, reads *chos rnams kyi chos nyid dbyings* while F, folio 17.a, has *chos rnams kyi chos nyid / chos gnas pa'i dbyings*, referring respectively to *dharmatā* and *dharmadhātu* (compare with Mvyut 1719: *chos gnas pa nyid*; *dharmasthititā*). I am reluctant to translate *dbyings* (*dhātu*) as "realm/domain" here because the meaning of *dhātu* as "constituent" makes so much sense, particularly when reading F, in which *dbyings* is glossed as *chos gnas pa*, "that which abides within phenomena," "that which is the support/source of phenomena," or "the condition of phenomena." Xuanzang's translation confirms the suggested translation: 唯有常常時恒恒時如來出世若不出世諸法法性安立法界安住 (CBETA, Taishō 676).

Chapter 5

«5.1» Then the bodhisattva Vishālamati asked the Blessed One, "Blessed One, when bodhisattvas who are skilled in the secrets of mind, thought, and cognition are called 'skilled in the secrets of mind, thought, and cognition,' what does it mean?[100] When they are designated in this way, what does it refer to?"

The Blessed One answered, "Vishālamati, you are asking this for the benefit and happiness of many beings, out of compassion for the world, and for the welfare, benefit, and happiness of all beings, including gods and humans. Your intention is excellent when questioning the Tathāgata on this specific point. Therefore, listen, Vishālamati. I will explain to you in which way bodhisattvas are skilled in the secrets of mind, thought, and cognition.

«5.2» "Vishālamati, when such and such beings are reborn and manifest[101] in this samsara comprised of six destinies, in any class of beings or

100. *ji tsam gyis*; *kiyant*. The complete sentence reads, "In what sense are they skilled in the secrets of mind, thought, and cognition?"

101. D: *blo gros yangs ba 'gro ba drug gi 'khor ba 'di na sems can gang dang gang dag sems can gyi ris gang dang gang du yang sgo nga nas skye ba'i skye gnas sam / yang na mngal nas skye ba'am / yang na drod gsher las skye ba'am / yang na rdzus te skye ba'i skye gnas su lus mngon par 'grub cing 'byung bar 'gyur ba der*. "For whatever sentient beings an individual existence (*ātmabhāva*) comes about and emerges in this saṁsāra comprising six destinations, in whatever community of beings, be it in [the mode of] egg-born, womb-born, moisture-born or spontaneous generation, there . . ." (Schmithausen 2014, 177, §149). Regarding *lus mngon par 'grub cing 'byung bar 'gyur ba*, one finds the Sanskrit equivalent *ātmabhāvam abhinirvartayati* for *lus mngon par 'grub 'gyur ba* (see Yokoyama and Hirosawa 1996). Schmithausen reads here, "For whatever sentient beings an individual existence (*ātmabhāva*) comes about and emerges" (Schmithausen 2014, 177, §149), but it seems to me that we could have had here a causative (*ātmabhāvam abhinirvartayanti*) with the literal meaning of producing or bringing about a [new] existence, in a word, being reborn (for an instance of this rendering, see Schmithausen 2014, 191n812). Otherwise, one would expect a syntactic particle in Tibetan after *sems can gang dang gang dag* to match Schmithausen's reading, "For whatever

state of birth, be it egg-born, womb-born, moisture-born, or spontaneously generated,[102] there is first a twofold appropriation: the appropriation of the physical sense faculties together with their supports, and the appropriation of mental imprints producing the elaboration of conventional expressions with regard to manifest characteristics, names, and conceptualizations. In dependence upon this twofold appropriation, the mind containing all the seeds matures, merges [with the embryo], grows, increases, and expands.[103] This twofold appropriation occurs in the realm of form but it does not appear in the realm of the formless.[104]

«5.3» "Vishālamati, this cognition is also called 'appropriating cognition' because it grasps and appropriates the body. It is also called 'subliminal cognition,' because it dwells and lies hidden in this body, sharing a common destiny. It is also called 'mind,' because it is accumulated[105] and developed by visual forms, sounds, smells, flavors, tangible objects, and phenomena.[106]

«5.4» "Vishālamati, taking this appropriating cognition as support and

---

sentient beings," particularly if one understands *'gro ba drug gi 'khor ba 'di na sems can gang dang gang dag* as not in apposition to *sems can gyi ris gang dang gang du*, which I think is the correct way to understand the expression.

102. I follow here the second possible interpretation of the correlative-relative syntactic structure of the sentence as suggested by Schmithausen (see Schmithausen 2014, 178, §150), in which *der* (*tatra*) is read as having a temporal connotation, rendered by the adverb "then."

103. D: *sa bon thams cad pa'i sems rnam par smin cing 'jug la rgyas shing 'phel ba dang yangs par 'gyur ro*. See Schmithausen 1987, 356n508, and 2014, 325n1490, for the Sanskrit reconstruction: *(*sarvabījakaṁ cittaṁ*) *vipacyate saṁmūrcchati vṛddhiṁ virūdhiṁ vipulatām apadyate*. See also Waldron 2003, 218, n. 13. Lamotte (1973, 65ff.) suggests *kalalatvena saṁmūrcchati* in his translation of the *Mahāyānasaṁgraha* I,34. The appended commentary describes how the appropriating cognition enters the mother's womb by uniting with the semen and the blood (*śukraśoṇita*). The embryo with which, from then on, the appropriating cognition shares a common destiny (*ekayogakṣema*) is the result of this "coagulation." On the topic, see Kritzer 2000.

104. See Waldron 2003, 94–95, for a translation of 5.2. See also Brunnhölzl 2018, 1305ff., regarding Asaṅga's and Wonch'uk's commentaries on Saṁdh. 5.2–7.

105. *kun tu bsags pa*; *ācita*. This explanation corresponds to an etymological analysis of the Sanskrit term *citta*. Xuanzang's translation reads 由此識色聲香味觸等積集滋長故 (CBETA, Taishō 676).

106. See Schmithausen 2014, 157ff., for an extensive discussion of the various testimonies and interpretations of this sentence. See also Waldron 2003, 95–96, for a translation of 5.3, and Tillemans 1997, 157–58, for a discussion of Powers' translation of 5.3. Powers translates the verb in the last sentence with an active form "because it collects and accumulates forms, sounds . . ." (Powers 1995, 71). It seems to me that, since this is an etymological explanation of *citta*, a passive is better in the present case.

basis, the six kinds of cognition,[107] that is, visual, auditive, olfactory, gustatory, tactile, and mental cognitions, arise. Among these, a visual cognition arises on the basis of the eye, which is connected with a visual cognition and a visual form. Simultaneously and in conformity with this visual cognition, a mental cognition that conceptualizes the object arises at the same time, having the same object. [Likewise,] Vishālamati, an auditive, olfactory, gustatory, or tactile cognition arises on the basis of a sense faculty connected to a cognition, such as the ear, nose, tongue, or body, and a sound, smell, flavor, or tangible object. Simultaneously and in conformity with this auditive, olfactory, gustatory, or tactile cognition, a mental cognition that conceptualizes the object arises at the same time, having the same object. If only one visual cognition arises at one time, then only one mental cognition that conceptualizes the object arises simultaneously, having the same object. If two, three, four, or five cognitions arise simultaneously, then also in that case, having the same object as the group of five cognitions, only one mental cognition that conceptualizes this object arises simultaneously.[108]

«5.5» "Vishālamati, it is like this: If the conditions for the arising of a single wave in a large stream of water are present, then only one wave arises.[109] If the conditions for the arising of two or many waves are present, then two or many waves arise.[110] However, the river [itself] neither stops as a stream of water nor becomes exhausted. If the conditions for the arising of a single reflection in a perfectly polished mirror are present, then only one reflec-

107. *rnam par shes pa'i tshogs drug po*, lit. "the sixfold group of cognitions."
108. Waldron's translation (Waldron 2003, 97) seems to follow the Sanskrit and Tibetan found in Sthiramati's *Triṁśikāvijñaptibhāṣyam* (see TrBh, 33.25–34.4, in Buescher 2007). However, the quote of Saṁdh. in this treatise is drawn from 5.5. It does not quite match the last sentence of 5.4. See D: *gal te rnam par shes pa'i tshogs gnyis sam / gsum mam bzhi lhan cig gam / lnga car lhan cig 'byung na yang der rnam par shes pa'i tshogs lnga po dag dang / spyod yul mtshungs pa rnam par rtog pa'i yid kyi rnam par shes pa yang gcig kho na lhan cig 'byung ngo.* Compare with TrBh, 33.26–27 (Buescher 2007): *gal te rnam par shes pa gnyis sam gsum mam lnga 'byung ba'i rkyen nye bar gnas par gyur na yang gnyis sam gsum mam lnga' bar du 'byung bar 'gyur ro.* Sanskrit: *saced dvayos trayānāṁ sacet pañcānāṃ vijñānām utpattipratyayaḥ pratyupasthito bhavati sakṛd yāvat pañcānāṃ pravṛttir bhavati.*
109. For a comparison with the Dunhuang edition of 5.5, as well as for a general evaluation of the relevance of this edition, see Schmithausen 2014, 419n1852.
110. D: *gal te rlabs gnyis sam gal te rab tu mang po dag 'byung ba'i rkyen nye bar gnas par gyur na rlabs rab tu mang po dag 'byung*, but VD, folio 54.a: *gal te rlabs gnyis sam gal te rab tu mang po dag 'byung ba'i rkyen nye bar gnas par gyur na rlabs kyang gnyis sam rab tu mang po dag 'byung*. S, folio 19.a, is in agreement with D here (*gnyis sam* is omitted).

tion arises.[111] If the conditions for the arising of two or many reflections are present, then two or many reflections arise.[112] However, the mirror neither transforms itself into the object corresponding to the reflection nor manifests reflections by being in close contact [with the reflected objects].[113] Vishālamati, similarly, taking this appropriating cognition as support and basis, as in the examples of the river and the mirror, if the conditions for the arising of one visual cognition are present, then only one visual cognition arises. If the conditions for the simultaneous arising of up to five cognitions are present, then up to five cognitions simultaneously arise.

«5.6»"Vishālamati, taking in this way the knowledge[114] of this doctrine as a support and basis, bodhisattvas are skilled in the secrets of mind, thought, and cognition. Yet when the Tathāgata designates the bodhisattvas as skilled in the secrets of mind, thought, and cognition, they are not designated as completely skilled merely on account of this. Vishālamati, I call bodhisattvas 'skilled in the ultimate' as soon as[115] they, by themselves and in their own experience,[116] neither perceive the appropriation nor the appropriating cognition but [instead perceive] in accord with the truth; as soon as they neither perceive the subliminal nor the subliminal cognition; neither the accumulated nor the mind;[117] neither the eye, nor the form, nor the visual cognition; neither the ear, nor the sound, nor the auditive cognition; neither the nose, nor the smell, nor the olfactory cognition; neither the tongue, nor the flavor, nor the gustatory cognition; and neither the

111. On the metaphor of the mirror in Buddhist texts, see Wayman 1974.

112. D: *gal te gzugs brnyan gnyis sam gal te rab tu mang po dag 'byung ba'i rkyen nye bar gnas par gyur na gzugs brnyan rab tu mang po dag 'byung*, but VD, folio 54.a: *gal te gzugs brnyan gnyis sam gal te gzugs brnyan rab tu mang po dag 'byung ba'i rkyen nye bar gnas pa gyur na gzugs brnyan yang gnyis sam rab tu mang po dag 'byung*.

113. Lamotte 1935, 186, translates *yongs su sbyor bar yang mi mngon* with "ne souffre aucun dommage."

114. *shes pa*, although it is worth noting that the Dunhuang manuscript reads *ye shes*. See Hakayama 1986, 11 E6 (3).

115. D: *blo gros yangs pa gang gi phyir byang chub sems dpa' rang gi so so nang gi len pa mi mthong / len pa'i rnam par shes pa yang mi mthong la / de yang dag pa ji lta ba bzhin du yin pa*. I am following here Schmithausen's reading of *gang gi phyir* (*yataḥ*) in the sense of "as soon as" (see Schmithausen 2014, 346–47, n. 1577). This interpretation is confirmed by F, folio 19.b, which reads *nam* instead of *gang gi phyir*.

116. *nang gi so sor rang rig pa*; *adhyātmaṁ prātyatmam* (see Schmithausen 2014, 346–47n1577). See F, folio 19.b: *nang gi so so rang*.

117. "Neither the accumulated nor the mind" is a pun on *ācita* and *citta*.

body, nor the tangible object, nor the tactile cognition. Vishālamati, I call bodhisattvas 'skilled in the ultimate' as soon as they, by themselves and in their own experience, neither perceive thought, nor phenomena, nor mental cognition but instead perceive in accord with the truth. Vishālamati, the Tathāgata designates as skilled in the secrets of mind, thought, and cognition the bodhisattvas who are skilled in the ultimate. Vishālamati, for this reason, bodhisattvas are skilled in the secrets of mind, thought, and cognition. Also, when the Tathāgata designates them as such, it is for this reason."

«5.7» Then, at that moment, the Blessed One spoke these verses:

> "Profound and subtle is the appropriating cognition.
> Containing all the seeds, it flows like a stream of water.
> I did not teach it to the immature,
> Lest they would imagine it to be a self."[118]

This was the chapter of Vishālamati—the fifth chapter.

118. Sanskrit verses are found in Buescher 2007, see TrBh, 34.2–3. Also translated into English in Waldron 2003, 101.

Chapter 6

«6.1» Then the bodhisattva Guṇākara asked the Blessed One, "Blessed One, when bodhisattvas who are skilled in the defining characteristics of phenomena are called 'skilled in the defining characteristics of phenomena,' what does it mean? Moreover, when the Tathāgata designates them as such, what does it refer to?"

«6.2» The Blessed One replied to the bodhisattva Guṇākara, "Guṇākara, for the benefit and happiness of many beings, out of compassion for the world, for the welfare, benefit, and happiness of all beings, including gods and humans, you are asking this. Your intention is excellent when questioning the Tathāgata on this specific point. Therefore, listen, Guṇākara, I will explain to you in which way bodhisattvas are skilled in the defining characteristics of phenomena.

«6.3» "Guṇākara, the defining characteristics of phenomena are three. What are these three? They are the imaginary defining characteristic, the other-dependent defining characteristic, and the actual defining characteristic.[119]

«6.4» "Guṇākara, what is the imaginary defining characteristic [of phenomena]? It is what is nominally and conventionally posited[120] as the

119. *yongs su grub pa'i mtshan nyid*; *parinispannalakṣaṇa*. I read these compounds as *karmadhārayas*, not as genitive *tatpuruṣas*. For an analysis of these compounds, see Schmithausen 2014, 359n1626.

120. *rnam par bzhag pa*; *vyavasthā*, which has the connotation of something's being agreed upon, represented, arranged, settled, decreed, or established.

essence or the distinctive [characteristic] of phenomena, even just[121] in order to designate[122] [them].[123]

«6.5» "Guṇākara, what is the other-dependent defining characteristic [of phenomena]? It is the dependent arising of phenomena. It is like this: 'When this is, that arises; because this arises, that arises.' It is also from '[in dependence upon ignorance as a condition,] conditioning mental factors [arise]' up to 'thus, the whole great mass of suffering comes to be.'

121. Frauwallner and Lamotte do not translate *ji tsam du* (see Frauwallner 1969, 285: "um sie im täglichen Sprachgebrauch zu bezeichnen" and Lamotte 1935, 188: "permettant de les mentionner dans le langage courant"). The Chinese term 乃至 in Xuanzang's translation (乃至為令隨起言說, CBETA, Taishō 676) corresponds to the Tibetan *ji tsam du* (for *yāvat* or *kiyat*), which I understand here in the sense of "at least, only, even just." Interestingly enough, the Go witness has *ci tsam gis* (see Go, folio 12.a); F, folio 20.a, reads *gang ji skad du*, and He, folio 77.a, returns *gang ji snyed du* (while *rjes su* is omitted) for *ji tsam du* in D.

122. The Tibetan *rjes su tha snyad gdags pa* and the Chinese 隨起言說 correspond to *anuvyavahāra*.

123. D: *ji tsam du rjes su tha snyad gdags pa'i phyir chos rnams kyi ngo bo nyid dam bye brag tu ming dang brdar rnam par gzhag pa gang yin pa'o*. Frauwallner's translation of this passage is slightly ambiguous and could be potentially misleading on account of the German preposition "nach": "Es ist jede Festsetzung eines Namens und einer Vereinbarung für die Gegebenheiten nach Wesen oder Besonderheit, um sie im täglichen Sprachgebrauch zu bezeichnen" (Frauwallner 1969, 286). If one reads this sentence as "a determination in terms of being and specific defining characteristic," then the translation is correct. However, if one reads it as meaning "the determination of . . . in accordance with / corresponding to [their] being or specific defining characteristic," then the translation becomes problematic since the point made in the text is precisely that there is no such thing. The determination (Festsetzung) of a name and convention for phenomena (für die Gegebenheiten) is not made according to the essence or defining characteristic of phenomena (nach Wesen oder Besonderheit). Hence the term "imaginary defining characteristic." If this determination occurred according to the essence of phenomena, it would be illogical to call this defining characteristic "imaginary." Lamotte's translation is therefore more accurate in the present case, although his rendering of *rnam par bzhags pa* (*vyavasthāna*) as a present participle qualifying *ming dang brda* slightly modifies the original meaning of the sentence. Sanskrit compounds with *vyavasthāna* can be read as instrumental *tatpuruṣa*, for example *saṁjñākaraṇavyavasthāna*, *mātrāvyavasthāna*, or *aṅgavyavasthāna*. Xuanzang translates this passage as 云何諸法遍計所執相。謂一切法名假安立自性差別。乃至為令隨起言說。(Taishō 676), in which *nāmasaṁketa* ("names and common references") seem at first glance to be the grammatical passive subject of the main verb of the clause (安立) or an adverb. In fact, F, folio 20.a, and He, folio 77.a, read *ming dang brdas rnam par bzhag pa* instead of *ming dang brdar rnam par bzhag pa* in D and other witnesses mentioned in the preceding notes. The terminative of the Tibetan *ming dang brdar* could be read adverbially in the sense of "nominally and conventionally" in the sense of "by means of / in terms of names and common references" for *nāmasaṁketa*.

«6.6» "Guṇākara, what is the actual[124] defining characteristic [of phenomena]? It is their true reality, namely, the unsurpassable, complete, and perfect awakening that is finally attained by bodhisattvas as they realize this [true reality] through their diligence and correct application of mind and then become perfectly familiar with the realization of this [true reality].[125]

124. Regarding the choice of terminology for *pariniṣpanna*, Edgerton mentions two possible meanings (see Edgerton 1953, 325): (1) "completely perfected" in the sense of "accomplished/attained," which corresponds to the second clause in the present definition (6.6) in which the *yong su grub pa* is glossed in the sense of *yang dag par 'grub pa* (D) and *yang dag par bsgrub pa* (F). (2) The second meaning of *pariniṣpanna* according to Edgerton is "absolute." The term is also translated into English as meaning "real." Understanding *pariniṣpanna* as "established" or "perfected" is indeed problematic. Reality in the sense of *tathatā* cannot be referred to as "perfected," because it is not perfectible. If it were, it would be conditioned (see Saṁdh. chapter 3). Likewise, *tathatā* cannot be termed "established" because if it were, it would be impermanent, but it is said to be the only permanent reality (see Saṁdh. chapter 4). As a consequence, it appears clearly from the context of the definition given above and from Edgerton's explanations that *pariniṣpannalakṣaṇa* refers to both the "character accomplished [by bodhisattvas]" in the sense of the accomplishment of the defining characteristic of the ultimate as the ultimate attainment of the bodhisattva's spiritual path, and the "absolute or real character" in the sense of reality itself (*tathatā*). As emphasized throughout Saṁdh., *pariniṣpanna-lakṣaṇa* is indeed none other than the defining characteristic of the ultimate (*don dam pa'i mtshan nyid*; *paramārthalakṣaṇa*), the object conducive to purification (*rnam par dag pa'i dmigs pa*; **viśuddhyālambana*). In the present translation, I opt for "actual," a term that fits well with the metaphors found in Saṁdh. chapter 6, to explain the three natures (Lamotte chose "absolu," and Frauwallner "vollkommen"). The term "actual" obviously induces a clear dichotomy between what is imaginary and what is real, which was most probably at the origin of these terminological choices in the source language. On the opposition between the imaginary and the actual by equating the imaginary with the unreal through the usage of the same terminology (i.e., *pariniṣpanna* and *parikalpa/parikalpita*), see 1.2.

125. The syntax of this sentence differs according to the various available editions of the text with little bearing on the meaning of the sentence. For example, compare D, VD, folios 55.a–b: *chos rnams kyi de bzhin nyid gang yin pa ste / byang chub sems dpa' rnams kyis rtun pa'i rgyu dang / legs par tshul bzhin yid la byas pa'i rgyus de rtogs shing de rtogs pa goms par byas pa yang dag par grub pas kyang bla na med pa yang dag par rdzogs pa'i byang chub kyi bar du yang dag par 'grub pa gang yin pa'o*; F, folio 20.a–b: *gang chos rnams kyi de bzhin nyid de / byang chub sems dpa' rnams kyis brtson ba'i rgyu dang / yang dag par tshul bzhin yid la byed pa'i rgyud gang rtogs par 'gyur ba yin te rtogs dang / bsgoms pa bsgrubs pas / bla na med pa yang dag par rdzogs pa'i byang chub kyi bar du yang dag par bsgrub pa'o*; and S, folio 20.b: *gang chos rnams kyi de bzhin nyid / gang byang chub sems dpa' rnams kyis brtson ba'i rgyu dang / yang dag par tshul bzhin yid la byed pa'i rgyus rtogs par 'gyur ba yin te / de rtogs pa goms par byas pa yang dag par grub pas kyang / bla na med pa yang dag par rdzogs pa'i byang chub kyi bar du yang dag par 'grub pa'o*. Frauwallner reads this passage in the following way: "Es ist die Soheit der Gegebenheiten, ihr Erschauen durch die Bodhisattva auf Grund ihrer Energie

«6.7» "Guṇākara, it is like this: you should consider the imaginary defining characteristic to be just like[126] the falsity of the visual aberrations [perceived] by someone suffering from the timira visual disorder.

"Guṇākara, it is like this: you should consider the other-dependent defining characteristic to be just like the manifest characteristics manifesting to this very person suffering from the timira disease, such as [actually nonexistent] hairs, flies, sesame seeds, [or patches of] blue, yellow, red, or white [in their visual field].

"Guṇākara, it is like this: you should consider the actual defining characteristic to be just like the original and unerring visual object seen by the same person when their vision is healthy and free from the visual aberrations resulting from the timira disease.

«6.8» "Guṇākara, it is like this: when a pure crystal is in contact with something blue, it appears to be a sapphire. Because people perceive it by mistake as a sapphire, they are deceived by it. When this pure crystal is in contact with something red, green, or yellow, it appears to be a ruby, an

---

und richtigen Beobachtung (*yoniśomanasikāraḥ*), und durch das Zustandekommen der Übung dieses Erschauens schließlich das Zustandekommen der hochsten vollkommenen Erleuchtung" (Frauwallner 1969, 286). Lamotte 1935, 189, is similar to Frauwallner's reading. It is plausible that Frauwallner simply followed Lamotte's translation of this passage. Schmithausen suggests that the relative clause starting with *gang byang chub* specifies the *tathatā*, which I agree with, although reading the two clauses defining *pariniṣpannalakṣaṇa* as being in apposition would not negate the fact that the second one merely specifies the first one (*tathatā*) as being that which is attained by bodhisattvas: "(Suchness) into which the bodhisattvas, in consequence of their zeal and in consequence of their appropriate contemplation, obtain direct insight (**prativedha*, cf. SaṁdhDh: *so sor chud pa*), and, through the accomplishment of the repeated practice of this insight, finally attain the Highest Perfect Awakening" (Schmithausen 2014, 540n2241). It is important here to note that *rtogs shing de rtogs pa goms par byas pa* stands on the same level in relation to *yang dag par grub pas*, which is not apparent in Schmithausen's translation. Thus, "obtain direct insight" (*de rtogs shing*) is part of a larger argument: *rtogs shing de rtogs pa goms par byas pa* (D) or *rtogs par 'gyur ba yin te rtogs dang / bsgoms pa bsgrubs pas* (F). This meaning unit should therefore not be put on the same level as *yang dag par 'grub pa gang yin pa'o* as it is in Schmithausen's translation, since it is one of the reasons why there is an accomplishment according to the available testimonies. Regarding the translation of *bar du* (*yāvat*), I followed Schmithausen's way of solving the problem. Powers understands it in its usual sense of "up to," but it does not work here, since this would imply that what are accomplished are also inferior realizations, to which Powers refers between square brackets as "stages"; see Powers 1995, 83. Schmithausen's reading of the second clause as specifying *tathatā* seems preferable.

126. *de lta bur ni*; *evam eva*.

emerald, or gold. Because people perceive it by mistake as a ruby, an emerald, or gold, they are deceived by it.

«6.9» "Guṇākara, it is like this: You should consider the mental imprint of conventions in terms of an imaginary defining characteristic[127] upon the other-dependent defining characteristic to be just like the contact of colors with a pure crystal. Thus, you should consider the perception of an imaginary defining characteristic [superimposed] on the other-dependent defining characteristic to be just like the mistaken perception of a sapphire, ruby, emerald, or gold [superimposed] on the pure crystal.

"Guṇākara, it is like this: You should consider the other-dependent defining characteristic to be just like this pure crystal itself. Thus, you should consider the actual defining characteristic as the permanent and immutable lack of any actuality or essence in the imaginary defining characteristic [superimposed] on the other-dependent defining characteristic,[128] just as there is permanently and immutably no actuality or essence in the defining characteristic of a sapphire, ruby, emerald, or gold [superimposed] on a pure crystal.

«6.10» Thus, Guṇākara, bodhisattvas distinctly perceive[129] the imaginary

127. Lamotte translates this term with "essentiellement fantaisiste"; see Lamotte 1935, 190. This is missing the point that this actually refers to the imaginary defining characteristic.
128. D; VD, folio 56.a: *gzhan gyi dbang gi mtshan nyid de / kun brtags pa'i mtshan nyid der rtag pa rtag pa'i dus dang / ther zug ther zug gi dus su yongs su ma grub cing ngo bo nyid med pa nyid kyis yongs su grub pa'i mtshan nyid blta bar bya'o*; F, folio 21.b: *gzhan gyi dbang de nyid la / kun brtag brtags pa'i mtshan nyid de rtag pa rtag pa'i dus dang / 'khor bar 'khor ba'i dus su ma grub cing rang bzhin med pa nyid ni / yongs su grub pa'i mtshan nyid du blta'o*; S, folio 21.b: *gzhan gyi dbang de nyid kun brtags pa'i mtshan nyid der rtag pa rtag pa'i dus dang / ther zug ther zug gi dus su yongs su ma grub cing rang bzhin med pa nyid ni / yongs su grub pa'i mtshan nyid du blta'o*. F and S are helpful here to interpret the syntax of D. The following simple emendation would improve the syntax of D: *gzhan gyi dbang gi mtshan nyid de la / kun brtags pa'i mtshan nyid der rtag pa rtag pa'i dus dang / ther zug ther zug gi dus su yongs su ma grub cing ngo bo nyid med pa nyid kyis yongs su grub pa'i mtshan nyid blta bar bya'o*. Lamotte's translation of 6.9 is more intelligible than that of Frauwallner. which is more literal and strictly follows the syntax found in D. Xuanzang's translation, which reads: 即依他起相上由遍計所執相於常常時於恆恆時無有真實無自性性圓成實性當知亦爾 (CBETA, Taishō 676). In my translation I chose to topicalize *yongs su grub pa'i mtshan nyid* (in agreement with D) because the purpose of this dialogue is to define the three defining characters.
129. *rab tu shes*; *prajānāti* with the meaning of *pratijānāti*; see Edgerton 1953, 357. Lamotte translates this term with "repose," which does not convey the meaning of *prajānāti*; see Lamotte 1935, 190. In the following paragraph, Lamotte uses the verb "connaître" for the same term.

defining characteristic on the basis of names denoting manifest characteristics.[130] They distinctly perceive the other-dependent defining characteristic on the basis of the erroneous conception[131] [that superimposes] an imaginary defining characteristic[132] on the other-dependent defining characteristic.[133] They distinctly perceive the actual defining characteristic on the basis of the nonexistence of any erroneous conception [that superimposes] an imaginary defining characteristic on the other-dependent defining characteristic.

«6.11» "Guṇākara, when bodhisattvas distinctly perceive the imaginary defining characteristic [superimposed] on the other-dependent defining characteristic of phenomena exactly as it is, they distinctly perceive the phenomena devoid of any defining characteristic exactly as they are. Guṇākara, when bodhisattvas distinctly perceive the other-dependent defining characteristic exactly as it is, they distinctly perceive the phenomena characterized by affliction exactly as they are. Guṇākara, when bodhisattvas distinctly perceive the actual defining characteristic exactly as it is, they distinctly perceive the phenomena characterized by purification exactly as they are. Guṇākara, when bodhisattvas distinctly perceive the phenomena devoid of a defining characteristic [superimposed] on the other-dependent

130. *mtshan ma dang 'brel pa'i ming la brten nas*. VD, folio 56.a: *ming dang 'brel ba'i mtshan ma la brten nas*.

131. *mngon par zhen pa*; *abhiniveśa*. Usually with a negative connotation; see Edgerton 1953, 53. Powers reads it as meaning "strongly adhering"; see Powers 1995, 87.

132. See the definition of the imaginary defining characteristic in 6.4: "Guṇākara, what is the imaginary defining characteristic? It is what is nominally and conventionally posited as the essence or the distinctive [characteristic] of phenomena, even just in order to designate [them]." See also 7.4: "Paramārthasamudgata, what is the essencelessness of all phenomena with regard to defining characteristics? It is the imaginary defining characteristic [of phenomena]. Why? Because as much as this defining characteristic is nominally and conventionally posited, it is not posited on the basis of an essence or a distinctive [characteristic]. Therefore, it is called the essencelessness of all phenomena with regard to defining characteristics."

133. See 6.5: "Guṇākara, what is the other-dependent defining characteristic [of phenomena]? It is the dependent arising of phenomena. It is like this: 'When this is, that arises; because this arises, that arises.' It is also from '[in dependence upon ignorance as a condition,] conditioning mental factors [arise]' up to 'thus, the whole great mass of suffering comes to be.'" And also 7.5: "Paramārthasamudgata, what is the essencelessness of all phenomena with regard to arising? It is the other-dependent defining characteristic of phenomena. Why? Because this is [the defining characteristic] arising on account of causes other [than itself] and not by itself. Therefore, it is called essencelessness with regard to arising."

defining characteristic exactly as they are, they abandon the phenomena characterized by affliction. Once they have abandoned the phenomena characterized by affliction, they will obtain the phenomena characterized by purification. Guṇākara, since bodhisattvas distinctly perceive in this way the imaginary, other-dependent, and actual defining characteristics of phenomena exactly as they are, they distinctly perceive the phenomena devoid of a defining characteristic, those characterized by affliction, and those characterized by purification exactly as they are.[134] Having distinctly perceived the phenomena devoid of a defining characteristic exactly as they are, they abandon the phenomena characterized by affliction. Once they have abandoned the phenomena characterized by affliction, they will obtain the phenomena characterized by purification. For all these reasons, bodhisattvas are skilled in the defining characteristics of phenomena. Moreover, when the Tathāgata designates the bodhisattvas as 'skilled in the defining characteristics of phenomena,' it is for these reasons."

«6.12» Then, at that moment, the Blessed One spoke these verses:

"Once the phenomena devoid of defining characteristics have been distinctly perceived,
The phenomena characterized by affliction will be abandoned.
Once the phenomena characterized by affliction have been abandoned,
The phenomena characterized by purification will be obtained.

"Careless beings, overcome by wrongdoing and indulging in laziness,
Do not realize the imperfection of conditioned phenomena.
Falling apart in the midst of fleeting phenomena,
They deserve[135] compassion."

This was the chapter of Guṇākara —the sixth chapter.

134. I read *mtshan nyid med pa dang / kun nas nyon mongs pa'i mtshan nyid dang / rnam par byang ba'i mtshan nyid* (D) as in the previous clauses, namely, as *bahuvrīhis*.
135. Lamotte 1935, 191: "Ils excitent la pitié." *A la rigueur*, one could have accepted "ils suscitent la pitié"!

Chapter 7

«7.1»At that time, the bodhisattva Paramārthasamudgata asked the Blessed One, "Blessed One, when I was alone in a secluded place, I had the following thought: 'The Blessed One also spoke in many ways of the defining characteristic specific to the five aggregates, mentioning the defining characteristic of their arising, disintegration, abandonment, and comprehension.[136] In the same way, he spoke of the twelve sense domains, dependent arising, and the four kinds of sustenance. The Blessed One also spoke in many ways of the defining characteristic of the four noble truths, mentioning the comprehension of suffering, the abandoning of the cause of suffering, the actualization of the cessation of suffering, and the practice of the path. The Blessed One also spoke in many ways of the defining characteristic specific to the eighteen constituents, mentioning their varieties, manifoldness, abandonment, and comprehension. The Blessed One also spoke in many ways of the defining characteristic specific to the four applications of mindfulness, mentioning their adverse factors, antidotes, practice, their arising from being non-arisen, their remaining after they arose, and their maintaining, resuming, or increasing. Similarly, he also spoke in many ways of the defining characteristic specific to the four correct self-restraints, the four bases of supernatural powers, the five faculties, the five forces, and the seven branches of awakening. The Blessed One also spoke in many ways of the defining characteristic specific to the eight branches of the path, mentioning their adverse factors, antidotes, and practices, their arising from being non-arisen and remaining after they arose, and their maintaining, resuming, or increasing.'

"When the Blessed One further said, 'All phenomena are without an

136. This enumeration follows the structure found in 4.2.

essence,[137] unborn, unceasing, primordially in the state of peace, and naturally in the state of nirvana,' what was the underlying intent of the Blessed One? I would like to ask the Blessed One about this point: what was the Blessed One thinking when he said, 'All phenomena are without an essence, unborn, unceasing, primordially in the state of peace, and naturally in the state of nirvana'?"

«7.2» The Blessed One replied to the bodhisattva Paramārthasamudgata, "Paramārthasamudgata, this reflection of yours arose virtuously and appropriately. It is excellent indeed. You are asking this for the benefit and happiness of many beings, out of compassion for the world, and for the welfare, benefit, and happiness of all beings, including gods and humans. Your intention is excellent when questioning the Tathāgata on this specific point. Therefore, listen, Paramārthasamudgata. I will explain to you what my underlying intent was when I declared, 'All phenomena are without an essence, unborn, unceasing, primordially in the state of peace, and naturally in the state of nirvana.'[138]

«7.3» "Paramārthasamudgata, the essencelessness of all phenomena has three aspects. Having in mind essencelessness regarding defining characteristics, essencelessness regarding arising, and essencelessness regarding the ultimate, I thus taught what is called the essencelessness of all phenomena.

«7.4» "Paramārthasamudgata, what is the essencelessness of all phenomena with regard to defining characteristics? It is the imaginary defining characteristic [of phenomena]. Why? Because as much as this defining characteristic is nominally and conventionally posited, it is not posited[139] on the basis of an essence or a distinctive [characteristic].[140] Therefore, it is called the essencelessness of all phenomena with regard to defining characteristics.

137. D: *thams cad ngo bo nyid ma mchis pa* for *chos thams cad ngo bo nyid ma mchis pa* (D, folio 16.b passim).

138. For a list of texts including this sentence, see Lamotte 1935, 198.

139. *rnam par gnas pa*; *vyavasthita* (Chinese: 安立).

140. See Lamotte's and Frauwallner's translations of this passage (Lamotte 1935, 194, and Frauwallner 1969, 291). Both read *rnam par gnas pa* ("établi," "beruht") as the main verb in both clauses, which is syntactically dubious. Xuanzang's translation concords with D: 善男子云何諸法無自性性謂諸法遍計所執相。何以故。此由假名安立為相非由自性安立為相 (CBETA, Taishō 676). The complete definition of *parikalpitalakṣaṇa* in 6.4: D should be kept in mind when translating the definition of the *lakṣaṇaniḥsvabhāvatā*: *yon tan 'byung gnas de la chos rnams kyi kun brtags pa'i mtshan nyid gang zhe na / ji tsam du rjes su tha snyad*

«7.5» "Paramārthasamudgata, what is the essencelessness of all phenomena with regard to arising? It is the other-dependent defining characteristic of phenomena. Why? Because this is [the defining characteristic] arising on account of causes other [than itself] and not by itself. Therefore, it is called essencelessness with regard to arising.

«7.6» "Paramārthasamudgata, what is the essencelessness of all phenomena with regard to the ultimate? Phenomena arising in dependence upon causes, which lack an essence on account of lacking an essence in terms of arising and also lack an essence on account of lacking an ultimate essence. Why? Because, Paramārthasamudgata, I showed that the referential object conducive to purification within phenomena is the ultimate, but the other-dependent defining characteristic is not the referential object conducive to purification. Therefore, this essencelessness is called essencelessness with regard to the ultimate.

"Moreover, Paramārthasamudgata, the actual defining characteristic of phenomena should also be referred to as essencelessness with regard to the ultimate. Why? Because, Paramārthasamudgata, the selflessness of phenomena is called the essencelessness of phenomena, which is the ultimate, but the ultimate is characterized by[141] the essencelessness of all phenomena. Therefore, it is called essencelessness with regard to the ultimate.[142]

«7.7» "Paramārthasamudgata, it is like this: consider essencelessness with regard to defining characteristics to be exactly like a [nonexistent] sky flower; consider essencelessness with regard to arising, as well as essencelessness with regard to the ultimate in one of its aspects, to be exactly like a magical illusion;[143] consider essencelessness with regard to the ultimate in its other aspect, which consists in the selflessness of phenomena and pervades everything, to be exactly like space, which consists in the essencelessness of form and pervades everything.[144]

---

gdags pa'i phyir chos rnams kyi ngo bo nyid dam bye brag tu ming dang brdar rnam par gzhag pa gang yin pa'o.

141. *rab tu phye ba*; *prabhāvita* (see Schmithausen 2014, 400n1770).

142. See Schmithausen 2014, 559. Schmithausen reads *paramārthaniḥsvabhāvatā* as "lack of own-being [that is] the ultimate reality."

143. For a discussion of the syntactic construction *gcig . . . gcig*, refer to Tillemans 1997, 161–64.

144. See Schmithausen 2014, 560, on the textual material pertaining to this sentence.

«7.8» "Paramārthasamudgata, with this threefold essencelessness in mind, I taught what is called the essencelessness of all phenomena. Paramārthasamudgata, having in mind essencelessness with regard to defining characteristics, I taught, 'All phenomena are without an essence, unborn, unceasing, primordially in the state of peace, and naturally in the state of nirvana.' Why? Because, Paramārthasamudgata, what lacks a specific defining characteristic is unborn. What is unborn is unceasing. What is unborn and unceasing is primordially in the state of peace. What is primordially in the state of peace is naturally in the state of nirvana. For what is naturally in the state of nirvana, there is nothing in the slightest that passes into the state of nirvana. Therefore, having in mind essencelessness with regard to defining characteristics, I taught, 'All phenomena are without an essence, unborn, unceasing, primordially in the state of peace, and naturally in the state of nirvana.'

«7.9» "Paramārthasamudgata, having in mind essencelessness with regard to the ultimate, which is characterized by selflessness, I taught, 'All phenomena are without an essence, unborn, unceasing, primordially in the state of peace, and naturally in the state of nirvana.' Why? Because essencelessness with regard to the ultimate, which is characterized by selflessness, indeed abides permanently and immutably. As the nature of phenomena, it is unconditioned and free from all afflictions. What permanently and immutably abides as the very nature of phenomena, being unconditioned, is unborn and unceasing due to being unconditioned. Because it is free from all afflictions, it is primordially in the state of peace and naturally in the state of nirvana.[145] Therefore, having in mind essencelessness with regard to the ultimate, which is characterized by selflessness, I taught, 'All phenomena are without an essence, unborn, unceasing, primordially in the state of peace, and naturally in the state of nirvana.'

«7.10» "Paramārthasamudgata, I did not designate three kinds of essencelessness because those in the world of beings consider that the imaginary essence and the other-dependent essence, as well as the actual essence, are different by nature.[146] Rather, I did so because they superimpose an imag-

145. See Schmithausen 2014, 561ff.

146. For a complete comparison of this passage across editions, see Kojirō Katō's forthcoming edition of the text. As an example, it is interesting to compare the syntax of D and F. D: *don dam yang dag 'phags pas ni sems can gyi khams na sems can rnams kyis kun brtags pa'i ngo bo nyid ngo bo nyid kyis tha dad par mthong zhing gzhan gyi dbang gi ngo bo nyid dang / yongs*

inary essence on the other-dependent essence and the actual essence and because they designate the other-dependent essence and the actual essence as the defining characteristics of an imaginary essence. While they designate them in this way, their minds,[147] which are saturated with designations, become confined to such designations and predisposed[148] toward them. On this basis, they wrongly conceive the other-dependent essence and the actual essence as the defining characteristics of an imaginary essence. Wrongly conceiving them in this way, with their wrong conception of the other-dependent essence as the defining characteristic of an imaginary essence acting as a cause and condition, they will give rise in the future to an other-dependent essence.[149] As a result of this, they will be beset by

---

su grub pa'i ngo bo nyid kyang ngo bo nyid kyis tha dad par mthong na / de'i phyir ngo bo nyid med pa nyid rnam pa gsum mi 'dogs kyi. Interestingly, L, S, and T are in agreement with D, as are C, J, N, P, VD, VG, and VP. Only F offers a variant reading (folio 25.b): *don dam yang dag 'phags sems can gyi khams ni / sems can rnams kyis kun brtags pa'i rang bzhin ngo bo nyid kyis tha dad par mi mthong / gzhan gyi dbang gi rang bzhin dang / yongs su grub pa'i rang bzhin yang ngo bo nyid kyis tha dad par yang mi mthong ste / de'i phyir ngas rang bzhin med pa rnams gsum du gzhag go*. F explains why the Buddha taught an *essencelessness* by referring to beings as not perceiving a distinct essence in the three natures: "Paramārthasamudgata, beings in the world of beings do not consider the imaginary essence as different from an essence. They do not even consider the other-dependent essence and the actual essence as different from an essence. As a consequence, I presented the threefold essencelessness." This does not make much sense. I therefore follow the reading found in D. Frauwallner chose to follow D very closely here. He takes as the subject of the verb *mi 'dogs* the Buddha, like Powers and Lamotte: "Ich habe . . . die dreifache Wesenlosigkeit nicht verkündet, weil die Lebewesen in der Sphäre der Lebewesen das vorgestellte Wesen seinem Wesen nach als etwas Verschiedenes ansehen, und weil sie das abhängige Wesen und das vollkommene Wesen seinem Wesen nach als etwas Verschiedenes ansehen." Lamotte's translation (Lamotte 1935, 196) reads, "Si j'expose [for *'dogs*] la triple Irréalité, ce n'est pas parce que les êtres, dans le monde des êtres, considèrent la nature imaginaire comme une nature distincte, ou les natures dépendante et absolue comme des natures distinctes. Au contraire . . ." With "au contraire," Lamotte expresses the adversative function of the particle *kyi* at the end of the clause *de'i phyir ngo bo nyid med pa nyid rnam pa gsum mi 'dogs kyi*. To achieve this, Lamotte reads *mi 'dogs* in an affirmative mode and in the negative the statement regarding beings, which is in agreement with Xuanzang's translation: 復次勝義生非由有情界中諸有情類別觀遍計所執自性為自性故。亦非由彼別觀依他起自性及圓成實自性為自性故我立三種無自性性。然由有情於依他起自性及圓成實自性上增益遍計所執自性故我立三種無自性性 (CBETA, Taishō 676).

147. *sems*; *citta*. This is one of the synonyms for the subliminal mind (*kun gzhi rnam par shes pa*; *ālayavijñāna*) as explained in chapter 5. See chapters 5 and 6 on the latent disposition of the mind through karmic seeds in the sense of conventions.

148. *bag la nyal*; *anuśaya*. In the sense of "adhering/sticking" and "being latent/inclined" here (see Schmithausen 2014, 687).

149. Powers' translation does not render the meaning of this sentence: "Due to these causes

the afflictions of defilements, karma, and birth. Because they will not pass beyond samsara, they will transmigrate and wander among hell beings, animals, hungry ghosts, gods, demigods, and humans for a very long time.

«7.11» "Among these beings, Paramārthasamudgata, some do not produce roots of virtue from the very beginning. They do not clear obstructions or bring their mental continuums to maturity. Their confidence in my teaching is limited and they have not accomplished the accumulations of merit and gnosis. I impart to those beings the teaching on essencelessness with regard to arising. Once they have heard this teaching, they understand that conditioned phenomena arising in dependence on causes are of an impermanent, unstable, and unreliable nature. They develop aversion and repulsion toward conditioned phenomena. Once they have done this, they turn away from wrongdoing. Not committing any wrongdoing, they establish themselves in virtue. With this as a cause, they produce the roots of virtue that were yet to be produced. They clear obstructions that were yet to be cleared. They bring their mental continuums, which were not yet mature, to maturity. As a result, their confidence in my teaching becomes vast, and they will accomplish the accumulations of merit and gnosis.

«7.12» "Although such beings have produced in this way roots of virtue up to the accomplishment of the accumulation of merit and gnosis, they do not understand essencelessness with regard to arising just as it is, as the essencelessness with regard to defining characteristics and the essencelessness with regard to the ultimate in its two aspects. For this reason, they will not be completely repulsed by all conditioned phenomena, completely free from desire, or completely liberated. They will not be completely liberated from all the afflictions of defilements, karma, and birth. It is therefore for them that the Tathāgata imparts the teaching on the essencelessness with regard to defining characteristics and the essencelessness with regard to the ultimate. He does so in order to make them feel repulsion toward all conditioned phenomena, as well as to free them from desire, to completely liberate them, and to take them perfectly[150] beyond the afflictions of defilements, karma, and birth.

«7.13» "Once they have heard this teaching, they do not wrongly con-

and conditions, in the future [this view of] the own-being of the other-dependent proliferates" (Powers 1995, 107). The other-dependent in the sense of dependent arising refers here to rebirth and future lives.

150. *yang dag par* ("perfectly") is important here, as it echoes the statement above, and with-

ceive the other-dependent essence as the defining characteristic of an imaginary essence. As a result, they accept the essencelessness with regard to arising as the essencelessness with regard to defining characteristics and the essencelessness with regard to the ultimate in its two aspects. They discern and understand it exactly as it is. It is like this: Their minds,[151] which are no longer saturated with designations, are not confined to these designations or predisposed toward them. As a result, by attaining the powers of wisdom in this life and perfectly cutting off the continuity [of the aggregates] into a future existence, they will put an end to the other-dependent defining characteristic. On this basis, they will be completely repulsed by all conditioned phenomena, completely free from desire, and completely liberated. They will be completely liberated from all the afflictions of defilements, karma, and birth.

«7.14»"Moreover, Paramārthasamudgata, even those belonging to the lineage of the hearers' vehicle attain nirvana, the unsurpassable happiness, through this very path and journey,[152] as do those belonging to the lineage of the solitary realizers' vehicle and the lineage of the tathāgatas. This is why it is the single path of purification for hearers, solitary realizers, and bodhisattvas. Since there is only a single purification, there is no other. Therefore, with this in mind, I taught the Single Vehicle. Yet it is not the case that those in the world of beings are not of various types corresponding to their capacities, be they weak, average, or sharp in accord with their nature.

«7.15»"Paramārthasamudgata, even if they were to exert themselves as all buddhas did,[153] individuals belonging to the hearers' lineage with the state of peace as their sole journey could not reach the heart of awakening and

---

out it the entire paragraph loses its meaning: to achieve perfect liberation, the teaching on essencelessness with regard to both defining characteristics and the ultimate is necessary.

151. L, S, T, and F (e.g., F, folio 27.a) logically confirm *shes pa*, which is interesting since it establishes a distinction between occurrences of *shes pa* and *ye shes*, which D does not do systematically (see Kojirō Katō's edition of chapter 7). The term here is a synonym for *sems*; see the parallel passage above in 7.10.

152. F, folio 27.a, has *lam 'di nyid dang 'grod pa 'di nyid kyis* instead of D: *lam 'di nyid dang sgrub pa 'di nyid kyis grub pa dang*. C, H, J, N, and K0774 also read *sgrub*; VD, VG, VP: *bsgrub*; L, S: *bgrod*; F, T: *'grod*. (cf. Kojirō Katō's edition).

153. *don dam yang dag 'phags nyan thos kyi rigs can gang zag zhi ba'i bgrod pa gcig pu pa ni sangs rgyas thams cad brtson pa dang ldan par gyur kyang byang chub kyi snying po la bzhag ste*. Brunnhölzl reads the qualifying clause *sangs rgyas thams cad brtson pa dang ldan par gyur* in quite a different way here: "even if all buddhas with [all] their effort were [to attempt] to establish persons with the śrāvaka disposition . . ." (Brunnhölzl 2018, 1522).

attain the unsurpassable, complete, and perfect awakening. Why? Because, having limited compassion and a great fear of suffering, they belong to a lineage that is by nature inferior. Thus, having limited compassion, they avoid striving for beings' welfare. Being afraid of suffering, they stay clear of the conditioning process of the mental factors.[154] However, I did not teach that avoiding striving for beings' welfare and staying clear of the conditioning process of the mental factors was the unsurpassable, complete, and perfect awakening. Therefore, these individuals are called those who have the state of peace as their sole journey.

«7.16»"I taught that hearers who evolve toward awakening belong to the category of bodhisattvas because, liberated from the obscuration of defilements and inspired by the tathāgatas, they liberate their minds from the obscuration of cognitive objects. It is [only] because they first liberated themselves from the obscuration of defilements for their own sake that the Tathāgata designated them as the lineage of hearers.

«7.17»"Thus, Paramārthasamudgata, there are beings with various degrees of confidence in my Dharma and my Vinaya, which are well proclaimed, well imparted, pure in their intention, and well communicated. In this teaching, Paramārthasamudgata, the Tathāgata, having in mind the three kinds of essencelessness, teaches through a discourse of provisional meaning: 'All phenomena are without an essence, unborn, unceasing, primordially in the state of peace, and naturally in the state of nirvana.'

«7.18»"Among such beings, Paramārthasamudgata, some have produced roots of virtue, purified their obscurations, and brought their mental continuum to maturity. They have much confidence in my teaching and have accomplished the accumulations of merit and gnosis. Once they have heard my teaching, they understand my explanations in accord with my underlying intent exactly as it is. Moreover, they recognize that this teaching is the truth.[155] Through their wisdom, they realize its meaning exactly as it is. By also engaging in the practice of this realization, they will very quickly attain the ultimate state. They will develop faith in these teachings, and think,

154. *'du byed mngon par 'du bya ba*; *saṁskārābhisaṁskaraṇa*. Compare with the Sanskrit sentence in Tucci's edition of *Bhāvanākrama* (Tucci 1971, 22): *ekāntasattvārtha-vimukhasya ekāntasaṃsārābhisaṃskāravimukhasya [nā]uttarā samyaksaṃbodhir uktā mayeti*, which has *saṃsārābhisaṃskāra* instead of *saṃskārābhisaṃskaraṇa* as found in Tibetan.
155. *chos*; *dharma*.

'Amazing! The Blessed One is completely and perfectly awakened. Through him, one becomes perfectly awakened with respect to all phenomena.'

«7.19» "Among such beings, some have not produced roots of virtue, purified their obscurations, and brought their mental continuums to maturity. Their confidence in my teaching is limited and they have not accomplished the accumulations of merit and gnosis. They are honest and sincere. Unable to evaluate and refute[156] [others' views], they do not consider their own as supreme. Once they have heard my teaching, although they do not understand my explanations in accord with my underlying intent exactly as it is, they still develop confidence and faith in these teachings: 'The Tathāgata's discourse is profound and has the appearance of profundity. [Because] emptiness is the topic of this discourse, it is difficult to perceive and difficult to understand. Being beyond judgment, it does not belong to the domain of speculation. It can [only] be known by intelligent scholars well versed in the subtle.'[157] They think, 'We do not understand the meaning of this sutra and these teachings that were taught by the Blessed One. Profound is the awakening of the Buddha and the nature of phenomena. Only the Tathāgata understands them. We, however, do not. The Dharma taught by the tathāgatas arises according to the various inclinations of beings. Their gnosis[158] and perception are infinite, whereas ours are merely like the [shallow] hoofprints left by a cow.' Filled with devotion for these discourses, they also write them down. Having written them down, they also keep them in mind, read them, propagate them, venerate them, expound them, recite them, and chant them aloud. However, because they do not understand these profound teachings in accord with my underlying intent, they are unable to engage themselves in the various aspects of practice. As a consequence of this, they will further develop their accumulation of merit and

156. *drang po dang drang po'i rang bzhin can / rtog pa dang sel mi nus pa*. Powers understands *rtog pa dang sel* as "to remove conceptuality" (Powers 1995, 117). F, folio 28.b, reads *brtag pa dang / bzhig pa mi nus pa*. The problem is that *sel* is a transitive verb. It is therefore syntactically difficult to take *rtog pa* as the object of *sel*. In the present case, Keenan's solution based on Chinese is interesting: "to make judgments" (Keenan 2000, 42).

157. *zhib mo brtags pa'i mkhas pa dang 'dzangs pas rig pa*; *sūkṣmaṃ nipuṇapaṇḍitavijñavedanīyaḥ* (see Mvyut 2918). Lit. "It is to be known." All Sanskrit synonyms for this sentence are found in Mvyut 2013–20.

158. In accordance with the multiple occurrences of this phrase in chapter 2, *shes pa* should be read here as *ye shes* in agreement with F.

gnosis, and those whose mental continuums are still immature will bring them to maturity.

«7.20» "Other beings have not perfectly completed these stages up to the great accumulation of merit and gnosis. They are dishonest and insincere. Capable of evaluating and refuting [others' views], they consider their own as supreme. Once they have heard my teaching, they do not understand my profound explanations in accord with my underlying intent exactly as it is. Although they have confidence in this teaching, they wrongly conceive it according to its literal meaning: 'All phenomena are only without an essence, only unborn, only unceasing, only primordially in the state of peace, and only naturally in the state of nirvana.' As a consequence of this, they acquire the view that all phenomena are inexistent and the view that they are without defining characteristics. Then, once they have acquired these views, they negate all phenomena by [negating] all defining characteristics, thereby negating the imaginary defining characteristic as well as the other-dependent and actual defining characteristics. Why is it said that they negate all three defining characteristics? Because, Paramārthasamudgata, if the other-dependent and actual defining characteristics are accepted, then the imaginary defining characteristic also will be distinctly perceived. Now, those who consider the other-dependent and actual defining characteristics as inexistent have already negated the imaginary defining characteristic. This is why they are called those who negate all three defining characteristics. They consider my teaching to be the truth while considering some nonsense to be its meaning. Those who consider my teaching to be the truth while considering some nonsense to be its meaning cling to my teaching as the truth while at the same time clinging to some nonsense as its meaning. Since they have confidence in my teaching, they will progress by developing virtuous qualities. However, because they wrongly conceive some nonsense to be the meaning of my teaching, they will stray from wisdom. Straying from wisdom, they will stray from the vast and immeasurable virtuous qualities.

«7.21» "Others hear from those beings that my teaching is the truth while some nonsense is its meaning. Then, delighted by this view, they accept that my teaching is the truth and some nonsense is its meaning. Thus, they wrongly conceive my teaching as the truth with some nonsense as its meaning. As a consequence of this, you should know that they will likewise stray from virtuous qualities.

«7.22» "Others who take no delight in this view are overcome by fear and anxiety when they hear that all phenomena are without an essence, unborn, unceasing, primordially in the state of peace, and naturally in the state of nirvana. They then say, 'These are not the words of the Buddha but the words of Māra!' Thinking in this way, they reject this discourse, disparage it, denigrate it, and criticize it. As a consequence of this, they will obtain the great misfortune as well as the great karmic obscuration [of rejecting the truth].[159] This is precisely why I said, 'Those who mislead the multitude of beings into obtaining the great karmic obscuration, who consider all defining characteristics as inexistent and teach some nonsense as the meaning of my teaching, are burdened with the great karmic obscuration [of rejecting the truth].

«7.23» "Paramārthasamudgata, among such beings, some have not produced roots of virtue, purified their obscurations, and brought their mental continuum to maturity. Their confidence in my teaching is limited, and they have not accomplished the accumulations of merit and gnosis. They are dishonest and insincere. Although they are unable to evaluate and refute [others' views], they consider their own as supreme. When they hear my teaching, they neither understand my explanations in accord with my underlying intent exactly as it is, nor do they develop confidence in this teaching. They accept that my teaching is not the truth and its meaning is some nonsense. They say, 'These are not the words of the Buddha but the words of Māra!' Thinking in this way, they reject this discourse, disparage it, denigrate it, criticize it, and distort [its meaning]. In many ways, they apply themselves to discarding, undermining, and subverting this discourse, considering as enemies those who are devoted to it. From the very beginning, they are affected by the karmic obscuration [of rejecting the truth]. As a consequence of this, they also cause [others] to be obscured by this karmic obscuration. Although it is easy to determine the beginning of this karmic obscuration, it is difficult to know how many myriad eons it will last.

"Thus, Paramārthasamudgata, those are the various degrees of confidence in my Dharma and my Vinaya,[160] which are well proclaimed, well imparted, pure in their intention, and well communicated."

159. See Lamotte 1935, 201n31: *las kyi sgrib chen po* refers here to *saddharmapratikṣepa-karmāvaraṇa*.

160. *chos 'dul ba*; *dharmavinaya* (read as a *dvandva*).

«7.24» Then, at that moment, the Blessed One spoke these verses:

"All phenomena are without an essence, unborn,
Unceasing, primordially in the state of peace,
And naturally in the state of nirvana.
What wise person would say this without an underlying intent?

"I have spoken of essencelessness
With regard to defining characteristics, arising, and the ultimate.
No wise person who understands my underlying intent
Will travel the path leading to corruption.

"There is only one path of purification for all beings,
As there is only one purification, not two.
This is why, even if there are various lineages of beings,
I proclaimed the Single Vehicle.

"In the world of beings, innumerable are
The solitary beings who attain nirvana,
While rare are those who have attained nirvana
And possess the energy and compassion to not turn away from beings.

"Subtle, inconceivable, and undifferentiated
Is the uncontaminated domain of those who are liberated.
Nondual and inexpressible, blissful and immutable,
It is the accomplishment of all [intentions], the release from all suffering and defilements."

«7.25» Then the bodhisattva Paramārthasamudgata said to the Blessed One, "Blessed One, the speech expounding the underlying intent of the buddhas is subtle, extremely subtle, profound, extremely profound, difficult to understand, and extremely difficult to understand. How marvelous, how wonderful it is!

"This is how I understand the meaning of the words spoken by the Blessed One: The manifest characteristic of conditioned phenomena, namely, the basis of the imaginary defining characteristic, the object of conceptualization,[161] is nominally and conventionally posited as an essential characteristic or a distinctive characteristic,[162] for example, as the aggregate of form, its arising, its cessation, its abandonment, or the comprehension of this aggregate. What is posited in this way is the imaginary defining characteristic. For this reason, Blessed One, you referred to essencelessness with regard to the defining characteristics of phenomena. The manifest characteristic of conditioned phenomena, namely, the basis of the imaginary defining characteristic, the object of conceptualization, is the other-dependent defining characteristic. For this reason, Blessed One, you referred to essencelessness with regard to both the arising of phenomena and the ultimate in one of its aspects.

"This is how I understand the meaning of the words spoken by the Blessed One: this very manifest characteristic of conditioned phenomena, namely, the basis of the imaginary defining characteristic, the object of conceptualization, is devoid of any actuality or essence as that which has an imaginary defining characteristic.[163] On account of this, this essencelessness or selflessness of phenomena, true reality, the referential object conducive to purification, is the actual defining characteristic. For this reason, Blessed One, you referred to the essencelessness of phenomena with regard to the ultimate in its other aspect.

"One should proceed in exactly the same way with the remaining aggregates as well as with each of the twelve sense domains, the twelve factors of conditioned existence, the four kinds of sustenance, and the six and eighteen constituents.

«7.26»"This is how I understand the meaning of the words spoken by

161. I read *rnam par rtog pa'i spyod yul kun brtags pa'i mtshan nyid kyi gnas 'du byed kyi mtshan ma* (D) as a *karmadhāraya*, which means that the last compound in the series of three should be topicalized. It seems to me that since the opposition between *nimitta* ("manifest characteristic") and *svabhāva* or *svalakṣaṇa* ("unique/specific/particular defining characteristic or essence") is central throughout the text, reading the compound in this way clarifies the meaning of this definition of the *parikalpita*, which basically results from the operation consisting in attributing an essence to appearance by means of verbal conventions.

162. This definition elaborates on the definition of *parikalpitasvabhāva* formulated in 6.4. In 6.5 and 6.7, that which has the defining characteristic of dependent arising is equated with manifest characteristic. On the basis of what is dependent on an other, essence is imputed in the sense of a real entity, independent of any other cause to exist as what it is. This corresponds to the imaginary defining characteristic.

163. Lamotte's translation is built on the same structure but inverts the main clauses of the sentence: In the *nimitta*, the *parikalpita* is unestablished. See Lamotte 1935, 204.

the Blessed One: The manifest characteristic of conditioned phenomena, namely, the basis of the imaginary defining characteristic, the object of conceptualization, is nominally and conventionally posited as an essential characteristic or a distinctive characteristic, for example, as the noble truth of suffering or the comprehension of suffering. For this reason, Blessed One, you referred to essencelessness with regard to the defining characteristics of phenomena. The manifest characteristic of conditioned phenomena, namely, the basis of the imaginary defining characteristic, the object of conceptualization, is the other-dependent defining characteristic. For this reason, Blessed One, you referred to essencelessness with regard to both the arising of phenomena and the ultimate in one of its aspects.

"This is how I understand the meaning of the words spoken by the Blessed One: This very manifest characteristic of conditioned phenomena, namely, the basis of the imaginary defining characteristic, the object of conceptualization, is devoid of any actuality or essence as that which has an imaginary defining characteristic.[164] On account of this, this essencelessness or selflessness of phenomena, true reality, the referential object conducive to purification, is the actual defining characteristic. For this reason, Blessed One, you referred to the essencelessness of phenomena with regard to the ultimate in its other aspect.

"As with the noble truth of suffering, one should proceed in exactly the same way with the other truths. As with the truths, so one should proceed in exactly the same way with each of the applications of mindfulness, the self-restraints, the bases of supernatural powers, the faculties, the forces, the branches of awakening, and the branches of the path.

«7.27»"This is how I understand the meaning of the words spoken by the Blessed One: The manifest characteristic of conditioned phenomena, namely, the basis of the imaginary defining characteristic, the object of conceptualization, is nominally and conventionally posited as an essential characteristic or a distinctive characteristic, for example, as correct concentration,[165] its adverse factors and antidotes, its practice, its arising from

164. Lamotte's translation is built on the same structure but inverts the main clauses of the sentence: In the *nimitta*, the *parikalpita* is unestablished. See Lamotte 1935, 204. D: *kun brtags pa'i mtshan nyid der yongs su ma grub*. I read *kun brtags pa'i mtshan nyid* as a *bahuvrīhi*: "that which has the imaginary defining characteristic" or "that which consists in / is characterized by the imaginary."

165. *yang dag pa'i ting nge 'dzin*; *samyaksamādhi*.

being non-arisen, its remaining after it arose, and its maintaining, resuming, increasing, or expanding. For this reason, Blessed One, you referred to essencelessness with regard to the defining characteristics of phenomena. The manifest characteristic of conditioned phenomena, namely, the basis of the imaginary defining characteristic, the object of conceptualization, is the other-dependent defining characteristic. For this reason, Blessed One, you referred to essencelessness with regard to both the arising of phenomena and the ultimate in one of its aspects.

"This is how I understand the meaning of the words spoken by the Blessed One: This very manifest characteristic of conditioned phenomena, namely, the basis of the imaginary defining characteristic, the object of conceptualization, is devoid of any actuality or essence as that which has an imaginary defining characteristic. On account of this, this essencelessness or selflessness of phenomena, true reality, the referential object conducive to purification is the actual defining characteristic. For this reason, Blessed One, you referred to the essencelessness of phenomena with regard to the ultimate in its other aspect.

«7.28»"Blessed One, thus it is said, for example, that dried ginger should be added to all medicinal powders and elixirs. Likewise, this teaching of definitive meaning expounded by[166] the Blessed One in reference to the statement 'All phenomena are without an essence, unborn, unceasing, primordially in the state of peace, and naturally in the state of nirvana'[167] should also be added to all the discourses of provisional meaning.[168]

166. D: *bcom ldan 'das nges pa'i don bstan pa 'di* should be read *bcom ldan 'das kyi* (or *kyis* as in VD) *nges pa'i don bstan pa 'di*, lit. "of the Blessed One," rendered here as "[expounded] by the Blessed One." *bcom ldan 'das* is omitted in L, S, T, and F; see Katō's edition of chapter 7.

167. Lamotte and Powers understand the statement "All phenomena are without an essence, unborn, unceasing, primordially in the state of peace, and naturally in the state of nirvana" to be the teaching of definitive meaning (see Lamotte 1935, 206, and Powers 1995, 135–37). However, the entire point of this chapter is that there is an underlying intent of definitive meaning to this statement. This is the reason why it is explained in the next paragraphs that a third turning of the wheel of Dharma was necessary.

168. D: *de bzhin du chos rnams kyi ngo bo nyid ma mchis pa nyid las brtsams / skye ba ma mchis pa dang / 'gag pa ma mchis pa dang / gzod ma nas zhi ba dang / rang bzhin gyis yongs su mya ngan las 'das pa nyid las brtsams nas / bcom ldan 'das nges pa'i don bstan pa 'di yang drang ba'i don gyi mdo sde thams cad du stsal bar bgyi pa lags so.* C, H, J, N, K0774, VG, VP, L, S, T, and F also read *stsal*; VD: *bstsal* (cf. Kojirō Katō's edition). Lamotte translates *stsal* with "se recommande" to create a parallel construction with the analogy of the dried ginger (see Lamotte 1935, 205). This somehow does not solve our problem. Powers translates *stsal bar*

"Blessed One, it is like this: for example, the canvas for a painting, whether blue, yellow, red, or white, is identical for all painted figures and thus perfectly clarifies their contours. Likewise, this teaching of definitive meaning expounded by the Blessed One in reference to the statement 'All phenomena are without an essence, unborn, unceasing, primordially in the state of peace, and naturally in the state of nirvana' is identical in all discourses of provisional meaning and thus perfectly clarifies their interpretable intent.

"Blessed One, it is like this: for example, adding clarified butter to all sorts of stews, meat dishes, and porridge is delicious. Likewise, it is delightful to add to all discourses of provisional meaning this teaching of definitive meaning expounded by the Blessed One in reference to the statement 'All phenomena are without an essence, unborn, unceasing, primordially in the state of peace, and naturally in the state of nirvana.'

"Blessed One, it is like this: for example, space is identical everywhere and, [being empty and free from all obstruction,] does not hinder any endeavor. Likewise, this teaching of definitive meaning expounded by the Blessed One in reference to the statement 'All phenomena are without an essence, unborn, unceasing, primordially in the state of peace, and naturally in the state of nirvana' is identical in all discourses of provisional meaning and does not hinder any endeavor in the course of the hearers', solitary realizers', or bodhisattvas' vehicle."

«7.29» Following these words, the Blessed One complimented the bodhisattva Paramārthasamudgata: "Excellent, Paramārthasamudgata, this is excellent! You have understood my explanation in accord with the Tathāgata's underlying intent. Your examples of the dried ginger, painting, clarified butter, and space perfectly illustrated its point. Paramārthasamudgata, so it is, and not otherwise. Therefore, keep in mind this teaching in this way."

«7.30» Then the bodhisattva Paramārthasamudgata spoke again to the Blessed One. "In the deer park of Ṛṣhivadana in Vārāṇasī, the Blessed One first set in motion the wonderful wheel of Dharma by teaching the four

---

gyi with a past tense "placed" (see Powers 1995, 137). Keenan 2000, 48, offers a literal rendering of Xuanzang's translation that is similar to the Tibetan version of the text (如是世尊依此諸法皆無自性無生無滅本來寂靜自性涅槃無自性性了義言教遍於一切不了義經皆應安處, CBETA, Taishō 676): "just so, World-Honored One, the explicit teaching that all things have no essence, no arising, and no passing away, are originally quiescent, and are essentially in cessation *must be put into all the scriptures of implicit meaning*."

noble truths to those who were engaged in the hearers' vehicle. Not a single god or human in the world had previously ever turned such a wheel of Dharma. However, this turning of the Dharma wheel by the Blessed One was surpassable and adapted to the circumstances. Being of provisional meaning,[169] it became a topic of dispute. Then, for those who were engaged in the Great Vehicle, you turned the second, even more wonderful, wheel of Dharma in the form of a teaching on emptiness: 'All phenomena are without an essence, unborn, unceasing, primordially in the state of peace, and naturally in the state of nirvana.' However, this turning of the Dharma wheel by the Blessed One was surpassable and adapted to the circumstances. Being of provisional meaning, it became a topic of dispute. Then, for those who were engaged in all vehicles,[170] you turned the third wonderful Dharma wheel of excellent discernment in reference to the statement 'All phenomena are without an essence, unborn, unceasing, primordially in the state of peace, and naturally in the state of nirvana.'[171] This turning of the Dharma wheel by the Blessed One was unsurpassable and not limited to the circumstances.

«7.31» "Blessed One, when sons or daughters of noble family have heard the teaching of definitive meaning taught by the Blessed One in reference to the statement 'All phenomena are without an essence, unborn, unceasing, primordially in the state of peace, and naturally in the state of nirvana,' they develop devotion for this teaching and commission its transcription into writing. Once it has been put into writing, they keep it in mind, read it, venerate it, propagate it, expound it, chant it aloud, contemplate it, and apply it in their practice. As they do so, how much merit will they produce?"

«7.32» The Blessed One answered, "Paramārthasamudgata, these sons and daughters of noble family will produce immeasurable and incalculable merit. Although it is difficult to illustrate this with examples, I will briefly

169. D: *drang ba'i don rtsod pa'i gzhi'i gnas su gyur pa lags la* in the sense of *drang ba'i don lags te / rtsod pa'i gzhi'i gnas su gyur pa lags la* as in *nges pa'i don lags te / rtsod pa'i gzhi'i gnas su gyur pa ma lags so* (see D, folio 25.a).

170. This is an important statement regarding the intent of the third turning of the wheel, which is to bring together those following the hearers' and the bodhisattvas' paths within a single vehicle.

171. By repeating the same statement to describe the second and third turnings, it is made clear that interpreting this statement in terms of emptiness alone is provisional. The underlying intent of the statement corresponds to the teaching found in the third turning.

explain it to you. Paramārthasamudgata, it is like this: Compared to the amount of earth, the amount of dirt at the tip of a fingernail does not come close to a hundredth, a thousandth, a one hundred thousandth of it, or anything implying calculation, partition, numeration, analogy, or comparison. Compared to the amount of water contained in the four great oceans, the amount of water contained in the hoofprint of an ox does not come close to a hundredth, a thousandth, a one hundred thousandth of it, or anything implying calculation, partition, numeration, analogy, or comparison. Likewise, Paramārthasamudgata, compared to the amount of merit accumulated by developing confidence in my teaching of definitive meaning up to applying it in one's practice, the amount of merit accumulated by developing confidence in my teaching of provisional meaning . . . up to applying it in one's practice does not come close to a hundredth, a thousandth, a one hundred thousandth of it, or anything implying calculation, partition, numeration, analogy, or comparison."

«7.33» The bodhisattva Paramārthasamudgata inquired, "Blessed One, what is the name of this teaching as a Dharma discourse that elucidates the Tathāgata's intent?[172] How should I keep it in mind?"[173]

The Blessed One answered: "Paramārthasamudgata, this is a teaching of definitive meaning on the ultimate. Therefore, keep it in mind as *The Teaching of Definitive Meaning on the Ultimate.*"

As the Blessed One expounded this teaching of definitive meaning on the ultimate, six hundred thousand beings produced the mind directed at the unsurpassable, complete, and perfect awakening;[174] three hundred thousand hearers purified the Dharma eye from impurities and contaminations; one hundred and fifty hearers who were without attachment liberated their minds from all outflows; and seventy-five thousand bodhisattvas attained the acceptance that phenomena are non-arisen.

This was the chapter of the bodhisattva Paramārthasamudgata—
the seventh chapter.

172. Lit. "Blessed One, what is the name of that which has been taught as a Dharma discourse ascertaining the [Tathāgata's] intent?"
173. *gzung bar bgyi*; *dhārayāmi* (cf. Sanskrit text in Matsuda 2013, 940 *ad* Lamotte 1935 VIII.41). I suggest reading *dhārayāmi*, which is a causative present of *dhṛ-*, as an optative here.
174. This refers to *byang chub kyi sems*; *bodhicitta*.

Chapter 8

«8.1» Then the bodhisattva Maitreya asked a question to the Blessed One, "Blessed One, when bodhisattvas practice mental stillness and insight in the Great Vehicle, what is their support and basis?"

The Blessed One answered, "Maitreya, their support and basis are the discourses teaching Dharma and the constant aspiration to attain the unsurpassable, complete, and perfect awakening.

«8.2» "The Blessed One taught that four things are the referential objects of mental stillness and insight: the image with conceptualization; the image without conceptualization; the point where phenomena end; and the accomplishment of the goal."

"Blessed One, how many referential objects of mental stillness are there?"

"There is [only] one, namely, the image without conceptualization."

"How many are the referential objects of insight?"

"There is only one, namely, the image with conceptualization."

"How many are the referential objects of both combined?"

"There are two, namely, the point where phenomena end and the accomplishment of the goal."

«8.3» "Blessed One, once bodhisattvas have taken as a support and basis these four things that are the referential objects of mental stillness and insight, how do they dedicate themselves to mental stillness? How do they become skilled in the practice of insight?"

"Maitreya, I have given to the bodhisattvas discourses teaching Dharma in the following twelve collections of teachings: sutras, discourses in prose and verse, prophecies, poetic discourses, aphorisms, discourses for specific beings, narratives, parables, discourses on previous lives, extensive discourses, teachings on miracles, and instructions. Once bodhisattvas have properly heard these explanations, once they have memorized them well, recited them, examined them, and understood them by means of discernment, they remain alone in seclusion and settle themselves in a state of inner absorption. Then they direct their attention in that (1) they direct their attention toward the teachings they have properly contemplated[175] and (2) continuously direct their attention inwardly toward the mind that is directing attention. As they repeatedly engage themselves in this way, their bodies and minds become flexible. The occurrence of this physical and mental flexibility is what is called mental stillness. This is how bodhisattvas dedicate themselves to mental stillness.

«8.4» "Once they have obtained[176] this physical and mental flexibility, they settle in this very state and abandon some aspects of mind [corresponding to mental stillness].[177] Then they apply themselves to analyzing the image that is the object of their concentration according to the teachings they have properly contemplated. Differentiating, discerning, considering, and examining in this way the cognitive aspects of the image that is the object of their concentration, accepting and wishing to do so, and distinguishing, scrutinizing, and investigating [this discerning mind in the same way] is what is called [the practice of] insight. This is how bodhisattvas are skilled in insight."

«8.5» "Blessed One, when bodhisattvas direct their attention inwardly toward the mind that takes the mind as its referential object but have not yet attained physical and mental flexibility, what do you call their practice of directing attention?"

"Maitreya, this is not yet mental stillness. So you should refer to it as a practice aspiring to mental stillness."

"Blessed One, when bodhisattvas direct their attention toward the image that is the object of their concentration according to the teachings they

175. This paragraph follows the pattern according to which *prajñā* is developed as *śrutamayī prajñā, cintāmayī prajñā, bhāvanāmayī prajñā*. Once the bodhisattvas have heard and contemplated what has been taught, they proceed with practice.

176. Read *thob* instead of *thos*. See F, folio 36.b: *lus shin tu sbyangs pa dang / sems shin tu sbyangs pa de dag thob pa de'i bar du* and *lus shin tu sbyangs pa dang / sems shin tu sbyangs pa de dag thob kyi bar du* (8.5).

177. D: *de lus shin tu sbyangs pa dang / sems shin tu sbyangs pa de thos nas de nyid la gnas te / sems kyi rnam pa spangs nas ji ltar bsams pa'i chos de dag nyid nang du ting nge 'dzin gyi spyod yul gzugs brnyan du so sor rtog par byed mos par byed do*. S, folio 37.b; F, folio 36.a: *des lus shin tu sbyangs pa dang / sems shin tu sbyangs pa de dag thos nas de nyid la gnas te / ji ltar bsams pa'i chos de dag nyid nang du ting nge 'dzin gyi spyod yul gzugs brnyan du sems kyi rnam pa spangs nas / so sor rtog cing byed mor byed do*.

have properly contemplated, but they have not yet attained physical and mental flexibility, what do you call their practice of directing attention?"

"Maitreya, this is not yet insight. So you should refer to it as a practice aspiring to insight."

«8.6» "Blessed One, should we refer to the path of mental stillness and the path of insight as being distinct or indistinct from one another?"

"Maitreya, we should refer to them as neither distinct nor indistinct. Why are they not distinct? Because mental stillness takes mind, which is the referential object of insight, as its object. Why are they not indistinct? Because insight takes a conceptual image as its referential object."

«8.7» "Blessed One, what image do bodhisattvas focus on as their object of concentration? Should we consider it as distinct from mind or not?"[178]

"Maitreya, we must consider that it is not distinct from mind. Why? Because this image is merely a representation. Maitreya, I have explained that cognition is constituted[179] by the mere representation that is the referential object [of this cognition]."[180]

"Blessed One, if this image that is the object of concentration is not distinct from the mind, how does this very mind investigate itself?"

178. For a detailed discussion of 8.7–9, refer to Schmithausen 2014, 391ff.

179. *rab tu phye ba*; *prabhāvita* in the compound **ālambanavijñaptimātraprabhāvita* (see Schmithausen 1984, 436; 2014, 400–1 passim). On the possible meanings of the Sanskrit term *prabhāvita* in the sense of "consisting of" or "characterized as" as opposed to "characterized by," refer to Schmithausen 2014, 400n1770.

180. The compound *dmigs pa rnam par rig pa tsam*; **ālambanavijñaptimātra* can be read as a *tatpuruṣa*: "the mere representation of a referential object," or as a *karmadhāraya*: "a referential object that is a mere representation" or "a mere representation as a referential object" (see Schmithausen 2014, 411). If we add to these possibilities the distinction between "characterized as / consists of" and "characterized by" mentioned by Schmithausen in reference to *prabhāvita* (see n.181), it is clear that this important statement can be interpreted in various ways that are consistent with the syntax of this sentence. If one wishes to read the compound **ālambanavijñaptimātra* as a *tatpuruṣa*, the phrase reads "the mere representation of a referential object." However, it seems to me that we should read this compound as a *karmadhāraya*, since the whole point of this paragraph is to answer Maitreya's original question about the nature of the image qua object. The answer to this question is that the image (*pratibimba*) that is the object of concentration is not distinct from mind because mind is constituted by a representation that is the actual object of this cognition. With regard to this issue, Xuanzang's translation reads 善男子當言無異何以故由彼影像唯是識故 善男子我說識所緣唯識所現故 (CBETA, Taishō 676), which is compatible with the suggested translation. For a complete analysis of these two sentences across selected Chinese and Tibetan editions, see Schmithausen 2014, 392ff., and Brunnhölzl 2018, 511n139, which contains a detailed summary of Schmithausen's analysis.

"Maitreya, [ultimately] no phenomenon whatsoever investigates any phenomenon at all. However, the mind that arises as [if it were conscious of an object] appears as [if it were investigating itself]. Maitreya, it is like this: based on a form [in front of a mirror], you see that same form on the clear surface of this mirror and realize that you are seeing a reflection, an image in which this reflection and the form [it is based on] appear to be distinct objects. Likewise, the mind arising as [if it were conscious of an object] and what is called its image, the object of concentration, appear as if they were distinct objects."[181]

«8.8» "Blessed One, should we say that mental images naturally present to beings, such as the appearance of material form and so forth, are also not distinct from mind?"[182]

"Maitreya, we should say that they are not distinct. However, foolish beings with erroneous ideas do not understand just as it is that [mental] images are mere representations. As a consequence, their minds are mistaken."

«8.9» "Blessed One, when do the bodhisattvas practice only insight?"

"Whenever they direct their attention[183] toward mental manifest characteristics[184] without interruption."

"When do the bodhisattvas practice only mental stillness?"

"Whenever they direct their attention toward the unimpeded mind without interruption."

"When do they combine both insight and mental stillness and unite them evenly?"

181. On VIII.7, see Brunnhölzl 2018, 512n141.

182. D: *bcom ldan 'das sems can rnams kyi gzugs la sogs par snang ba sems kyi gzugs brnyan rang bzhin du gnas pa gang lags pa de yang sems de dang tha dad pa ma lags zhes bgyi'am*; S, folio 38.b: *bcom ldan 'das sems can rnams kyi sems kyi gzugs brnyan rang bzhin du gnas pa / gzugs la sogs pa gang lags de yang sems de dang tha dad pa ma lags shes bgyi'am*; F, folio 37.a: *bcom ldan 'das sems can rnams kyi sems kyi gzugs brnyan rang bzhin du gnas pa / gzugs la tshogs pa de dag kyang sems de dang tha dad pa ma lags shes bgyi'am*.

183. D: *mtshan nyid la byed pa*. F, folio 37.b: *mtshan nyid yid la byed pa*.

184. *sems kyi mtshan nyid* but *sems kyi mtshan ma* would be better here since Maitreya inquires about *mtshan ma* right after this. Unfortunately, Xuanzang's translation does not contribute to solving this quandary since 相 can refer to both *lakṣaṇa* and *nimitta* (see 若相續作意唯思维心相, CBETA, Taishō 676). However, the structure of the paragraph in which questions are asked about definitions of terms found in the Buddha's previous answer in 8.8 indicates that we should emend *sems kyi mtshan nyid* to *sems kyi mtshan ma*.

"Whenever they direct their attention toward the one-pointedness of mind."

"Blessed One, what is a mental appearance?"

"Maitreya, this is the referential object of insight, the conceptual image that is the object of concentration."

"What is the unimpeded mind?"

"Maitreya, it is the referential object of mental stillness, the mind that takes the image as an object."

"What is one-pointedness of mind?"

"[One-pointedness of mind is] realizing in regard to the image that is the object of concentration, 'This is merely a representation,' and, on realizing that, directing one's attention toward true reality."[185]

«8.10» "Blessed One, how many kinds of insight are there?"

"Maitreya, there are three: insight arising from manifest characteristic, insight arising from inquiry, and insight arising from awakening."[186]

"What is insight arising from manifest characteristic?"

"It is the insight in which attention is directed exclusively toward a conceptual image, the object of concentration."

"What is insight arising from inquiry?"

"It is the insight in which attention is directed in order to perfectly understand whatever phenomena were not yet understood by means of wisdom."[187]

"What is insight arising from awakening?"

"It is the insight in which attention is directed on whatever phenomena one perfectly understood by means of wisdom in order to attain the happiness of liberation."

«8.11» "How many kinds of mental stillness are there?"

185. Based on the definitions above, it appears that one-pointedness of mind refers to the state in which manifest characteristics (the object of the practice of insight), representation (the object of the practice of mental stillness), and emptiness (the nature of reality as explained in the previous chapters) are in unity.

186. *so sor rtog pa* in the sense of "comprehension/realization" (*pratibodha*).

187. Compare D: *de dang der shes rab kyis shin tu legs par ma rtogs pa'i chos de dag nyid shin tu legs par rtogs par [F.28.a] bya ba'i phyir yid la byed pa'i lhag mthong gang yin pa'o* with S, folio 39.b: *gang de dang des shes rab kyis legs par ma rtogs pa'i chos de dag nyid legs par rtogs par bya ba'i phyir de nyid yid la byed pa'i lhag mthong ngo* and F, folio 38.a: *gang shes rab kyis legs par ma rtogs pa'i chos de dang de dag la legs par rtogs par bya ba'i phyir de nyid yid la byed pa'i lhag mthong ngo.*

"There are three kinds of mental stillness corresponding to the unimpeded mind. Maitreya, it is also said to be of eight kinds: the first, second, third, and fourth meditative absorptions, the domain of the infinity of space, the domain of infinite cognition, the domain of nothingness, and the domain of neither conception nor lack of conception. It is also of four kinds: immeasurable loving-kindness, immeasurable compassion, immeasurable joy, and immeasurable equanimity."

«8.12» "Blessed One, you have mentioned 'mental stillness and insight that are established in Dharma' and 'mental stillness and insight that are not established in Dharma.' What do these terms mean?"

"Maitreya, the mental stillness and insight that are established in Dharma are the mental stillness and insight whose object is in agreement with manifest characteristic as presented in the teachings that bodhisattvas have understood and contemplated.

"You should know that the mental stillness and insight that are not established in Dharma are the mental stillness and insight whose object, being unrelated to the teachings that bodhisattvas have understood and contemplated, is based on other instructions or precepts, such as taking as referential objects putrefying or festering corpses as well as any other similar objects, the impermanence of all conditioned phenomena, the suffering [inherent to all conditioned phenomena], the selflessness of all phenomena, and nirvana as the state of peace.[188]

"Maitreya, regarding this, I consider those bodhisattvas who follow the teaching based on the mental stillness and insight established in Dharma to possess sharp faculties. As for those faithfully following the teaching based on the mental stillness and insight that are not established in Dharma, I consider them to possess inferior faculties."

«8.13» "Blessed One, you also mentioned 'the mental stillness and insight with a specific[189] teaching as a referential object' and 'the mental stillness and insight with a universal teaching as a referential object.' What do these terms mean?"

188. The last four meditation objects represent the four seals of Dharma (*phyag rgya bzhi*; *caturmudrā*).

189. *ma 'dres pa'i chos*. On *ma 'dres pa'i chos* and *'dres pa'i chos*, see Brunnhölzl 2018, 561n322. Brunnhölzl translates *'dres pa'i chos* as "dharmas in fusion." Considering dharmas without fusing them means considering them individually. However, 8.14 seems to indicate that *dharma* is used here in the sense of "teaching" rather than "phenomenon."

"Maitreya, suppose that bodhisattvas practice the mental stillness and insight that take as a referential object an individual teaching, such as a specific discourse, among all the teachings they have understood and contemplated. This is called mental stillness and insight with a specific teaching as a referential object.

"Now, suppose that bodhisattvas unify, condense, subsume, or gather teachings from various discourses into a single one, thinking that all these teachings converge toward true reality, lean toward true reality, and tend toward true reality; converge toward awakening, lean toward awakening, and tend toward awakening; converge toward nirvana, lean toward nirvana, and tend toward nirvana; and converge toward a shift in one's basis of existence,[190] lean toward a shift in one's basis of existence, and tend toward

190. *gnas gyur pa*; *āśrayaparivṛtti*. I chose to translate this technical term with "shift in one's basis [of existence]" or "shift of the basis [of existence]" instead of "transformation of the basis" as is usually the case. The *āśrayaparivṛtti* in Saṁdh. is an attainment that is obtained after the *ālayavijñāna* has ceased (see Schmithausen 1987, 198, and Schmithausen 2014, 37). In this sutra, the *ālaya* therefore does not seem to be equated with the *āśraya*. In chapter 10, the basis is evoked in relation to the truth body (*dharmakāya*). According to 10.2 and 8.35.11, it appears that the basis one possesses once all corruption has been eliminated is none other than the truth body after it has been purified of adventitious defilements (see Xing 2005, 97), at least in the case of the bodhisattvas. The *dhāraṇī* in 10.8 makes it clear that conceptions of being defiled or purified have in fact no *raison d'être*. From the perspective of true reality, they are completely adventitious. As stated by the Buddha at the conclusion of 10.8, bodhisattvas exchange the body afflicted by corruption for the body of truth or actual body, the *dharmakāya*. In line with this interpretation, *āśraya* is read as a quasi-synonym for *kāya* as in the expression *āśrayapādātṛ* (on this term, see Schmithausen 2014, 331, §272.1). This reading seems to be confirmed, for example, in YBhtP'i 30b4f (see ibid., 521–22, §483), which explains the *āśrayaparivṛtti* as the completely purified *dharmadhātu*, which is permanent and inconceivable. Schmithausen adds, "At the same time, it [this passage of the YBht] stresses the permanence of *āśrayaparivṛtti* (in the ontological perspective), precluding thereby a causal process in the strict sense." Elsewhere, Schmithausen refers to this term as "the [accomplished] *āśrayaparivṛtti* or purification of the *tathatā*" (Schmithausen 2014, 527, 536ff.). While there is certainly a multiplicity of interpretations with regard to this complex matter, it seems to me that this reading is precisely what is meant in Saṁdh. In that sense, *āśrayaparivṛtti*, as a result (*phala*), corresponds to an unveiling (see Schmithausen 2014, 537) or purification of the basis in the form of a return, a restoration, a restitution, or a reentry into the *dharmakāya*, *tathatā*, or *dharmadhātu*. The synonyms given in the list above (true reality, awakening, and nirvana) show that *āśrayaparivṛtti* does not refer to afflicted dharmas, which would be the case if the *ālayavijñāna* was meant here. To conclude this discussion, it seems on the basis of Sakuma's work (Sakuma 1990) that we are in the presence of (at least) two models of *āśrayaparivṛtti*: (1) an originally ontological model, as found in the *Śrāvakabhūmi*, in which the psychophysical base (lit. the basis of existence) of the person

a shift in one's basis of existence. Thinking that all these teachings actually refer to the immeasurable and infinite virtuous truth,[191] they direct their attention [toward their referential object]. This is [called] mental stillness and insight with a universal teaching as a referential object."

«8.14»"Blessed One, you also mentioned mental stillness and insight 'with a fairly universal teaching as a referential object,' 'with a highly universal teaching as a referential object,' and 'with an infinitely universal teaching as a referential object.' What do these terms mean?"

"Maitreya, suppose the bodhisattvas gather together [the meaning of] each of the twelve collections of my teaching, from the sutras up to the extensive discourses, the teachings on miracles, and the instructions. Having done so, they direct their attention toward this referential object. This should be known as the mental stillness and insight with a fairly universal teaching as a referential object.

"When the bodhisattvas gather together[192] all the teachings or discourses they have understood and contemplated and then direct their

practicing *śamatha* and *vipaśyanā* is transformed, as *dauṣṭhulya* is replaced by *praśrabdhi*; and (2) a cognitive or epistemic model using this originally ontological terminology to express the purification of the *tathatā*. In this model, the purification as an elimination of the *dauṣṭhulya* alone is the manifestation of the *dharmakāya* that is not the creation of a causal process transforming an entity conceived in ontological terms, as repeatedly stated throughout the later chapters of Saṁdh. In this latter model, the cognitive purification of the *tathatā* as a causal process can only make sense from the perspective of conventional truth (see chapter 3). From the ultimate standpoint of realization, nothing was ever purified by anyone (cf. *dhāraṇī* in 10.8). As a consequence of this (and following William Waldron's suggestion), I would like to make clear that the "shift in one's basis of existence" referred to in Saṁdh. is a cognitive restoration of the basis in which the attainment of gnosis plays a central role *from the perspective of conventional truth*. In the present context, one should therefore refrain from interpreting the term *āśrayaparivṛtti* as implying any ontological commitment to the process thereby described. To conclude on this point, I understand *āśrayaparivṛtti* in Saṁdh. as implying a "doctrine of (re-)embodiment" as explained in Radich 2007, 1109ff. At the end of the path, one has as a basis of existence the truth body in lieu of the body afflicted by corruption as mentioned above, hence the notion of a shift.

191. *chos*; *dharma*.

192. D: *byams pa mdo'i sde nas shin tu rgyas pa'i sde dang / rmad du byung ba'i chos kyi sde dang / gtan la bab par bstan pa'i sde'i bar dag so sor gcig tu bzlums te . . . [F.29.a] mdo'i sde la sogs pa de dag nyid ji snyed bzung ba dang / bsams pa so sor gcig tu bzlums te yid la byed pa ni 'dres pa chen por gyur pa'i chos la dmigs pa yin par rig par bya'o*. F, folio 39.a: *so sor gcig tu bsdu ba te . . . bsam pa de dag nyid gcig tu bsdu ba byas te*. I followed F and did not translate *so sor* in the sentence pertaining to the highly universal teaching (*'dres pa chen por gyur pa'i chos*).

attention onto this referential object, this should be known as the mental stillness and insight with a highly universal teaching as a referential object.

"When the bodhisattvas gather together the teachings imparted by the tathāgatas that refer to the infinite truth,[193] the infinite words and letters expressing it, and the ever-increasing infinite wisdom and eloquence of the tathāgatas, and then direct their attention toward this referential object, this should be known as the mental stillness and insight with an infinitely universal teaching as a referential object."

«8.15» "Blessed One, how do bodhisattvas obtain mental stillness and insight with a universal teaching as a referential object?"

"Maitreya, you should know that they obtain them through five causes: (1) At the time of directing their attention, they destroy all supports of corruption in every moment. (2) After giving up the variety of conditioned phenomena, they rejoice in the joy of Dharma. (3) They perfectly know the immeasurable and unceasing brilliance of Dharma in the ten directions. (4) They bring together, without conceptualizing them, the manifest characteristics that are imbued with the accomplishment of the goal and in harmony with the element conducive to purification. (5) In order to attain, perfect, and accomplish the truth body, they seize the most supreme and auspicious cause."

«8.16» "Blessed One, how should we know at which point the bodhisattvas cognize and obtain the mental stillness and the insight that have a universal teaching as a referential object?"

"Maitreya, you should know that they cognize them on the first bodhisattva stage, Utmost Joy, and obtain them on the third stage, Illuminating. Maitreya, in spite of this, even beginners among bodhisattvas should not abstain from training in them and directing their attention toward their referential object."

«8.17» "Blessed One, in what way do mental stillness and insight become a concentration associated with mental engagement[194] and investigation? In what way do they become a concentration not with mental engagement but with investigation only? In what way do they become a concentration without either mental engagement or investigation?"

"Maitreya, when mental stillness and insight attend to experiences of the

193. On this point, see 8.13 above.

194. *rtog pa*; *vitarka*. For the translation of *vitarka* and *vicāra*, see Cousins 1992, 147.

manifest and coarse[195] manifest characteristics mentioned in the teachings the bodhisattvas have understood, investigated, and examined, this is the concentration associated with mental engagement and investigation.

"When mental stillness and insight do not consist in attending the experiences corresponding to the manifest and coarse manifest characteristics mentioned in their teachings but consist in being merely mindful of manifest characteristics, namely, in attending the experience of subtle manifest characteristics,[196] this is a concentration not with mental engagement but with investigation only.

"When mental stillness and insight consist in practicing by directing one's attention toward the experience of the effortless Dharma with regard to each and every manifest characteristic mentioned in these teachings, this is a concentration without either mental engagement or investigation.

"Moreover, Maitreya, mental stillness and insight arising from inquiry consist in a concentration associated with mental engagement and investigation. The mental stillness and insight arising from awakening is a concentration not with mental engagement but with investigation only.[197]

"The mental stillness and insight taking a universal teaching as its referential object consist in a concentration without either mental engagement or investigation."

«8.18»"Blessed One, what is the cause of mental stillness? What is the cause of setting the mind? What is the cause of equanimity?"

"Maitreya, when one feels excited or feels one might become excited, one directs one's attention toward phenomena that induce sorrow and the unimpeded mind.[198] This is what is called the cause of mental stillness.

"Maitreya, when one feels drowsy or feels one might become drowsy, one directs one's attention toward phenomena that induce joy and mental manifest characteristics.[199] This is what is called the cause of setting the mind.

195. See F, folio 40.a: *gsal zhing che bar myong ba'i rjes su dpyod pa*. This construction is also found in the following sentences in F.

196. Lit. "experienced as subtle" according to F, or "the experience of the subtle" according to D.

197. On this point, see 8.10.

198. See 8.9: "What is the unimpeded mind?" "Maitreya, it is the referential object of mental stillness, the mind that takes the image as an object."

199. See 8.9: "Maitreya, this is the referential object of insight, the conceptual image that is the object of concentration."

"Maitreya, whether one is devoted to mental stillness or insight only, or practices them in union, when one applies one's mind without being affected by these two secondary defilements,[200] [namely agitation and drowsiness,] one directs one's attention spontaneously. This is what is called the cause of equanimity."

«8.19» "Blessed One, the bodhisattvas who practice mental stillness and insight possess the analytical knowledge of designations as well as the analytical knowledge of the objects of designation.[201] In what way do they possess these analytical knowledges?"

"Maitreya, the analytical knowledge of designations comprises five points: names, phrases, letters, their individual apprehension, and their collective apprehension. What is a name? It is that which superimposes a so-called essential or distinctive characteristic on the phenomena conducive to affliction and purification for the sake of communication. What is a phrase? It is that which is based on a collection of those very names taken as its support and basis in order to designate objects of affliction and purification. What are letters? They are phonemes acting as the basis for both names and phrases. What is the analytical knowledge that apprehends them individually? It is the analytical knowledge resulting from directing one's attention toward a specific referential object. What is the analytical knowledge that apprehends them collectively? It is the analytical knowledge resulting from directing one's attention toward a general referential object. When all these five points are put together, this should be known as the analytical knowledge of designations. This is how bodhisattvas possess the analytical knowledge of designations.

«8.20» "Maitreya, the analytical knowledge of the objects of designation comprises ten points: the diversity of things and the nature of things;[202] the apprehending subject and the apprehended object; the abodes and objects

200. *nye ba'i nyon mongs*; *upakleśa*.

201. These two expressions refer to *dharmapratisaṁvid* and *arthapratisaṁvid*. Lamotte and Powers opted for "object" and Keenan for "meaning" for *artha*, while *dharma* is usually translated with "Dharma." For an interpretation of the term in the sense of the translation suggested above, refer to Nance 2012, 58–59, 72, 74–75, 135, 227–28, and 233–35. The same interpretation is found in Lamotte 1970, 1617ff.: *dharma* is translated with "designation" and *artha* with "chose."

202. *ji lta ba bzhin du yod pa nyid*; *yathāvadbhāvikatā*. On *yāvadbhāvikatā* and *yathāvadbhāvikatā*, see Takasaki 1966, 173.

of enjoyment; wrong view and correct view; and the object conducive to affliction and the object conducive to purification.

"Maitreya, all[203] the various divisions of phenomena conducive to affliction and purification according to their aspects represent the diversity of things, namely, the fivefold enumeration of the aggregates, the sixfold enumeration of the internal sense domains, the sixfold enumeration of the external sense domains, and so on.

"Maitreya, the true reality of all these very phenomena conducive to affliction and purification is itself the nature of things. It has seven aspects:[204] (1) the true reality of arising in the sense that all conditioned phenomena are without beginning and end; (2) the true reality of defining characteristics in the sense that everything, person or phenomenon, is without a self; (3) the true reality of representations in the sense that all conditioned phenomena are mere representations;[205] (4) the true reality of existence in the sense of the truth of suffering that I have taught; (5) the true reality of mistaken action[206] in the sense of the truth of the origin of suffering that I have taught; (6) the true reality of purification in the sense of the truth of cessation [of suffering] that I have taught; (7) the true reality of correct action in the sense of the truth of the path that I have taught.

"Maitreya, on account of the true reality of arising, defining characteristics, and existence, all beings are similar and equal. Maitreya, on account of the true reality of defining characteristics and representations, all phenomena are similar and equal. Maitreya, on account of the true reality of purification, the awakening of the hearers, the awakening of the solitary realizers, and the unsurpassable, complete, and perfect awakening are similar and equal. Maitreya, on account of the true reality of correct action, similar and equal too are the wisdoms encompassed by the mental stillness and insight that take as a referential object a universal teaching that has been heard, contemplated, and practiced.[207]

203. *mthar thug pa*; *paryanta*, in the sense here of "entirety."

204. For the Sanskrit of these seven, see Nagao 1964, 43.

205. See F, folio 41.a: *rnam par rig pa'i de bzhin nyid ni gang / 'du byed rnam par rig pa tsam mo.*

206. *log par sgrub pa*; *mithyāpratipatti*. In F, *sgrub pa* is translated with *nan tan* (see for example F, folio 41.b).

207. D: *byams pa de la yang dag par sgrub pa'i de bzhin nyid des ni thos pa thams cad 'dres pa'i chos la dmigs pa'i zhi gnas dang lhag mthong gi bsdus pa'i shes rab mtshungs shing mnyam mo.*

"Maitreya, the apprehending subject consists in the phenomena of the five physical sense domains, mind, thought, cognition, and mental states.

"Maitreya, the apprehended object consists in the six external sense domains. In addition, Maitreya, apprehending subjects are also apprehended objects.

"Maitreya, the objects corresponding to abodes are the worlds of beings, which manifest wherever there are beings: as one, one hundred, one thousand, or one hundred thousand villages; as one, one hundred, one thousand, or one hundred thousand continents; as one, one hundred, one thousand, or one hundred thousand great continents of Jambudvīpa; as one, one hundred, one thousand, or one hundred thousand times the four great continents; as one, one hundred, one thousand, or one hundred thousand universes of a thousand worlds; as one, one hundred, one thousand, or one hundred thousand bichiliocosms; as one, one hundred, one thousand, one hundred thousand, ten million, one billion, ten billion, one hundred billion, or ten trillion trichiliocosms; as one, one hundred, one thousand, one hundred thousand times an incalculable number of them; or as many as the number of atoms present in one hundred thousand times an incalculable number of trichiliocosms.

"Maitreya, I have taught that objects of enjoyment are the assets and belongings owned by beings for the sake of their enjoyment.

"Maitreya, a wrong view is a mistaken conception, thought, or view conceiving the impermanent as permanent, suffering as happiness, impurity as purity, or selflessness as self with regard to notions such as an apprehending subject.

"Maitreya, a correct view, being the opposite of a wrong view, is its antidote.

"Maitreya, the object conducive to affliction is of three kinds: the object conducive to the affliction comprising the defilements of the three worlds, to the affliction of karma, and to the affliction of arising.

"Maitreya, the object conducive to purification consists of all that is in

F, folio 41.b: *byams pa gang yang dag pa'i nan tan de bzhin nyid des ni thos pa dang bsams pa dang / bsgoms pa'i 'dres pa la dmigs pa'i zhi gnas dang lhag mthong gis yongs su zin pa'i shes rab mtshungs shing mnyam mo*. Xuanzang's translation confirms the reading found in D: 聽聞正法緣總境界勝奢摩他毘缽舍那所受慧平等平等 (CBETA, Taishō 676). However, F makes sense from the perspective of the meaning of this chapter.

harmony with awakening on account of being free indeed from the three sorts of affliction.

"Maitreya, you should know that all objects of designation are included in these ten points.

«8.21» "Moreover, Maitreya, the analytical knowledge of these objects of designation comprises five items. What are they? They are the topics to be comprehended, the objects of designation to be comprehended, comprehension, the result of comprehension, and the communication of this result.

"Maitreya, the topics to be comprehended consist of anything that is knowable or perceptible, such as what is referred to as the aggregates, the internal and external sense domains, and so forth.

"Maitreya, the objects of designation to be comprehended consist of [all] cognitive objects, however diverse they appear and as they really are: the conventional and the ultimate; shortcomings and qualities; conditions and time; the defining characteristics of arising, abiding, and disintegrating; sickness, old age, and death; suffering, the origin of suffering, the cessation of suffering, and the path leading to the cessation of suffering; true reality, the ultimate limit of existence, and the domain of truth; condensed and detailed teachings; categorical, analytical, interrogative, and dismissive answers; and secret instructions and proclamations. You should know that these are the objects of designation to be comprehended.

"Maitreya, comprehension is grasping both the topics and the objects of designation to be comprehended, any factor that is in harmony with awakening, such as the applications of mindfulness, the correct self-restraints, and so forth.

"Maitreya, the result of comprehension consists of disciplining and completely eliminating desire, anger, and delusion, as well as in actualizing the results of the path of the recluse together with the virtuous qualities of the hearers and tathāgatas I have described as mundane and supramundane, ordinary and extraordinary.

"Maitreya, communicating this result consists in revealing what brings about liberation[208] on the basis of[209] the very teachings one has actualized, as well as in propagating these teachings for the sake of others.[210]

208. See Z, folio 38.a: *rnam par grol bar byed* instead of D: *rnam par grol bar shes*.
209. See Z, folio 37.b, F, folio 43.a: *chos de dag nyid la* instead of D: *chos de dag nyid las*.
210. We find slightly variant readings in F and D. D: *byams pa de la rab tu rig par byed pa ni*

"Maitreya, you should know that all objects are subsumed within these five points.

«8.22» "Maitreya, the bodhisattvas' analytical knowledge of the objects of designation includes four topics. What are they? They are mental appropriation, experience, affliction, and purification. Maitreya, you should know that all the objects of designation are also included within these four topics.

«8.23» "Maitreya, the bodhisattvas' analytical knowledge of the objects of designation is also presented according to three topics. What are they? They are letters, meanings, and contexts.

"Maitreya, you should understand the letters as forming collections of names.

"Maitreya, meanings comprise ten aspects: the defining characteristic of true reality, the defining characteristic of comprehension, the defining characteristic of abandonment, the defining characteristic of realization, the defining characteristic of practice, the defining characteristic consisting of these very five defining characteristics, the defining characteristic of the relation between the support and the supported, the defining characteristic of the phenomena undermining comprehension and so forth, the defining characteristic of the phenomena in harmony with comprehension, and the defining characteristic of the benefits and shortcomings resulting from having comprehension or not.

"Maitreya, there are five contexts: the context of the surrounding universe, the context of beings, the context of Dharma, the context of discipline, and the context of methods of discipline.

"Maitreya, you should know that all objects of designation are also included within these three topics."

«8.24» "Blessed One, what differences are made between the comprehension of the objects of designation that is produced by the wisdom arising from hearing the Dharma, the comprehension of the objects of designation that is produced by the wisdom arising from contemplating the Dharma, and the comprehension of the objects of designation that is produced by the wisdom arising from practicing mental stillness and insight?"

---

mngon sum du byas pa'i chos de dag nyid las rnam par grol bar shes pa dang / gzhan dag la yang rgya cher ston pa dang / yang dag par ston pa gang yin pa ste. F, folio 43.a: *byams pa de la shes par byed pa ni gang mngon sum du byas pa'i chos de dag nyid la rnam par grol bar shes pa dang / rgya cher yang gzhan la ston cing 'chad pa dang / yang dag par ston pa'o.*

"Maitreya, through the wisdom arising from hearing the Dharma, the bodhisattvas rely on the literal meaning of words but not on their underlying intent, which they do not understand; although they are in harmony with liberation, their comprehension is [limited to] the objects of designation that do not liberate them.

"Maitreya, through the wisdom arising from contemplating the Dharma, the bodhisattvas do not rely exclusively on the literal meaning of words but also on the underlying intent, which they understand; although they are in great harmony with liberation, their comprehension is [still limited to] the objects of designation that do not liberate them.

"Maitreya, through the wisdom arising from practicing mental stillness and insight, the bodhisattvas, relying, or not, on the literal meaning of words, rely on the underlying intent, which they understand by means of an image, an object of concentration corresponding to a cognitive object; they are in great harmony with liberation, and their comprehension includes the objects of designation that liberate them. Maitreya, such is the difference between them."

«8.25» "Blessed One, what is the gnosis[211] of the bodhisattvas who practice mental stillness and insight and who comprehend designations as well as objects of designation? What is their perception?"

"Maitreya, I have explained their gnosis[212] and perception in many ways, but I will give you a concise explanation. Gnosis consists in the mental stillness and insight that take a universal teaching as a referential object. Perception consists in the mental stillness and insight that take a specific teaching as a referential object."

«8.26» "Blessed One, as bodhisattvas practice mental stillness and insight, which kinds of manifest characteristic do they discard? How do they direct their attention to achieve this?"

"Maitreya, they discard the manifest characteristic of designations and objects of designation by directing their attention on true reality. They discard names by not taking the essence of names as a referential object and by not paying attention to the manifest characteristic that constitutes their basis. You should know that, just as it is with names, so it is also with words,

211. In accord with F, folio 44.b, *shes pa* should be read here also as *ye shes*.
212. The phrase is repeated throughout the text. Here *shes pa* should be read as *ye shes*, a reading confirmed by F.

letters, and all objects of designation. Maitreya, they discard letters, meanings, and contexts by not taking their essence as a referential object and by not paying attention to the manifest characteristic that constitutes their basis."[213]

«8.27» "Blessed One, is manifest characteristic also discarded with regard to the analytical knowledge of the object of designation corresponding to true reality?"

"Maitreya, if the analytical knowledge of the object of designation corresponding to true reality does not have a manifest characteristic and does not take a manifest characteristic as its referential object, then what would be discarded in that case? Maitreya, the analytical knowledge of the object of designation corresponding to true reality disposes of all the manifest characteristics of designations and objects of designation. But I did not teach that anything at all could dispose of this analytical knowledge."

«8.28» "Blessed One, you have explained by way of analogy that it is impossible to discern one's own manifest characteristics[214] in a container filled with muddy water, a dirty mirror, or an agitated pond surface, but that it is possible in a container filled with clear water, a well-polished mirror, or a quiet pond. You have explained that, likewise, the mind of those who do not practice cannot know true reality exactly as it is, whereas the mind of those who do practice can indeed. In reference to this statement, what is this mental inspection?[215] What true reality do you have in mind here, and what is the meaning of this statement?"

"Maitreya, I spoke those words in reference to the three kinds of mental inspection: the mental inspection arising from hearing the Dharma, the mental inspection arising from contemplating the Dharma, and the mental inspection arising from practicing the Dharma. I taught this having in mind the true reality of representations."[216]

«8.29» "Blessed One, how many kinds of manifest characteristics did you

213. See 8.23, in which the three *arthapratisaṁvid* are letters, meanings, and contexts.
214. *mtshan ma* corresponds here to a reflection (*gzugs brnyan*; *pratibimba*).
215. *so sor brtags pa*; *pratisaṁkhyā*. D: *zhes bka' stsal pa gang lags pa de la sems kyis so sor brtag pa ni gang lags*.
216. *rnam par rig pa'i de bzhin nyid*; see 8.20.2, in which the true reality of representations corresponds to the fact that "all conditioned phenomena are mere representations." In the preceding sentence, I added the term "truth" (*dharma*) to render a frequent collocation that clarifies the meaning of this statement.

teach to the bodhisattvas who possess the analytical knowledge of designations and objects of designation and who engage in eliminating manifest characteristics?"

"Maitreya, there are ten kinds of manifest characteristics, and these bodhisattvas eliminate them by means of emptiness. What are these ten?

"The diverse manifest characteristics in the way of words and letters through which designations and objects of designation are analytically known—these manifest characteristics are eliminated by means of the emptiness of all phenomena.[217]

"The manifest characteristics corresponding to a continuum of arisings and cessations or abidings and transformations through which the object designated as the true reality of existence is analytically known—these manifest characteristics are eliminated by means of the emptiness of defining characteristic and by the emptiness of what is without beginning and end.

"The manifest characteristics resulting from the belief in a perduring self or the thought 'I am,' through which the object designated as the apprehending subject is analytically known—these manifest characteristics are eliminated by means of the emptiness of the inner subject and the emptiness of what is not taken as a referential object.[218]

"The manifest characteristics resulting from the belief in objects of enjoyment through which the object designated as the apprehended object is analytically known—these manifest characteristics are eliminated by means of the emptiness of the outer object.[219]

"The manifest characteristics of pleasure within the inner subject and of beauty regarding the outer object through which courtesans[220] and possessions are analytically known as objects of enjoyment—these manifest char-

217. Lamotte reads *chos dang don* respectively as "Dharma" and "chose" ("thing"); see Lamotte 1935, 225. Powers reads them as "doctrine" and "meaning"; see Powers 1995, 189. However, as explained above (see 8.19–21), I understand these two technical terms to refer to "designation" and "objects of designations." Lamotte's rendering of the syntax of the entire passage appears to be inaccurate: "Pour celui qui. . . , il y a . . ."

218. See 8.20.3.

219. See 8.20.4.

220. *skyes pa dang / bud med kyi bsnyen bkur*, probably for *upasthāna-kāri/-kārikā*, "(a woman) serving, doing service to (a man, sexually; said of a courtesan)"; see Edgerton 1953, 143.

acteristics are eliminated by means of the emptiness of the outer object and the emptiness of essence.

"The innumerable manifest characteristics through which objects of designation corresponding to states of existence are analytically known—these manifest characteristics are eliminated by means of the great emptiness.

"With formlessness as a support, the manifest characteristics of the liberation brought about by inner peace are analytically known—these manifest characteristics are eliminated by means of the emptiness of conditioned phenomena.

"The manifest characteristic of the selflessness of persons and phenomena, the manifest characteristic of what is merely a representation, and the manifest characteristic of the ultimate through which the object of designation corresponding to the true reality of defining characteristics is analytically known—these manifest characteristics are eliminated by means of the emptiness of the limitless, the emptiness of the substanceless, the emptiness of essence of the substanceless, and the emptiness of the ultimate.

"The manifest characteristics of what is unconditioned and changeless through which the object of designation corresponding to the true reality leading to purification[221] is analytically known—these manifest characteristics are eliminated by means of the emptiness of the unconditioned and the emptiness devoid of rejection.

"The manifest characteristics of emptiness resulting from directing one's attention toward this very emptiness as an antidote to manifest characteristics are eliminated by means of the emptiness of emptiness."

«8.30» "Blessed One, when bodhisattvas eliminate these ten kinds of manifest characteristics, which manifest characteristics do they eliminate, and from which binding manifest characteristics will they be free?"

"Maitreya, by eliminating the object of concentration, the manifest characteristic corresponding to an image,[222] bodhisattvas will be free from manifest characteristics consisting in the manifest characteristics of affliction, which they will also eliminate.

221. In the case of **viśuddhyālambana*, one can read the Sanskrit compound as a genitive or dative *tatpuruṣa*; see Schmithausen 2014, 363n1648 and 362n1644. I read *rnam par dag pa'i de bzhin nyid* as **viśuddhitathatā* in accord with Schmithausen 2014, 362–63, §306.5, and n. 1647.

222. *gzugs brnyan*; *pratibimba*; see 8.1–10 for the meaning of the image in the context of contemplative practice.

"Maitreya, you should know that these various kinds of emptiness are the direct antidotes to these various kinds of manifest characteristic. But it is not the case that each of them is not an antidote to all manifest characteristics. Maitreya, it is like this: ignorance does not [directly] bring about all afflictions up to old age and death [with regard to the twelve factors of conditioned existence]. Yet, because it is indeed the closely or very closely related condition [for their arising, it does bring them about indirectly]. This is why it is taught that ignorance directly brings about conditioning mental factors. You should consider the present topic in the same way.

«8.31»"Blessed One, what is it that bodhisattvas realize in the context of the Great Vehicle? What is then inherent to the defining characteristic of emptiness that causes bodhisattvas to not deviate from it because of pride?"

Then the Blessed One said, "Excellent, Maitreya. You question the Tathāgata on this point so that bodhisattvas will not deviate from emptiness. This is excellent indeed. Why? Because, Maitreya, bodhisattvas who deviate from emptiness will also deviate from the entire Great Vehicle. Therefore, listen well, Maitreya, and I will explain to you what is inherent to the defining characteristic of emptiness.

"Maitreya, emptiness as taught in the Great Vehicle means that the other-dependent and actual defining characteristics are completely devoid of the imaginary defining characteristic of affliction and purification and that bodhisattvas do not take this imaginary defining characteristic as a referential object."[223]

«8.32»"Blessed One, how many types of concentration are included within mental stillness and insight?"

"Maitreya, you should know that they include all the types of concentration of the hearers, bodhisattvas, and tathāgatas that I have taught."

"Blessed One, from which causes do mental stillness and insight arise?"

"Maitreya, they arise from a pure discipline and a pure view resulting from hearing and contemplating [the Dharma] as their causes."

"Blessed One, please explain what their results are."

"Maitreya, a pure mind and a pure wisdom are their results. You should

223. See Schmithausen 2014, 366n1664, quoting YBht P'i 83a5f: *de de la mi dmigs pa gang yin pa* and F, folio 46.b: *de'ang mi dmigs pa* instead of D, folio 34.b: *de la de dmigs pa gang yin pa*.

know that all mundane and supramundane virtuous qualities of the hearers, the bodhisattvas, and the tathāgatas are also their results."

"Blessed One, what is the activity of mental stillness and insight?"

"Maitreya, they liberate one from the two kinds of bonds: the bonds of manifest characteristic and the bonds of corruption."

«8.33» "Blessed One, among the five obstacles mentioned by the Blessed One, which are obstacles to mental stillness, which are obstacles to insight, and which are obstacles to both?"

"Maitreya, caring[224] about the body and objects of enjoyment is an obstacle to mental stillness. Not obtaining instructions from noble beings as desired is an obstacle to insight. Living in a state of confusion and being content with bare necessities are obstacles to both.[225] On account of the first of these, one will not exert oneself. On account of the second, one will not exert oneself through to the completion of practice."

"Blessed One, among the five obstructions mentioned by the Blessed One, which are obstructions to mental stillness, which are obstructions to insight, and which are obstructions to both?"

"Maitreya, agitation and remorse are obstructions to mental stillness. Laziness, lethargy, and doubts are obstructions to insight. Craving for desired objects and malicious thoughts are obstructions to both."

"Blessed One, when is the path of mental stillness purified?"

"At the time when agitation and remorse have been conquered."

"Blessed One, when is the path of insight purified?"

"At the time when laziness, lethargy, and doubts have been conquered."[226]

«8.34» "Blessed One, how many kinds of mental distractions will bodhisattvas engaged in mental stillness and insight experience?"

224. *lus dang longs spyod la lta ba*; 顧戀身財.

225. This reference remains obscure. Could this point be directed at outcast bodhisattvas (*byang chub sems dpa' gdol ba*; *bodhisattvacāṇḍāla*), namely, bodhisattvas taking pride in detachment who practice in the way of hearers? See Conze 1975, 438ff.?

226. D has *bcom ldan 'das ci tsam gyis na zhi gnas kyi lam yongs su dag pa lags / byams pa gang gi tshe rmugs pa dang gnyid legs par rab tu choms par gyur pa'o / / bcom ldan 'das ji tsam gyis na lhag mthong gi lam yongs su dag pa lags / byams pa gang gi tshe rgod pa dad 'gyod pa legs par rab tu choms par gyur pa'o*, but one should read *bcom ldan 'das ci tsam gyis na zhi gnas kyi lam yongs su dag pa lags / byams pa gang gi tshe rgod pa dad 'gyod pa legs par rab tu choms par gyur pa'o / / bcom ldan 'das ji tsam gyis na lhag mthong gi lam yongs su dag pa lags / byams pa gang gi tshe rmugs pa dang gnyid dang the tshom legs par rab tu choms par gyur pa'o*. See F, folio 47.a, which seems to indicate that the list of terms in D is incomplete and in the wrong order.

"Maitreya, they will experience five kinds of mental distractions: the mental distraction with regard to the way one directs one's attention, the mental distraction with regard to outer objects, the mental distraction with regard to the inner subject, the mental distraction produced by manifest characteristics, and the mental distraction resulting from corruption.

"Maitreya, if bodhisattvas forsake the way attention is directed in the Great Vehicle[227] and fall into the way hearers and solitary realizers direct their attention, then this is mental distraction regarding the way one directs one's attention.

"If bodhisattvas let their minds wander among the five external objects of desire, entertainments, manifest characteristics, conceptualizations, defilements, secondary defilements, and external referential objects, then this is mental distraction with regard to outer objects.

"If bodhisattvas sink into laziness and lethargy, experience the taste of absorption, or become stained by any secondary defilement related to absorption, then this is mental distraction with regard to the inner subject.

"If bodhisattvas direct their attention toward the manifest characteristic that is the inner subject's object of concentration by relying upon the manifest characteristics of outer objects, then this is mental distraction produced by manifest characteristics.

"If bodhisattvas become conceited by identifying themselves with the body afflicted by corruption with regard to sensations arising in the course of directing the inner subject's attention, this is mental distraction ensuing from corruption."

«8.35» "Blessed One, for which obstacles do mental stillness and insight serve as antidotes from the first stage of the bodhisattva path up to the stage of a tathāgata?"

"Maitreya, on the first stage, mental stillness and insight are antidotes to the defilement of bad destinies as well as to the affliction of karma and birth.

"On the second stage, they are antidotes to the arising of confusion resulting from subtle transgressions.

"On the third stage, they are antidotes to attachment for desirous objects.

"On the fourth stage, they are antidotes to craving for absorption and Dharma.

227. *theg pa chen po dang ldan pa; mahāyānapratisaṁyukta.*

"On the fifth stage, they are antidotes to the exclusive rejection of samsara and exclusive inclination toward nirvana.

"On the sixth stage, they are antidotes to the abundant arising of manifest characteristics.

"On the seventh stage, they are antidotes to the subtle arising of manifest characteristics.

"On the eighth, they are antidotes to exerting oneself toward what is without manifest characteristic as well as to not having mastery over manifest characteristics.

"On the ninth, they are antidotes to not having mastery in teaching the Dharma in every aspect.

"On the tenth, they are antidotes to not having obtained the perfect analytical knowledge of the truth body.

"Maitreya, on the stage of a tathāgata, mental stillness and insight are antidotes to the extremely subtle defiling obstructions and the even more subtle cognitive obstructions.[228] By fully eliminating these obstructions, one abides within the truth body that has been completely purified. As a consequence, one obtains the realization of the object corresponding to the accomplishment of the goal—the gnosis and vision that are utterly free from attachment and hindrance."[229]

228. *nyon mongs pa dang shes bya'i sgrib pa*; *kleśajñeyāvaraṇa*.

229. The reading of this passage found in D is problematic on account of the double *la* particle in the second part of the sentence: *de legs par bcom pas thams cad la chags pa med pa dang / thogs pa med pa'i shes pa dang / mthong ba thob cing dgos pa yongs su grub pa'i dmigs pa la chos kyi sku shin tu rnam par dag pa la gnas pa yin no*. Compare with VD, folio 77.a: *de legs par bcom pas chos kyi sku shin tu rnam par dag pa la gnas pa na / dgos pa yongs su grub pa'i dmigs pa la / thams cad du chags pa med pa dang / thogs pa med pa'i shes pa dang mthong ba thob po*. K0771, folio 39.a: *de legs par bcom pas thams cad la chags pa med pa dang / thogs pa med pa'i shes pa dang / mthong ba thob cing dgos pa yongs su grub pa'i dmigs pa la cha shas kyi sku shin tu rnam par dag pa la gnas pa yin no*. S, folio 51.b: *de legs par bcom pa'i phyir / chos kyi sku shin tu rnam par dag pa la gnas pas / dgos pa yongs su grub pa'i dmigs pa la thams cad du mi thogs mi chags pa'i ye shes mthong ba rab tu thob bo*. F, folio 48.a: *de bcom pa'i phyir chos kyi sku shin tu rnam par dag pa la gnas pas / dgos pa yongs su grub pa'i dmigs pa la thams cad du mi thogs mi chags pa'i ye shes mthong ba rab tu thob po*. Bd, folio 54: *de legs par bcom pas chos kyi sku shin tu rnam par dag pa la gnas pa na/ dgongs pa yongs su grub pa'i dmigs pa thams cad la chags pa med pa dang / thogs pa med pa'i shes pa dang / mthong ba thob po*. L, folio 48.a: *de bcom pa'i phyir / chos kyi sku shin tu rnam par dag pa la gnas pas/ dgos pa yongs su grub pa'i dmigs pa la thams cad du mi thogs mi chags pa'i ye shes mthong ba rab tu thob bo* (similar to F, folio 48.a). He, folio 102b: *de bcom ldan pa'i phyir chos kyi sku shin tu rnam par dag pa la gnas pas dgongs pa yongs su grub pa'i dmigs pa dang / thams cad du mi thogs mi chags pa'i ye shes mthong ba rab tu*

«8.36» "Blessed One, in what way do bodhisattvas obtain mental stillness and insight so that they will attain the unsurpassable, complete, and perfect awakening?"[230]

"Maitreya, once bodhisattvas have obtained mental stillness and insight, they consider the seven aspects of true reality.[231] With their minds concentrated on the doctrine that has been heard and contemplated, they direct their attention inwardly toward the true reality that has been well[232] understood, contemplated, and focused upon. As they direct their attention in this way on true reality, their minds then remain in complete equanimity[233] toward each and every subtle manifest characteristic that manifests, not to mention coarse ones.

'thob po. First, a few general remarks: K0774 follows the syntax of D with an important variation: *cha shas kyi sku* instead of *chos kyi sku* in D. In some other editions, such as F, L, and H, as well as in Bd (which seems to be a compromise between D and K0774, on one side, and F and L on the other side), the syntax of the sentence is quite distinct from D and K0774; see for example VD in which entire blocks of text are found in a different order. In addition, we find in other minor variant readings, such as *dgongs pa* in apposition to *yongs su grub pa'i dmigs pa* (see Bd) instead of the more usual *dgos pa*. I therefore suggest the following emendations: One should read *ye shes mthong ba* instead of *shes pa dang / mthong ba* since we find in various forms the well-known collocation *ma chags ma thogs pa'i ye shes mthong ba* in Mvyut: *'das pa'i dus la ma chags ma thogs pa'i ye shes gzigs par 'jug go*; *'das pa'i dus la ma chags ma thogs pa'i ye shes mthong ba 'jug pa*, *atīte 'dhvany asaṅgam apratihataṁ jñānadarśanaṁ pravartate* (Mvyut 151) or *da ltar gyi dus la ma chags ma thogs pa'i ye shes gzigs par 'jug go*; *da ltar gyi dus la ma chags ma thogs pa'i ye shes mthong ba 'jug pa*, *pratyutpanne 'dhvany asaṅgam apratihatam jñānadarśanaṁ pravartate* (Mvyut 153). Based on the fact that *jñānadarśana* results from having discarded the obstructions, a doctrine already present in the Pāli tradition, F and L probably give a better account of the logical sequence of this passage: (1) first, obstructions are eliminated; (2) thereupon, one remains in the *dharmakāya*, which has been completely purified from these obstructions; (3) as a consequence of this, the insight into the accomplishment of the goal/intention, which is the real object, arises together with gnosis free from attachment and hindrance. In this context, *jñānadarśana* is interpreted as a *dvandva* ("gnosis and vision"). My suggestion for this passage would thus be quite close to Bd, folio 54: *de legs par bcom pas chos kyi sku shin tu rnam par dag pa la gnas pa na* (or *gnas pas*) */ dgos pa yongs su grub pa'i dmigs pa la thams cad du chags pa med pa dang / thogs pa med pa'i ye shes mthong ba thob po.*

230. Some editions (e.g., F) include *ji ltar* in the second clause: "once bodhisattvas have obtained mental stillness and insight, how do they attain the unsurpassable, complete, and perfect awakening?" The difference is not significant because the attainment of the fourth object of mental stillness and insight, the accomplishment of the goal, corresponds to the attainment of awakening (see 8.2).

231. See 8.20.2.

232. F, folio 48.b reads *legs par rtogs pa* instead of D, which has simply *bzung ba*.

233. *lhag par btang snyoms*; *adhyupekṣya*.

"Maitreya, these subtle manifest characteristics include the manifest characteristics appropriated by mind; the manifest characteristics of experiences, representations, affliction, and purification; the internal or external manifest characteristics and those that are both internal and external; the manifest characteristics related to the notion that one must act for the benefit of all beings; the manifest characteristics of knowledge and suchness; the manifest characteristics of the four noble truths of suffering, the origin of suffering, the cessation of suffering, and the path;[234] the manifest characteristics of the conditioned, the unconditioned, the permanent, the impermanent, and the nature inherent to what is subject to suffering and change or what is not subject to change; the manifest characteristic distinct or indistinct from the defining characteristic specific to the conditioned; the manifest characteristic of everything as a result of having the notion of 'everything' in reference to anything; and the manifest characteristic of the selflessness of the person and of phenomena. The bodhisattva's mind remains in complete equanimity toward all these manifest characteristics as they manifest.

"Continually practicing in this way, they will in due time purify their minds from obstacles, obstructions, and distractions. In the course of this practice, the seven aspects of the cognition that is personal and intuitive, the gnosis[235] that is the awakening[236] to the seven aspects of true reality, will arise. Such is the bodhisattvas' path of seeing. By obtaining it, bodhisattvas have entered the faultless state of truth,[237] are born into the lineage of tathāgatas, and, upon obtaining the first stage, enjoy all the advantages of this stage. Because they have already obtained mental stillness and insight, they have attained their two referential objects: the image with conceptualization and the image without conceptualization. Thus, having obtained the path of seeing, they attain the point where phenomena end.[238]

234. See 8.20.
235. F, folio 49.a, *ye shes* instead of *shes pa* in D.
236. D reads *de la nang gi so so'i bdag nyid la so sor rang rig pa de bzhin nyid rnam pa bdun so sor rtog pa'i shes pa rnam pa bdun skye bar 'gyur te*. Compare with F, folio 49.a: *de bzhin nyid rnam pa bdun bden bden pa'i rnam pa nang gi so so rang gis shes par bya ba rab tu rtogs pa'i ye shes skye bar 'gyur te*. I think F is more in the spirit of this paragraph than D. The notion of *so sor rtog pa'i shes pa* is at odds with *nang gi so so'i bdag nyid la so sor rang rig pa*, to which it stands in apposition in D. Instead, I'd rather read here *rab tu rtogs pa'i ye shes* as found in F.
237. *yang dag pa nyid skyon med pa* (D) or *yang dag pa mi 'gyur ba* (F); *samyaktvaniyama*.
238. These are the first three of the four objects of mental stillness and insight as explained in 8.2. The fourth is the accomplishment of the goal.

"In the higher stages, they enter the path of practice and direct their attention toward their threefold referential object.[239] It is like this: in the way one uses a smaller wedge to pull out a larger one and thus drives out a wedge by means of a wedge, they eliminate all manifest characteristics related to affliction by eliminating internal manifest characteristics. When they eliminate them, they also eliminate corruption. By getting rid of manifest characteristic and corruption, they gradually purify their minds in the higher stages in the way gold is refined. They will attain the unsurpassable, complete, and perfect awakening and also obtain the realization of the object corresponding to the accomplishment of the goal.[240] Thus, Maitreya, once bodhisattvas have achieved mental stillness and insight in this way, they will attain the unsurpassable, complete, and perfect awakening."

«8.37» "How do bodhisattvas practice so that they accomplish the great powers of a bodhisattva?"

"Maitreya, the bodhisattvas who are skillful with regard to these six topics accomplish the great powers of a bodhisattva: (1) the arising of the mind, (2) the underlying condition of the mind, (3) the emergence from the mind, (4) the increase of the mind, (5) the decrease of the mind, and (6) skillful means.

"How are they skillful with regard to the arising of the mind? They are skillful with regard to the arising of the mind as it is if they know the sixteen ways in which mind arises:[241] (1) the representation that is a support and receptacle, for example, the appropriating cognition;[242] (2) the representation that is a variegated image of a referential object, for example, the mental cognition of conceptualizations that simultaneously apprehends forms and so on, or that simultaneously apprehends outer and inner objects, or that in a single instant simultaneously settles in several states of concentration, perceives numerous buddha fields, or sees many tathāgatas—being nothing but the mental cognition of conceptualizations; (3) the representation taking limited manifest characteristics as its object, for example, the mind

239. This refers to the first three objects of mental stillness and insight; see 8.2.

240. See 8.35.11 above for a more detailed elucidation of this point.

241. Lit. "They are skillful with regard to the arising of the mind as it is if they know the sixteen points of the arising of the mind. The sixteen points of the arising of the mind are the arising of . . ."

242. See 5.3.

related to the [realm of] desire; (4) the representation taking vast manifest characteristics as its object, for example, the mind related to the [realm of] form; (5) the representation taking immeasurable manifest characteristics as its object, for example, the mind related to the domain of limitless space and limitless cognition; (6) the representation taking subtle manifest characteristics as its object, for example, the mind related to the domain of nothingness; (7) the representation taking ultimate manifest characteristics as its object, for example, the mind related to the domain of neither conception nor lack of conception; (8) the representation that does not have manifest characteristic [as its object], for example, the supramundane mind and the mind having cessation as its object; (9) the representation involving suffering, for example, the mind of hell beings; (10) the representation involving mixed sensations, for example, the mind experienced in the [realm of] desire; (11) the representation involving joy, for example, the mind belonging to the first and second meditative absorptions; (12) the representation involving bliss, for example, the mind belonging to the third meditative absorption; (13) the representation involving neither suffering nor bliss, for example, the mind belonging to the fourth meditative absorption up to the domain of neither conception nor lack of conception; (14) the representation involving defilements, for example, the mind associated with defilements and secondary defilements; (15) the representation involving virtue, for example, the mind associated with faith and so on; and (16) the neutral representation, for example, the mind that is not associated with either defilement or virtue.

"How are they skillful with regard to the underlying condition of the mind? They are skillful when they cognize the true reality of representations as it truly is.[243]

"How are they skillful with regard to the emergence from the mind? They are skillful when they cognize as they truly are the two bonds, namely, the bonds of manifest characteristic and corruption.

"How are they skillful with regard to the increase of the mind? They are skillful when they cognize as such the arising and increase of the mind at the moment when the mind that is the antidote to manifest characteristic and corruption arises and increases.

"How are they skillful with regard to the decrease of the mind? They

243. See 8.20.2.

are skillful when they cognize as such the decrease and decline of the mind at the moment when the mind afflicted by the adverse factors of manifest characteristic and corruption decreases and declines.

"How are they skilled in terms of means? They are skillful when they practice the eight liberations, the eight domains of mastery, and the ten domains of totality.

"Maitreya, in this way bodhisattvas have accomplished, do accomplish, and will accomplish the great powers of a bodhisattva."

«8.38» "The Blessed One said that all sensations have come to complete cessation in the domain of the nirvana with no aggregates remaining. What then are those sensations?"[244]

"Maitreya, in brief, two kinds of sensations cease: (1) the sensations[245] arising from corruption incumbent on being alive and (2) the sensations arising from their resulting objects.

"Among those, the sensations arising from corruption related to one's existence are of four kinds: (1) sensations arising from physical corruption, (2) sensations arising from nonphysical corruption, (3) sensations arising from corruption currently brought to fruition, and (4) sensations arising from corruption not yet brought to fruition.

"Sensations arising from corruption brought to fruition refer to present sensations, whereas sensations arising from sensations not yet brought to fruition refer to sensations that are the causes for future sensations.

"The sensations of their resulting objects are also of four kinds: (1) sensations related to places, (2) sensations related to necessities, (3) sensations related to enjoyments, and (4) sensations related to relations.

"Moreover, there are sensations in the domain of the nirvana with aggregates remaining. Although these include sensations not yet brought to fruition,[246] their opposites, the experience of sensations arising from present sensations, have not completely ceased. They are experienced as a mixture

244. D reads *yang dag pa'i tshor ba*, probably in the sense of *yang dag pa'i don gyi* (or *la*) *tshor ba*, but F, folio 50.a, has instead *'gag par 'gyur ba'i tshor ba* (but the sentence in F is not built according to a pronominal relative-correlative structure as it is in D).

245. D reads *rig pa* in the sense of *rnam par rig pa*, while F, folio 50.a, has *tshor ba* instead, which makes more sense in the present context. This reading is supported by Xuanzang's reading: 一者所依粗重受二者彼果境界受 (CBETA, Taishō 676), in which 受 refers to *vedanā*. I therefore emended the entire paragraph accordingly.

246. In the sense of sensations being the cause for future sensations as explained above (see 8.38.1.iv).

of pleasant and unpleasant sensations. Both kinds of sensation already brought to fruition have completely ceased. Only the category of sensations arising from present sensations are experienced. In the domain of the nirvana with no aggregates remaining, even this will cease when one passes into parinirvana. This is why I said that all sensations have come to a complete cessation in the domain of the nirvana with no aggregates remaining."

«8.39» Thereupon, the Blessed One spoke these words to the bodhisattva Maitreya: "Maitreya, you questioned the Tathāgata with determination and skill regarding the perfect and pure path of yoga. This is excellent. I taught that this path of yoga is perfect and pure, and exactly[247] so I have taught and will teach all the perfect buddhas of the past and the future. The sons and daughters of noble family should devote themselves to this path with great effort."[248]

«8.40» Then, at that moment,[249] the Blessed One spoke these verses:

"This presentation of the teachings by means of designations
Is thoughtful and of great significance for [the practice of this]
  yoga.[250]
Those who, by relying on this Dharma,
Correctly devote themselves to this yoga will attain awakening.[251]

"Those who, seeking liberation, study the entire Dharma
By looking for faults and disputing it
Are, Maitreya, as far from this yoga

247. Sanskrit reads *evam eva*; see Matsuda 2013, 940 *ad* Lamotte XIII.39.
248. D: *rigs kyi bu rnams dang / rigs kyi bu mo dag gis 'di la shin tu brtson par bya ba'i rigs so* Sanskrit: *ayam atra kulaputraiḥ kuladuhitṛbhir vā tīvravyāyāmair bhavituṁ* (see Matsuda 2013, 940 *ad* Lamotte VIII.39).
249. *de'i tshe, tasyāṁ velāyam* (cf. Sanskrit text in Matsuda 2013, 940 *ad* Lamotte VIII.39).
250. D: *chos rnams gdags pa rnam gzhag gang yin pa / / de ni rnal 'byor bag yod don chen yin*; in Sanskrit: *dharmāna prajñaptivyavasthito yo hi yoge pramattā na mahā*[*rtha*] *so hī* (see Matsuda 2013, 940 *ad* Lamotte VIII.40). The sentence is built according to a correlative-relative structure *yaḥ . . . sa. . .* , literally "that which is . . . is . . ." The Sanskrit here is of a hybrid nature as pointed out by Matsuda. Instead of *pramattā na*, *apramāda* would be expected for the Tibetan *bag yod*.
251. D: *gang dag chos der brten nas rnal 'byor 'dir / / yang dag brtson pa de dag byang chub 'thob*; Sanskrit: *taṁ dharmaṁ niśrāya ye atra yoge samyakprayukta te labha(ṁ)ti bodhi* (see Matsuda 2013, 940 *ad* Lamotte VIII.40).

As is the sky from the earth.[252]

"Wise[253] and skilled in the real meaning[254] of benefiting beings
Is the one who does not strive to benefit beings thinking they will reward him.[255]
The one expecting a reward will indeed[256] not obtain
The joy that is both[257] supreme and free from covetousness.[258]

"Those who grant Dharma instructions [to obtain] desirable objects
Have renounced desirable objects and yet[259] still accept them.
Although these fools have obtained the priceless and faultless[260] jewel of Dharma,
They wander like beggars.[261]

"Therefore, with great effort
Strive to abandon disputation, distractions, and mental elaborations.
In order to liberate the world of beings including the gods,
Devote yourself to this yoga."

«8.41» Then, the bodhisattva Maitreya asked the Blessed One, "Blessed

252. D: *gang dag glags lta de skad rgol ba las / thar bar lta ba chos kun chub byed pa / / byams pa de dag rnal 'byor 'di las ni/ /thag ring gnas sa ring ba ji bzhin no*; Sanskrit: *upāraṁbhaprekṣā iti vādamokṣaprekṣā ye dharmaṁ sarva pu /* (see Matsuda 2013, 940 *ad* Lamotte VIII.40).
253. *blo ldan*; *dhīmān* (cf. Sanskrit text in Matsuda 2013, 940 *ad* Lamotte VIII.40).
254. The Tibetan reads *sems can don zhes* while the Sanskrit has *satvārthasāra* (cf. Sanskrit text in Matsuda 2013, 940 *ad* Lamotte VIII.40). *Sāra* means both "real meaning"/"quintessence" and "wealth"/"riches."
255. D: *blo ldan sems can don zhes de dag las / / lan byed rig nas sems can don brtson min*; Sanskrit: *satvārthasāro na tu kāra tebhyaṁ viditva satvārthaprayukta dhīmān*.
256. *Eva* in Sanskrit (see Matsuda 2013, 940 *ad* Lamotte VIII.40).
257. . . . *ca* . . . *ca* in Sanskrit (see Matsuda 2013, 940 *ad* Lamotte VIII.40).
258. *zang zing med pa*; *nirāmiṣa* (in the sense of "disinterested, not expecting a reward"; see Matsuda 2013, 940 *ad* Lamotte VIII.40 for the Sanskrit term).
259. Sanskrit: *punar* (see Matsuda 2013, 940 *ad* Lamotte VIII.40).
260. *Anagharatna* (cf. Sanskrit text in Matsuda 2013, 940 *ad* Lamotte VIII.40).
261. *spongs zhing rgyu*; *caraṁti bhikṣāṁ* (cf. Sanskrit text in Matsuda 2013, 940 *ad* Lamotte VIII.40). The term *bhikṣā* literally corresponds to the French concept of "mendicité."

One, what is the name of the teaching imparted in this Dharma discourse that elucidates the Tathāgata's intent? How should I keep it in mind?"[262]

The Blessed One answered, "Maitreya, this is a teaching of definitive meaning on yoga. Keep it in mind as *The Teaching of Definitive Meaning on Yoga*." As the Blessed One expounded this teaching, six hundred thousand beings produced the mind directed at the unsurpassable, complete, and perfect awakening, three hundred thousand hearers purified the Dharma eye from impurities and contaminations; one hundred and fifty hearers who were without attachment liberated their minds from all outflows; and seventy-five thousand bodhisattvas attained the state wherein their attention was directed toward the great yoga.[263]

This was the chapter of the bodhisattva Maitreya—the eighth chapter.

262. *gzung bar bgyi*; *dhārayāmi* (cf. Sanskrit text in Matsuda 2013, 940 *ad* Lamotte VIII.41). I suggest reading *dhārayāmi*, which is a causative present, as an optative here.

263. This concluding passage is similar to the one concluding chapter 7 (see 7.33).

Chapter 9

«9.1» Then the bodhisattva Avalokiteshvara addressed the Blessed One. "Blessed One, the ten stages of the bodhisattva are called (1) Utmost Joy, (2) Stainless, (3) Illuminating, (4) Radiant, (5) Hard to Conquer, (6) Manifest, (7) Far Reaching, (8) Immovable, (9) Excellent Intelligence, and (10) Cloud of Dharma. When taken together with the eleventh, [called] Buddha Stage, in how many kinds of purification and subdivisions are they included?"

«9.2» The Blessed One answered, "Avalokiteshvara, you should know that they are included in four kinds of purification and eleven subdivisions.

"Avalokiteshvara, you should know that the first stage is included in the purification of intention; the second, in the purification of superior discipline; and the third, in the purification of superior mind; while stages four to eleven are included in the purification of superior wisdom, which gradually leads to perfection from stage to stage. These stages are thus included in four kinds of purification.

«9.3» "What are the eleven levels—the subdivisions including the ten stages of the bodhisattva and the Buddha Stage?

"On the first level consisting of actions based on superior[264] devotion, bodhisattvas cultivate superior devotion and patience[265] by engaging in the ten practices related to Dharma.[266] Once they have passed beyond this stage, they will enter the faultless state of truth of the bodhisattvas.[267]

264. Sanskrit reads *adhimukti*; see Matsuda 1995, 67.

265. Sanskrit reads *suparibhāvitādhimuktikṣanti*; see Matsuda 1995, 67.

266. See 7.31: "they develop devotion for this teaching and commission its transcription into writing. Once it has been put into writing, they keep it in mind, read it, venerate it, propagate it, expound it, chant it aloud, contemplate it, and apply it in their practice."

267. D reads *shin tu bsgoms pa'i phyir bzod pas sa de las yang dag par 'das nas byang chub sems dpa'i yang dag pa nyid skyon med pa la 'jug go*. The term *bzod pas* appears to be out of place

"Although the first level is accomplished by these practices, the second level is not, because the bodhisattvas are still unable to act while being aware of confusion resulting from subtle transgressions. By striving to accomplish this level, they will succeed.

"Although the second level is accomplished by this practice, the third level is not, because the bodhisattvas are still unable to settle into a perfect mundane concentration and recollect what they have heard. By striving to accomplish this level, they will succeed.

"However, the fourth level is not thereby accomplished, because the bodhisattvas, who frequently engage in practicing the awakening factors[268] in the way they obtained them, are still unable to settle their minds due to attachment to states of absorption and to the teaching.[269] By striving to accomplish this level, they will succeed.

"Although the fourth level is accomplished through this practice, the fifth level is not, because the bodhisattvas are still unable to fully examine the truths or settle in superior equanimity regarding samsara and nirvana, which they exclusively reject or focus upon, respectively. They are still unable to practice the awakening factors in conjunction with skillful means. By striving to accomplish this level, they will succeed.

"Although the fifth level is accomplished by this practice, the sixth level is not, because even once they have recognized the activities of conditioned states for what they are, the bodhisattvas are still unable to maintain for long an aversion toward them. They are also still unable to remain for long directing their attention toward what lacks manifest characteristics. By striving to accomplish this level, they will succeed.

---

here and should have been found in the preceding clause, as is the case in the Sanskrit text, which in addition contains no parallel to *phyir*.

268. *byang chub kyi phyogs dang mthun pa'i chos*; *bodhyaṅga*. D, folio 39.b reads *byang chub kyi phyogs dang 'thun ba'i chos ji ltar thob pa dag gis*, but F, folio 52.a, has *byang chub kyi phyogs kyi chos ji ltar thob pa de dag la*.

269. D: *'bad pas yan lag des yongs su rdzogs pa yin yang byang chub kyi phyogs dang 'thun ba'i chos ji ltar thob pa dag gis de la mang du gnas par bya ba dang / snyoms par 'jug pa la sred pa dang / chos la sred pa las sems lhag par btang snyoms su 'jug mi nus pas*. The expression *de la mang du gnas par bya ba* corresponds to *tadbahulavihārin*. Sanskrit: *na tu śaknoti yathāpratilabdhair bodhipakṣair dharmais tadbahulavihārī samāpattidharmatṛṣṇāyāś ca cittam adhyupekṣituṁ* (see Matsuda 1995, 68). The subject is singular masculine. I used a plural for bodhisattva in this chapter to avoid the gender issue since bodhisattvas include both males and females.

"Although the sixth level is accomplished by this practice, the seventh level is not, because the bodhisattvas are still unable to remain without hindrance and interruption while directing their attention toward what lacks manifest characteristic. By striving to accomplish this level, they will succeed.

"Although the seventh level is accomplished by this practice, the eighth level is not, because the bodhisattvas are still unable to rest in equanimity while striving to abide in what lacks manifest characteristic. They are also still unable to attain mastery over manifest characteristic. By striving to accomplish this level, they will succeed.

"Although the eighth level is accomplished by this practice, the ninth level is not, for the bodhisattvas are still unable to masterfully teach the Dharma in all its aspects by using synonyms, definitions, explanations, and categories. By striving to accomplish this level, they will succeed.

"Although the ninth level is accomplished by this practice, the tenth level is not, for the bodhisattvas are still unable to obtain the analytical knowledge of the perfect truth body. By striving to accomplish this level, they will succeed.

"Although the ninth level is accomplished by this practice, the tenth level is not, for the bodhisattvas are still unable to obtain the gnosis and vision that are utterly free from attachment and hindrance regarding all cognitive objects.[270] By striving to accomplish this level, they will succeed.

"Since this level is accomplished by this practice, all levels are accomplished. Avalokiteshvara, you should know that all the stages are included in these eleven levels."

«9.4» "Blessed One, why is the first stage called Utmost Joy? Why are the other stages up to the Buddha Stage called what they are?"

"The first stage is called Utmost Joy because there is a supreme and immense joy in attaining the immaculate and sublime purpose, the supramundane mind.

"The second stage is called Stainless because it is free from all stains consisting in [even] subtle transgressions or faulty discipline.[271]

"The third stage is called Illuminating because it is the very state of

270. See 8.35.11. Sanskrit has a locative singular: *jñeye*; see Matsuda 1995, 68.

271. Sanskrit reads *sarvasūkṣāpattidauṣṭhulyamalavigatām*; see Matsuda 1995, 69.

concentration and recollection imbued with the immeasurable light of gnosis.[272]

"The fourth stage is called Radiant because the fire of gnosis produced by the practice of the awakening factors is set ablaze[273] in order to burn the fuel of afflictions.

"The fifth stage is called Hard to Conquer because it is difficult indeed to master the practice of these very awakening factors in conjunction with skillful means.[274]

"The sixth stage is called Manifest because the activity of conditioning mental factors becomes manifest, as does the bodhisattvas' attention that is repeatedly directed toward what lacks manifest characteristic.

"The seventh stage is called Far Reaching because once the bodhisattvas engage for a long time without hindrance and interruption while directing their attention toward what lacks manifest characteristic, this stage is connected with the subsequent stages of purification.

"The eighth stage is called Immovable because what lacks manifest characteristic is spontaneously accomplished and the bodhisattvas are unshaken by the manifestation of defilements resulting from manifest characteristic.

"The ninth stage is called Excellent Intelligence because the bodhisattvas obtain a vast intelligence that flawlessly masters all aspects related to teaching the Dharma.

"The tenth stage is called Cloud of Dharma because the body afflicted by corruption, which is as empty as the sky, is pervaded and covered by the accumulation of Dharma[275] that is like a [great] cloud.[276]

272. Sanskrit has *apramāṇajñānāvabhāsena*. It seems that *jñāna* has been translated by *shes pa* in D while the more frequent corresponding Tibetan term *ye shes* is usually found in F. Sanskrit: *apramāṇajñānāvabhāsena sanniśrayatām upādāya tasya samādhes tasyāś ca śrutadhāraṇyās tṛtīyā bhūmiḥ prabhākarīty ucyate* (see Matsuda 1995, 69).

273. The Sanskrit fragment (see Matsuda 1995, 69) does not contain the Sanskrit equivalent for *me'i 'od*, which is most probably *agnyarci*, as suggested by Matsuda. In this case, understanding *'od/arci* as "flame" makes more sense. I translated *arcibhūtatva* as "set ablaze."

274. See 9.3.5.

275. *chos kyi tshogs*; *dharmasaṁbhāra*. The Sanskrit (see Matsuda 1995, 69) differs from the Tibetan (Go, folio 35.a reads *chos kyi tshogs*, just like the more recent witnesses): *nabhopamsya dauṣṭhulyakāyasya mahāmeghopamena dharmakāyena spharanāc chādanatām upadāya daśamī bhūmir dharmameghaty ucyate*. The process described here corresponds to the *āśrayaparāvṛtti* (i.e., the shift in one's basis of existence), which is completed on the eleventh stage.

276. I follow Wonch'uk's *ṭīkā* (vol. thi, folio 269.a) regarding the meaning of the analogy with the sky/space (*nam mkha' lta bu*): *gnas ngan len gyi lus nam mkha' lta bu la chos kyi sku*

"The eleventh stage is called Buddha Stage because once one has abandoned the most subtle defiling and cognitive obstructions, one completely and perfectly awakens and knows all aspects to be known,[277] without attachment and hindrance."

«9.5» "Blessed One, how many kinds of delusion and adverse factors of corruption are there on these stages?"

"Avalokiteshvara, there are twenty-two kinds of delusion and eleven adverse factors of corruption:

"On the first stage, there is the delusion of wrongly conceiving the person and phenomena, the delusion of bad destinies, and the adverse factor of the corruption resulting from these.

"On the second stage, there is the delusion of confusion resulting from subtle transgressions, the delusion related to the various aspects of the maturation of karma, and the adverse factor of the corruption resulting from these two.

"On the third stage, there is the delusion of desire, the delusion of perfectly remembering what was heard, and the adverse factor of the corruption resulting from these.

"On the fourth stage, there is the delusion of attachment to the states of absorption, the delusion of attachment to Dharma, and the adverse factor of the corruption resulting from these.

"On the fifth stage, there is the delusion of attending to samsara as exclusively negative or positive, the delusion of attending to nirvana as exclusively negative or positive, and the adverse factor of the corruption resulting from these.

"On the sixth stage, there is the delusion of making manifest the activity of conditioning mental factors, the delusion of the many manifesting

---

yongs su rdzogs pa sprin chen po lta bus khyab cing khebs pas de'i phyir bcu pa ni chos kyi sprin gyis zhes bya'o zhes bya ba ni bcu pa chos kyi sprin rnam par bshad pa'o / / 'di ltar bdag dang chos su 'dzin pas yongs su bsgos pa'i sa bon gang yin pa de ni las su mi rung ba'i phyir gnas ngan len zhes bya'o / / stong pa nyid rnam pa gnyis dang / bdag med pa'i don la sgrib pa'i phyir mdo las nam mkha' lta bu'o zhes gsungs so / / sa bcu po de la chos kyi dbyings rnam pa bcu'i chos kyi sku yongs su rdzogs pa ni sprin chen po dang mtshungs te / chos kyi dbyings mngon du gyur pa ni chos kyi sku yongs su rdzogs pa dang / bsgoms pa las byung ba'i chos kyi sku gnas ngan len nam mkha' lta bu la khebs pa'i phyir chos kyi sprin zhes bya'o.

277. *shes bya'i rnam pa thams cad* [*mkhyen pa*]; *jñeyasarvākāra*[*jñatā-*] (see Matsuda 1995, 69).

manifest characteristics, and the adverse factor of the corruption resulting from these.[278]

"On the seventh stage, there is the delusion of the manifestation of subtle manifest characteristics, the delusion toward skillful means since one's attention is exclusively directed toward what lacks manifest characteristic, and the adverse factor of the corruption resulting from these.

"On the eighth stage, there is the delusion of exerting oneself toward what lacks manifest characteristic, the delusion of not having mastery over manifest characteristics, and the adverse factor of the corruption resulting from these.

"On the ninth stage, there is the delusion of having mastery in the boundless teaching and expression of Dharma, the delusion of having mastery in continuously keeping it in mind in terms of wisdom and eloquence,[279] the delusion of having command of eloquent speech, and the adverse factor consisting in the corruption resulting from these two types of delusion.

"On the tenth stage, there is the delusion with regard to the sublime superior knowledge, the delusion of engaging in what is secret and subtle, and the adverse factor consisting of the corruption resulting from these two.

"On the Buddha Stage, there is the delusion of the extremely subtle attachment to cognitive objects, the delusion of the extremely subtle hindrance related to defilements, and the adverse factor consisting of the corruption resulting from these two.

"Avalokiteshvara, this is a presentation of the stages according to twenty-two kinds of delusion and eleven types of corruption. The unsurpassable, complete, and perfect awakening does not have any of them."

"In which case,[280] Blessed One, the unsurpassable, complete, and perfect awakening, the most sublime blessing and result, is truly wondrous! Once bodhisattvas have torn the great net of delusion in this fashion and gone beyond the vast jungle of corruption, they will awaken to the complete and perfect enlightenment.[281]

278. On the opposition between affliction and purification in this sentence, see Lamotte 1935, 240–41n13.

279. On the relation between *pratibhāna* and *dhāraṇī*, see Braarvig 1985.

280. *gang la*; *yatredānīm* (see Matsuda 1995, 70).

281. The variant reading found in F differs significantly from the Sanskrit edited by Matsuda in comparison to the Tibetan translation in D. I translated this passage from the Sanskrit (see

«9.6» "Blessed One, through how many kinds of purifications are these stages presented?"

"Avalokiteshvara, they are presented through eight purifications: (1) the purification of intention, (2) the purification of the mind, (3) the purification of compassion, (4) the purification of the perfections, (5) the purification of the vision of buddhas and of their veneration, (6) the purification of bringing beings to maturity, (7) the purification of birth, and (8) the purification of power.

"Avalokiteshvara, you should know that the purifications on the first stage, from the purification of superior intention up to the purification of power, as well as the purifications on the higher stages including the Buddha Stage, from the purification of superior intention up to the purification of power, become more and more intense.[282] Thus, if one excepts the purification of birth on the Buddha Stage, the qualities on the first stage seem similar to those of the higher stages. However, you should know that the qualities of each higher stage are superior to those on the former stage. You should also understand that the qualities on the ten stages of a bodhisattva can be surpassed, whereas the qualities on the Buddha Stage are unsurpassable."

«9.7» "Blessed One, why did you declare that, among all kinds of birth, the birth of a bodhisattva is supreme?"

"Avalokiteshvara, it is supreme for four reasons: (1) it accomplishes the great purification of one's roots of virtue, (2) it is appropriated as a result of mental inspection, (3) it is imbued with the compassion that protects all beings, and (4) it is not itself afflicted, but it repels the afflictions of others."

Matsuda 1995, 70): *(āścaryā bhaga)van yāvad mahānuśaṁsā mahāphalā anuttarā samyaksaṁbodhī yatredānīm evaṁ ma(hā)saṁmohajālaṁ saṁpracālya mahac ca dauṣṭhulyagahanaṁ samatikramya bodhisattvā anuttarāṁ samyaksaṁbodhim abhisaṁbudhyaṁte.* D: *bcom ldan 'das gang la de ltar / byang chub sems dpa' rnams de ltar kun tu rmongs pa'i dra ba chen po rab tu dral zhing de'i gnas ngan len thibs po chen po las yang dag par 'das te / bla na med pa yang dag par rdzogs pa'i byang chub mngon par rdzogs par 'tshang rgya ba'i bla na med pa yang dag par rdzogs pa'i byang chub ji tsam du phan yon che zhing 'bras bu che ba ni ngo mtshar lags so.* F, folio 54.b: *bcom ldan 'das ji tsam du bla na med pa yang dag par rdzogs pa'i byang chub de 'bras bu che zhing legs pa che ba dang / de ltar gti mug chen po'i dra ba gsal nas ngan len che zhing sdug pa las yang dag par 'das te / byang chub sems dpa' rnams bla na med pa yang dag par rdzogs pa'i byang chub mngon par rdzogs par 'tshang rgya ba ni ngo mtshar che'o.*

282. D: *chos rnam par dag pa dang / ches shin tu rnam par dag pa yin par rig par bya'o*; compare with K0774, folio 55.b: *ches rnam par dag pa dang / ches shin tu rnam par dag pa yin par rig par bya'o.*

«9.8» "Blessed One, why did you declare that bodhisattvas practice with a vast aspiration, are sublime, have a sublime aspiration, and possess the force of aspiration?"

"Avalokiteshvara, [I declared this] for four reasons: (1) bodhisattvas are skilled with respect to the blissful state of nirvana, (2) they are able to attain it swiftly, (3) they have given up both this swift attainment and this blissful state, and (4) without wavering or being compelled,[283] they mentally produce the aspiration to go for a long time through many kinds of suffering for the sake of beings. Therefore, I said that bodhisattvas possess a vast aspiration, a sublime aspiration, and the force of aspiration."

«9.9» "Blessed One, how many foundations of training do the bodhisattvas have?"

"Avalokiteshvara, they have six: generosity, discipline, patience, diligence, meditative absorption, and wisdom."

"Blessed One, among those six, how many constitute the training in superior discipline, how many constitute the training in superior mind, and how many constitute the training in superior wisdom?"

"Avalokiteshvara, you should know that the first three constitute the training in superior discipline, meditative absorption constitutes the training in superior mind, wisdom constitutes the training in superior wisdom, and diligence is present in each of these trainings."

"Blessed One, how many of these foundations of training constitute the accumulation of merit? How many constitute the accumulation of gnosis?"

"Avalokiteshvara, the training in superior discipline constitutes the accumulation of merit. The training in superior wisdom constitutes the accumulation of gnosis. Diligence and meditative absorption are present in both."

"Blessed One, how do bodhisattvas train in these six foundations of training?"

"Avalokiteshvara, they train in these six foundations of training according to five points: (1) by having devotion from the beginning for the teaching of the pure Dharma, for the teaching of the six perfections, and for the collection of teachings on the bodhisattva [path]; (2) by accomplishing next the wisdom arising from hearing, contemplating, and practicing [the truth] through the ten activities related to Dharma; (3) by preserving the

283. D: *dgos pa med* for *nirupalepa* (see Mvyut 6672)? F, folio 55.b: *dgongs pa med pa*. D and Xuanzang's translation agree: 無緣無待發大願心 (CBETA, Taishō 676).

awakening mind; (4) by relying upon a virtuous friend; and (5) by continuously practicing virtue."

"Blessed One, why are the foundations of training known in terms of a sixfold classification?"

"Avalokiteshvara, there are two reasons: (1) they benefit beings and (2) they are antidotes to defilements. You should know that, among them, three benefit beings while three are antidotes to defilements.

"Through their generosity, bodhisattvas benefit beings by providing them with what is necessary to life; through their discipline, they benefit beings by not impoverishing them, harming them, or ridiculing them; and through their patience, they benefit beings by enduring impoverishment, harm, and ridicule. Thus, they benefit beings through these three foundations of training.

"Through their diligence they apply themselves to the virtue that completely overcomes defilements and eliminates them, since defilements are unable to deflect them from this practice; through their meditative absorption they destroy defilements; and through their wisdom they put an end to their latent dispositions. Thus, these three foundations of training are antidotes to defilements."

«9.10» "Blessed One, why are the other perfections known in terms of a fourfold classification?"

"Avalokiteshvara, it is because they assist these six perfections:

"With the first three perfections, bodhisattvas benefit beings. Then they establish beings in virtue through the skillful means consisting of the four methods of conversion. Therefore, I taught that the perfection of skillful means assists the first three perfections.

"Avalokiteshvara, suppose the bodhisattvas are unable to practice at all times in this life as a result of their many defilements. Suppose they are unable to focus their minds within due to the weakness of their superior intention as a result of their limited experience[284] and aspiration. Suppose they are unable to accomplish the supramundane wisdom because they did not practice the meditative absorption based on the referential objects corresponding to the teachings on the bodhisattva path that they have heard. However, since they have accumulated merit, even to a limited extent, they produce with their minds the aspiration that their defilements will

284. D: *khams*, but F, folio 56.b, reads *mkhas pa*.

decrease in the future. This is the perfection of aspiration. Because defilements decrease and bodhisattvas are able to exert their diligence through this perfection, the perfection of aspiration therefore assists the perfection of diligence.

"Then, relying on a noble being and on hearing the Dharma, they attain the state in which they direct their attention on discipline. Once they have turned away from having a superior intention whose power is limited, they obtain the power of intention of the heavenly realms.[285] This is the perfection of power. Because bodhisattvas are able to focus on their minds through this perfection, the perfection of power therefore assists the perfection of meditative absorption.

"The bodhisattvas settle in meditative absorption as they practice the referential objects corresponding to the teachings on the bodhisattva path that they have heard. This is the perfection of wisdom. Because bodhisattvas are able to accomplish supramundane wisdom through this perfection, the perfection of gnosis therefore assists the perfection of wisdom."

«9.11» "Blessed One, why should one know that the six perfections are taught in this order?"

"Avalokiteshvara, it is because the former is the support on which the latter is established, and so on and so forth. By not fixating on their bodies and possessions, bodhisattvas acquire discipline. By maintaining their discipline, they take possession of patience. Through patience, they engage in diligence. By having engaged in diligence, they establish meditative absorption. Once meditative absorption is established, they will obtain the supramundane wisdom."

«9.12» "Blessed One, of how many kinds are these perfections?"

"Avalokiteshvara, each of these perfections is of three kinds:

285. D; K0774, folio 47.b: *khams gya nom pa* (syn. *khams bzang po*), *praṇītadhātu*(*kam*) (see Mvyut 7670), 妙界 (see Yokoyama, Kōitsu, and Takayuki Hirosawa, eds., *Sanskrit-Tibetan Index for the Yogâcārabhūmi-śāstra*, accessed August 29, 2016, http://www.buddhism-dict.net/cgi-bin/xpr-ddb.pl? q=%E5%A6%99%E7%95%8C). As a translation for this term, Lamotte 1935, 245, suggests "complexion" and Powers 1995, 243, gives "constituents." However, F, folio 57.a, has *dam pa'i dbyings su* instead of *khams gya nom pa las*. Obermiller 1933, 207n3, gives us the context in which *gya nom pa* (*praṇīta*) is usually used: "Emancipation, in the sense that (the extinction of Phenomenal Existence) represents the state of bliss and purity (which is completely free from the defiling forces of the Phenomenal World)." Xuanzang's translation reads 亦能獲得上界勝解 (CBETA, Taishō 676), in which 上界 refers to the formless and form realms.

"The three kinds of generosity are the gift of Dharma, the gift of material objects, and the gift of fearlessness.

"The three kinds of discipline are the discipline that turns away from what is not virtuous, the discipline that engages in virtue, and the discipline that engages in benefiting beings.

"The three kinds of patience are the patience of enduring harm, the patience of not considering [one's own] suffering, and the patient acceptance of Dharma by means of reflection.[286]

"The three kinds of diligence are the diligence that is like armor, the diligence to practice virtue, and the diligence to benefit beings.

"The three kinds of meditative absorption are the meditative absorption of blissful abiding that, nonconceptual and peaceful, is an antidote to defilements and suffering, the meditative absorption that brings about good qualities, and the meditative absorption that accomplishes the welfare of beings.

"The three kinds of wisdom are the wisdom that takes the conventional truth as its referential object, the wisdom that takes the ultimate truth as its referential object, and the wisdom that takes the welfare of beings as its referential object."

«9.13» "Blessed One, why are the perfections called 'perfections'?"

"Avalokiteshvara, this is for five reasons. The perfections are without

286. *chos la nges par rtog pa'i bzod pa*; *dharmanidhyānakśānti*. The term *kśānti* is used here in the sense of "acceptance." In the *Kīṭāgiri sutta* (M. I, 480), the phrase *dhammanijjhānakkhanti* is glossed in the following way: "Monks, I do not say that the attainment of gnosis is all at once. Rather, the attainment of gnosis is after gradual training, gradual action, gradual practice. And how is there the attainment of gnosis after gradual training, gradual action, gradual practice? There is the case where, when confidence has arisen, one visits the teacher. Having visited, one grows close. Having grown close, one lends ear. Having lent ear, one hears the Dhamma. Having heard the Dhamma, one remembers it. Remembering, one penetrates the meaning of the teachings. Penetrating the meaning, one comes to an agreement through pondering the teachings." *Kathañca bhikkhave anupubbasikkhā anupubbakiriyā anupubbapaṭipadā aññārādhanā hoti: idha bhikkhave saddhājāto upasaṅkamati, upasaṅkamanto payirupāsati, payirupāsanto sotaṁ odahati, ohitasoto dhammaṁ suṇāti, sutvā dhammaṁ dhāreti, dhatānaṁ dhammānaṁ atthaṁ upaparikkhati, atthaṁ upaparikkhato dhammā nijjhānaṁ khamanti, dhammanijjhānakkhantiyā sati chando jāyati, chandajāto ussahati, ussahitvā tuleti, tulayitvā padahati, pahitatto samāno kāyena ceva paramaṁ saccaṁ sacchikaroti, paññāya ca naṁ paṭivijjha passati.*" (Translation and citation are from Punnaji 2017).

attachment, disinterested, free from faults, nonconceptual, and dedication of merit:

"Being without attachment, they are completely devoid of attachment to factors adverse to themselves.

"Being disinterested, they are free from thoughts fixating on results or on some reward obtained from their accomplishment.

"Being free from faults, they are not involved with afflicted phenomena and lack unskillful means.

"Being nonconceptual, they are free from any literal assumption of having a defining characteristic specific to them.

"Being dedication of merit, they are the aspiration for the result of the bodhisattva path by having produced and accumulated[287] these perfections."

«9.14» "Blessed One, what are the factors adverse to the perfections?"

"Avalokiteshvara, you should know that there are six factors: (1) considering as beneficial the joy produced by desirable objects, (2) indulging in pleasurable activities through one's body, speech, or mind, (3) not enduring contempt with patience, (4) invoking merit to justify one's lack of diligence, (5) being distracted by occupations, entertainment, and people, and (6) considering as beneficial the conventional mental elaborations arising from what one sees, hears, thinks, or is conscious of."

«9.15» "Blessed One, what is the result of the maturation of these perfections?"

"Avalokiteshvara, you should know that there are six: (1) great wealth, (2) rebirth in pleasant destinies, (3) happiness and satisfaction from peace and concord, (4) sovereignty over beings, (5) the absence of physical harm, and (6) renown of having great powers."

«9.16» "Blessed One, how are these perfections involved with afflicted phenomena?"

"Avalokiteshvara, they are involved through four practices: (1) the practice of the perfections without compassion, (2) the improper practice of the perfections, (3) the irregular practice of the perfections, and (4) the negligent practice of the perfections.

"The improper practice of the perfections occurs when the practice of one of these perfections impairs the practice of the other perfections."

287. *byas shing bsags pa*; 造作增長; *kṛta-upacita*.

«9.17» "Blessed One, what are unskillful means?"

"Avalokiteshvara, the bodhisattvas assist beings by means of these perfections. If they do not establish beings in virtue once they have pulled them from nonvirtuous states and instead are satisfied to merely provide material objects to them, this is unskillful means. Why? Avalokiteshvara, one does not assist beings by merely doing this. It is like this: excrements, whether in large or small quantity, cannot be made to smell good by any method[288] whatsoever. Likewise, no method that merely supports beings with material objects can make happy those who are suffering, because their nature is to experience the suffering arising from being conditioned.[289] In contrast, establishing them in virtue is the best and only way to benefit them."

«9.18» "Blessed One, how many kinds of purification are [included] in these perfections?"

"Avalokiteshvara, I did not state that there were other purifications apart from the five kinds [I have already mentioned].[290] However, in relation to what I have already explained, I will clarify for you the (1) general and (2) specific purifications included in the perfections.

"You should know that the general purifications that are common to all perfections include seven points: (1) bodhisattvas do not seek to make a profit from others through the teachings on the bodhisattva path; (2) they do not produce wrong conceptions with regard to these teachings; (3) with respect to these teachings, they do not give rise to indecision or doubts as to whether they will attain awakening or not; (4) they do not praise themselves, nor do they blame others or despise them; (5) they do not generate arrogance or carelessness; (6) they are not satisfied with only limited or inferior attainments; and (7) they are not stingy or envious of others because of these teachings.

"You should know that the purifications specific to each perfection also include seven points:

"The seven points of the purification included in the perfection of generosity are as follows: (1) bodhisattvas practice generosity that is the puri-

288. *rnam grangs* is used here as a synonym for *thabs*.

289. Lit., "Likewise, beings who are suffering from being subject to the suffering resulting from being conditioned cannot be made happy by any method consisting in merely assisting them with material objects."

290. According to Lamotte and Keenan, this refers to 9.13: "The perfections are without attachment, disinterested, free from faults, nonconceptual, and dedication of merit."

fication of generosity through the purification[291] of the object that is the gift, and (2–7) they practice generosity that is the purification of generosity through the purification of discipline, view, mind, speech, knowledge, and stains. Thus, as I have just explained, the purifications included in the perfection of generosity that bodhisattvas obtain and practice constitute the seven aspects of the purification of generosity.

"The seven points of the purification included in the perfection of discipline are as follows: (1) bodhisattvas are skilled in all aspects of the foundation of training related to vows, (2) they are skilled in removing transgressions, (3) their discipline is free from doubts, (4) they have a firm discipline, (5) they maintain discipline in all circumstances, (6) they engage in discipline at all times, and (7) they engage in the training by correctly practicing the foundations of training. These are the seven aspects of the purification of discipline.

"The seven points of the purification included in the perfection of patience are as follows: (1) when confronted with any kind of adversity, bodhisattvas do not waver, for they are confident in the maturation of their karma; (2) they do not engage in harming others by abusing, insulting, striking, intimidating, or criticizing them in order to retaliate; (3) they do not hold grudges; (4) when accused,[292] they do not give rise to defilements; (5) they themselves do not indulge in accusations; (6) they do not practice patience with a mind that is fearful of consequences or interested in material gain; and (7) they do not fail to accomplish others' benefit. These are the seven purifications of patience.

"The seven points of the purification included in the perfection of diligence are as follows: (1) bodhisattvas understand the equanimity of diligence; (2) with reference to diligence, they neither praise themselves nor deprecate others; (3–6) they are powerful, diligent, enthusiastic, and resolute; and (7) they never cease to be diligent with respect to virtuous qualities. These are the seven purifications of diligence.

291. Translating *rnam par dag pa* with "purity" does not work here as can be seen in the case of the following purifications (2–7), which are formulated according to the exact same lexicographical and syntactical structure as (1).

292. *shag kyis 'chags*; *codanā*; 諫誨 (see Yokoyama, Kōitsu, and Takayuki Hirosawa, eds., *Sanskrit-Tibetan Index for the Yogâcārabhūmi-śāstra*, accessed August 30, 2016, http://www.buddhism-dict.net/cgi-bin/xpr-ddb.pl? q=%E8%AB%AB%E8%AA%A8). For *codanā*, see Edgerton 1953, 234.

"The seven points of the purification included in the perfection of meditative absorption are (1) the meditative absorption in the concentration that understands manifest characteristic, (2) the perfect meditative absorption in concentration, (3) the meditative absorption in the concentration that has these two aspects, (4) the meditative absorption in the spontaneously arising concentration, (5) the meditative absorption in the concentration without support, (6) the meditative absorption in the concentration that produces flexibility, and (7) the meditative absorption in the concentration on the boundless practice of the referential objects corresponding to the teachings on the bodhisattva path. These are the seven purifications of meditative absorption.

"The seven points of the purification included in the perfection of wisdom are as follows: (1) Once they have abandoned the extremes of superimposition and negation by means of wisdom, bodhisattvas emerge [from cyclic existence] through the middle path. (2) On account of this wisdom, they realize the very meaning of the gate to liberation exactly as it is, namely, the threefold gate to liberation: emptiness, wishlessness, and absence of manifest characteristics. (3) They realize exactly as it is the very meaning of essence, namely, the threefold essence: the imaginary, the other-dependent, and the actual. (4) They realize exactly as it is the very meaning of essencelessness, namely, the threefold essencelessness regarding defining characteristics, arising, and the ultimate. (5) They realize exactly as it is the very meaning of the conventional truth in relation to the five sciences.[293] (6) They realize exactly as it is the very meaning of the ultimate truth with respect to the seven aspects of true reality. (7) They frequently abide in the unique approach of the nonconceptual state free of mental elaborations. By means of the insight that takes countless universal teachings as its referential object, they correctly accomplish the attainment resulting from the practice of the teachings that are in harmony with Dharma. You should know that these are the seven purifications of meditative absorption."

«9.19» "Blessed One, what is the function of each of these five purifications?"

"Avalokiteshvara, you should know that the five functions are as follows: (1) Having no attachment, the bodhisattvas continuously practice the per-

293. *rigs pa'i gnas lnga po; pañcavidyā.* The five sciences are grammar, logic, philosophy, medicine, and crafts.

fections in this life. Because they practice them with enthusiasm, they are conscientious. (2) Being disinterested, they obtain the cause for the careful practice of these perfections in their future lives. (3) Free of any wrongdoing, they practice the perfect, pure, and stainless perfections. (4) Unburdened by conceptions, they swiftly perfect the perfections through their skillful means. (5) Because they transfer their merit, they will attain in all their future lives the inexhaustible perfections together with the desirable results produced by the maturation of their karma, until they obtain the unsurpassable, complete, and perfect awakening."

«9.20» "Blessed One, what is the vastness of the bodhisattvas' practice of these perfections?"

"Avalokiteshvara, bodhisattvas are without attachment and disinterested, and they transfer their merit."

"In what way are they without afflictions?"

"They are free of any wrongdoing and conceptions."

"In what way are they stainless?"

"They act as they mentally inspect."

"In what way are they immovable?"

"They are said to be immovable because this is the nature of those who have entered the stages of a bodhisattva."

"In what way are the perfections utterly pure?"

"Avalokiteshvara, they are included within the tenth stage and the Buddha Stage."

«9.21» "Blessed One, why is the desirable result of the maturation resulting from the practice of the perfections always inexhaustible[294] in the case of the bodhisattvas? Why do they obtain this inexhaustibility through the perfections?"

"Avalokiteshvara, it is because they practice each perfection[295] in dependence upon the others."

«9.22» "Blessed One, why is it that bodhisattvas do not have faith in the desirable result of the maturation resulting from the practice of the perfections in the way that they have faith in the perfections?"

"Avalokiteshvara, this is due to five reasons: (1) The perfections are the cause for the highest bliss and happiness, (2) they are the cause for the ben-

294. *ma 'tshal ba* (D), *mi zad pa* (F); *akṣaya*.
295. D: *sar grub pa*.

efit of oneself and others, (3) they are the cause for the desirable result of their maturation in future lives, (4) they are the foundation of the freedom from afflictions, and (5) they have the nature of immutability."

«9.23» "Blessed One, what are their specific powers?"

"Avalokiteshvara, you should know that their specific powers have the following four qualities: (1) When the bodhisattvas practice the perfections, they eliminate adverse factors, such as greed, faulty discipline, mental agitation, laziness, distraction, and wrong views; (2) they will attain the unsurpassable, complete, and perfect awakening; (3) in this life they will benefit themselves as well as beings; and (4) in future lives they will attain the desirable result of their maturation, which is vast and inexhaustible."

«9.24» "Blessed One, from what cause do these perfections arise? What are their result and benefit?"

"Avalokiteshvara, the perfections have compassion as their cause. As for result, they have the desirable result of their maturation and the result of accomplishing the benefit of beings. As for benefit, they have the great benefit of accomplishing the great awakening."

«9.25» "Blessed One, if the bodhisattvas have inexhaustible resources as well as compassion for beings, why are there poor people in the world?"

"Avalokiteshvara, this is nothing but the fault resulting from beings' own karma. If it were not so, if no obstruction were brought about by beings' own faults, bodhisattvas could at all times engage in compassionate activities toward them. As bodhisattvas have inexhaustible resources, how could the vision of suffering manifest? Avalokiteshvara, it is like this: hungry ghosts whose bodies are tormented by thirst perceive the waters of the ocean as a dry and barren place. This is not the fault of the ocean but the fault resulting from the maturation of nothing but these hungry ghosts' own karma. Likewise, the absence of result is not the fault of the bodhisattvas' generosity, which is like the ocean, but the fault of beings themselves, the fault resulting from the karma of those who are like hungry ghosts."

«9.26» "Blessed One, through which perfection do bodhisattvas apprehend essencelessness?"[296]

"Avalokiteshvara, they apprehend it through the perfection of wisdom."

"Blessed One, when they apprehend essencelessness through the perfec-

296. In D consistently expressed through the term *ngo bo nyid*, while in F *rang bzhin* is used instead.

tion of wisdom, why then do they not apprehend that essencelessness has an essence?"[297]

"Avalokiteshvara, I did not declare that essencelessness is apprehended by means of an essence.[298] However, if one does not use expressions to teach, it is impossible to explain that this essencelessness is inexpressible and cognized intuitively. On this basis, I said that they perceive essencelessness."

«9.27» "Blessed One, what is called perfection, immediate perfection,[299] and great perfection?"

"Avalokiteshvara, bodhisattvas possess virtuous qualities, generosity and so on, which they have practiced over immeasurable periods of time. But when defilements arise in them, they are unable to overcome them and, instead, are overcome by them. Thus, this inferior and intermediate aspiration on the stage where one proceeds by means of aspiration is called perfection.

"Then bodhisattvas possess virtuous qualities that they have practiced during further immeasurable periods of time. When defilements arise in them, these bodhisattvas overcome them and cannot be overcome by them. Thus, taking hold of these qualities beginning with the first stage is called immediate perfection.

"Next, bodhisattvas possess virtuous qualities that they have practiced during even longer immeasurable periods of time. In the bearer of such qualities, no defilement arises at all. Thus, taking hold of these qualities beginning with the eighth stage is called great perfection."[300]

297. D: *ngo bo nyid dang bcas pa nyid kyang ci'i slad du mi 'dzin lags*. F, folio 62.a: *rang bzhin ma mchis pa'i rnams kyang ci'i slad du mi 'dzin*.
298. D: *spyan ras gzigs dbang phyug nga ni ngo bo nyid kyis ngo bo nyid med pa nyid 'dzin par mi smra mod kyi*. Compare with F, folio 62.a: *spyan ras gzigs dbang phyug nga ni rang bzhin med pa nyid la / rang bzhin med par mi bzhad de*; VD, folio 89.a: *spyan ras gzigs dbang phyug nga ni ngo bo nyid med pa nyid kyis ngo bo nyid 'dzin par mi smra mod kyi*; and Xuanzang's translation: 我終不說以無自性性取無自性性 (CBETA, Taishō 676). The meanings of these translations can be interpreted as being similar, although their phrasing is quite different.
299. *nye ba'i pha rol tu phyin pa*. The prefix *nye ba* (for the upasarga *upa-*) refers here to proximity, intimacy, and immediacy (as defilements manifest in the present case). Reading this term as "subsidiary" or "secondary" does not make sense since the three kinds of transcendence are presented in increasing order from the lesser to the greater.
300. See 9.4.8: "The eighth stage is called Immovable because what lacks manifest characteristic is spontaneously accomplished and the bodhisattvas are unshaken by the manifestation of defilements resulting from manifest characteristic." See also 9.5.8.

«9.28» "Blessed One, how many kinds of latent dispositions toward defilements are there on the stages?"

"Avalokiteshvara, there are three:[301]

"The latent dispositions that destroy the factors conducive to the manifestation of defilements are as follows: on the first five stages, the factors conducive to the manifestation of innate defilements are non-innate defilements. At that point, these factors do not manifest. As a consequence, these latent dispositions are called latent dispositions that destroy the factors conducive [to the manifestation of defilements].

"The latent dispositions of limited power are as follows: on the sixth and seventh stages, subtle aspects of the latent dispositions manifest and, through practice, are suppressed. Therefore, as a consequence of this subtle manifestation, these latent dispositions are called latent dispositions of limited power.

"The subtle latent dispositions are as follows: on the eighth stage and above, defilements do not manifest at all because there only remain cognitive obstructions to be cleared. Therefore, these latent dispositions are called subtle latent dispositions."

«9.29» "Blessed One, how many kinds of elimination of corruption characterize these latent dispositions?"[302]

"Avalokiteshvara, there are three kinds:[303] (1) the elimination of superficial corruption characterizes the first and the second type of latent dispositions,[304] (2) the elimination of deeper corruption characterizes the third type of latent dispositions, and (3) since the elimination of the innermost corruption is the state in which there are no latent dispositions at all, I have taught that it is the Buddha Stage."

«9.30» "Blessed One, after how many eons are these types of corruption eliminated?"

"Avalokiteshvara, they are abandoned within three incalculable periods of time—within immeasurable eons, seasons, moons, half-moons, days and nights, days, half days, hours, minutes, seconds, or split seconds."

301. F has only two aspects; see F, folio 63.a. Xuanzang's translation has three: 善男子略有三種 (CBETA, Taishō 676).

302. For Schmithausen's translation of 9.29, see Schmithausen 2014, 563.

303. Regarding the fact some editions have *gnyis* ("two") and others *gsum* ("three"); see Schmithausen 2014, 563nn2311–12.

304. See 9.28.1–2.

«9.31» "Blessed One, how should the defining characteristic, the fault, and the positive quality of defilements arising in bodhisattvas be known?"

"Avalokiteshvara, defilements arising in bodhisattvas have the defining characteristic of nondefilement. Why? Because they fully realize the domain of truth, which is only determined on the first stage. On account of this, the defilements of bodhisattvas arise only with full awareness, not unconsciously. Therefore, [defilements arising in bodhisattvas have] the defining characteristic of nondefilements.

"Because they do not have the capacity to produce suffering in [bodhisattvas'] own [mental] continuums, they are faultless.

"Because they are the cause dispelling the suffering from the world of beings, they have boundless positive qualities."

"Blessed One, if even the defilements arising in this way in bodhisattvas outshine the roots of virtue produced by all beings, hearers, and solitary realizers to such an extent, what need is there to mention their other positive qualities? The supreme value of the bodhisattvas' awakening is truly amazing!

«9.32» "Blessed One, what was your underlying intention when you declared that the vehicle of the hearers and the Great Vehicle constitute the Single Vehicle?"

"In the vehicle of the hearers, I taught the essence of various phenomena, such as the five aggregates, the six internal sense domains, the six external sense domains, and so forth. In the Great Vehicle, I presented exactly these same phenomena by teaching them in terms of a single principle, the domain of truth. Therefore, I did not declare that [these two] vehicles are distinct from one another. Those who conceptualize these teachings exclusively according to their literal meaning also conceptualize these [two] vehicles as being distinct—some by superimposing, others by negating. As a consequence, they think that the two vehicles are contradictory[305] and thus refute one another. This is what I had in mind when I taught the Single Vehicle."

«9.33» Then, at that moment, the Blessed One spoke these verses:

305. See the verses below in D: *de dag 'gal ba snyam du sems pa na / / rnam par rmongs nas blo gros sna tshogs 'gyur.*

"The very teachings on the nature of various phenomena
Taught in the lower and higher vehicles
Are teachings of a single principle.
This is why I did not declare the vehicles to be distinct from one another.

"Those who conceptualize according to the literal meaning of the teachings
Think that these vehicles are contradictory
As a result of their superimpositions and negations,
And so from delusion arise various opinions.

"The buddhas taught as the Great Vehicle
What is included within the stages of a bodhisattva and a buddha,
The names of these stages, and their adverse factors, specific arising, aspiration, and training.
Those who will exert themselves in this will become buddhas."

Then the bodhisattva Avalokiteshvara asked the Blessed One, "Blessed One, what is the name of the teaching imparted in this Dharma discourse that elucidates the Tathāgata's intent? How should I keep it in mind?"

The Blessed One answered, "Avalokiteshvara, this is a teaching of definitive meaning on the stages and the perfections. Keep it in mind as *The Teaching of Definitive Meaning on the Stages and the Perfections*. As the Blessed One expounded this teaching, seventy-five thousand bodhisattvas obtained the bodhisattva's concentration, the light of the Great Vehicle.

This was the chapter of the bodhisattva Avalokiteshvara—the ninth chapter.

Chapter 10

«10.1» Then the bodhisattva Mañjushrī addressed the Blessed One, "Blessed One, when you mention 'the truth body of the tathāgatas,' what is the defining characteristic of this truth body of the tathāgatas?"

The Blessed One answered, "Mañjushrī, the truth body of the tathāgatas is characterized when one has fully achieved a shift in one's basis of existence, the emergence [from cyclic existence] through the practice of the stages and the perfections.[306] Because of the two [following] reasons, you should know that this truth body is characterized by inconceivability: (1) it is beyond mental elaborations and is not produced by intentional action,[307] (2) whereas beings are fixated on mental elaborations and produced by intentional action."

«10.2» "Blessed One, is the shift in the hearers' and solitary realizers' basis of existence also designated as the truth body?"

"Mañjushrī, it is not."

"Blessed One, how should it be called?"

"Mañjushrī, it should be called the liberation body.[308] With regard to the liberation body, the tathāgatas are similar and equal to the hearers and solitary realizers, but, on account of the truth body, they are distinctively superior to them. This being so, they are also distinctively superior to them in terms of the distinctively immeasurable aspect of their positive qualities. This is not easy to illustrate with examples."

306. See translation of VinSg 16 in Sakuma 1990, 202: "Der Dharmakāya der Tathāgatas ist dadurch charakterisiert, daß die [ihn konstituierende] 'Umgestaltung der Grundlage' daraus hervorgegangen ist, daß man die [Bodhisattva-]Stufen und Vollkommenheiten durch intensive Übung gemeistert hat."

307. *mngon par 'du bya ba med pa*; *anabhisaṁskāraṇa*.

308. On *vimuktikāya*, see Radich 2007, 1254ff.

«10.3» "Blessed One, how should we consider those who have the characteristic of manifesting themselves through the birth of a tathāgata?"

"Mañjushrī, those who have the characteristic of the emanation body[309] resemble those who manifest in the world realms. You should see them as those whose characteristic is to be established by the sovereign power[310] of the buddhas, being fully adorned with the ornaments of the tathāgatas' qualities. The truth body does not have this manifestation of arising."

«10.4» "Blessed One, how should we consider the skillful means employed by the emanation body [for the sake of liberating beings from cyclic existence]?"[311]

"Mañjushrī, being conceived in a family renowned to be powerful or honorable in all the buddha fields of the trichiliocosm, taking birth, growing up, enjoying desirable objects, leaving home, displaying immediately the practice of austerities, renouncing them, and displaying all the stages of the complete and perfect awakening should be considered as the skillful means of the emanation body."

"Blessed One, through which teachings emanating from their sovereign power do the tathāgatas bring to maturity those spiritually immature beings who have been converted? How do they liberate spiritually mature beings by means of the very referential object [taught in the Great Vehicle]?"

"Mañjushrī, they bring them to maturity through three teachings: the sutras, the Vinaya, and the mātṛkās."

«10.5» "Blessed One, what are the sutras, the Vinaya, and the mātṛkās?"

"Mañjushrī, it is like this: sutras are teachings that gather the subject matter of various Dharma methods in four, nine, or twenty-nine topics.

"What are the four topics? They are (1) what was heard, (2) taking refuge, (3) the training, and (4) the awakening.

"What are the nine topics? They are (1) concepts of sentient beings, (2) their possessions, (3) their birth, (4) their existence after birth, (5) their affliction and purification, (6) their diversity, (7) the teacher, (8) the teaching, and (9) the assembly.

"What are the twenty-nine topics? They are the topics related to afflic-

309. As with the compound in the opening question above, I read *sprul pa'i sku'i mtshan nyid* (*nirmāṇakāyalakṣaṇa*) as a *bahuvrīhi*.

310. *byin gyis brlabs*; *adhiṣṭhita*.

311. F, folio 65.a: *bstan pa la*.

tion: (1) [the phenomena] included in the conditioned, (2) their progressive activity, (3) the cause of their arising in future lives once they have been conceptualized as a person, and (4) the cause of their arising in future lives once they have been conceptualized as phenomena.

"They are also the topics related to purification: (5) the referential objects that are taken as reference points;[312] (6) the exertion in [the practice of] these very [objects]; (7) mental abiding;[313] (8) blissful abiding in this very life; (9) the referential objects that liberate from all suffering; (10) the three kinds of comprehension, which are the comprehension of the basis of error, the comprehension of the basis of error with respect to beings' conceptions for nonpractitioners, and the comprehension of the basis of humility for those who practice Dharma; (11) the basis of practice; (12) the actualization [of practice];[314] (13) the practice; (14) [the practice] as the central activity; (15) its aspects; (16) its referential objects; (17) the skills in the investigation of what already has been eliminated and what has not yet been eliminated; (18) [the factors] that are distractions from practice; (19) [the factors] that are not distractions from practice; (20) the source of nondistraction; (21) the yoga of clear mindfulness[315] that is protected by[316] the practice; (22) the benefit of practice; (23) its stability; (24) the unification with the lord of the noble [practice]; (25) the unification with its retinue and entourage; (26) the realization of true reality; (27) the attainment of nirvana; (28) the fact that the well-expounded Dharma and Vinaya are superior to the correct views of mundane beings and all nonpractitioners; and (29) the impairments resulting from not practicing. Thus, Mañjushrī, without practicing the well-expounded Dharma and Vinaya, impairments will ensue, and this is not because one has faulty views.

312. *dmigs pa la nye bar gtod pa.*

313. D: *sems can gnas pa*, but F, folio 65.b, reads *sems gnas pa*, which corresponds to Xuanzang's translation: 心安住事 (CBETA, Taishō 676).

314. *mngon du bya ba*; *sākṣātkāra.*

315. *gsal ba*; *paṭu* (?). See Mvyut 6695: *spyod pa mi gsal ba*; *apaṭupracāraḥ*. Another possibility for *gsal ba* would be *saṁprakhyāna*. Edgerton gives as synonym *asaṃmoṣa* ("absence of confusion"). As an equivalent for *saṁprakhyāna*, a Tibetan synonym of *gsal ba* is *dran pa*. See Edgerton 1953, 83 and 576.

316. D: *bsgom pa las yongs su skyob pa'i sbyor ba gsal ba*. Compare with F, folio 66.a: *bsgom pas yongs su skyob pa'i sbyor ba gsal ba.*

«10.6» "Mañjushrī, the Vinaya is my teaching on prātimokṣha for hearers and bodhisattvas, as well as that which is associated with it."

"Blessed One, how many topics are included in [the teaching on the] prātimokṣha of bodhisattvas?"

"Mañjushrī, there are seven topics: (1) the teachings on the ceremony of taking [the vows of the bodhisattva discipline], (2) the teachings on the basis of serious downfalls,[317] (3) the teachings on the basis of transgressions, (4) the teachings on the nature of transgressions, (5) the teachings on the nature of what are not transgressions, (6) the teachings on the emergence from transgressions, and (7) the teachings on the abandonment of the vows.

«10.7» "Mañjushrī, the mātṛkās are the teachings that I imparted and categorized into eleven topics. What are these eleven topics? They are (1) the defining characteristic of the conventional, (2) the defining characteristic of the ultimate, (3) the defining characteristic of referential objects consisting of the awakening factors, (4) the defining characteristic of their features; (5) the defining characteristic of the[ir] nature, (6) the defining characteristic of their result, (7) the defining characteristic of the description of the experience of them, (8) the defining characteristic of the factors disrupting them,[318] (9) the defining characteristic of the factors conducive to them, (10) the defining characteristic of the defects related to them, and (11) the defining characteristic of their benefit.

"Mañjushrī, consider that the defining characteristic of the conventional has three subtopics: (1) the teaching on persons, (2) the teaching on the imaginary nature, and (3) the teaching on the activity, movement, and action of phenomena.

"Consider the defining characteristic of the ultimate in terms of the teaching on the seven aspects of true reality.[319]

"Consider the defining characteristic of referential objects in terms of the teaching on all the things corresponding to cognitive objects.

"Consider the defining characteristic of [their] features in terms of the teaching on the eight features of the analysis of cognitive objects. What

317. *pham pa'i gnas lta bu*[*'i chos*]; *pārājayikasthānīya*[*dharmāḥ*]. See Edgerton 1953, 342.
318. *bar du gcod pa'i chos*; *antarāyikadharmāḥ* (see Mvyut 9324).
319. See 8.20.2.

are these eight? They are (1) the truth of cognitive objects, (2) their determination,[320] (3) their faults, (4) their positive qualities, (5) the methods for analyzing, (6) the processes related to them, (7) the principles of reason, and (8) the condensed and extensive presentations of cognitive objects.

"With respect to these eight points, the truth of cognitive objects is true reality.

"The determination of cognitive objects consists in establishing the person or the imaginary essence or in establishing categorical, analytical, interrogative, and dismissive answers as well as secret instructions.[321]

"The faults of cognitive objects are the defects of phenomena related to affliction, which I have taught in several ways.

"The positive qualities of cognitive objects are the benefits arising from phenomena related to purification, which I have taught in several ways.

"The methods for analyzing cognitive objects include six points: (1) the method for analyzing the meaning of true reality; (2) the method for analyzing attainments; (3) the method for analyzing explanations; (4) the method for analyzing the elimination of the two extremes; (5) the method for analyzing the inconceivable; and (6) the method for analyzing the underlying intention.

"The processes related to cognitive objects are the three times, the three defining characteristics of the conditioned, and the four conditions.

"There are four principles of reason in the analysis of cognitive objects: (1) the principle of reason based on dependence, (2) the principle of reason based on cause and effect, (3) the principle of reason based on logical proof, and (4) the principle of reason based on the nature of phenomena itself.

"The arising of conditioned phenomena and the causes for their being expressed through conventions, as well as related causal conditions, constitute the principle of reason based on dependence.

"The causes that will bring about a result,[322] a completion, or an action

320. D, folio 50.b: *gnas pa*. F, folio 67.a: *rnam par bzhag pa*. They are synonyms for *vyavasthāna*.

321. See 8.21, in which the exact same enumeration is found. See D, folio 31.b: *mgo gcig tu lan gdab pa dang / rnam par dbye ba dang / dris te lan gdab pa dang / gzhag pa dang / gsang ba dang*.

322. *'thob pa*. Usually "obtainment" or "attainment."

once phenomena have arisen, as well as related causal conditions, constitute the principle of reason based on cause and effect.

"The causes establishing the meaning and bringing about the valid understanding of the thesis,[323] the demonstration, and the statement of a proof, as well as related causal conditions, constitute the principle of reason based on logical proof.[324] This logical proof is, moreover, of two kinds: valid and invalid. Among these, five are characterized as valid[325] and seven as invalid. What are the five logical proofs characterized as valid? They are the logical proofs characterized by (1) a perception that is a direct cognition of the thing to establish,[326] (2) a perception that is a direct cognition of something existing in dependence on the thing to establish,[327] (3) a demonstration through an instance belonging to the same class,[328] (4) an actual demonstration, and (5) a citation from a valid scripture.[329]

323. D: *so so'i shes pa*; compare with F, folio 67.a: *dam bcas* for the Sanskrit *pratijñā*. Yoshimizu opts for "objects that are known" (see Yoshimizu 2010, 142), although it is clear that *so so'i shes pa* is the literal translation into Tibetan of *pratijñā*.

324. Yoshimizu 2010, 142, reads the correlative/relative sentence (*yat . . . tat . . .* ; . . . *gang dag yin pa de dag* . . .) as meaning "Whatever is. . . , that is . . ." Alternatively, this grammatical construction could be literally translated with the following syntactic structure: "That which is . . . is . . ." While Yoshimizu's translation is technically correct, reading *gang dag yin pa* in the sense of "whatever" in the present case is unnecessary since this grammatical structure is usually used to give a definition of a technical term. As a consequence, we do not need to mirror the Sanskrit correlative/relative structure in English. The result is a more simple and fluid rendering of the text.

325. In this paragraph, I read the compounds ending with *lakṣaṇa* as *bahuvrīhis*. Yoshimizu translated these compounds as *tatpuruṣas*. It seems to me that reading them as *bahuvrīhis* makes the entire passage much easier to understand.

326. *de mngon sum du dmigs pa'i mtshan nyid*; *tatpratyakṣopalabdhilakṣaṇa* (see Mvyut 4405).

327. *de la gnas pa mngon sum du dmigs pa'i mtshan nyid*; *tadāśritya pratyakṣopalabdhilakṣaṇa* / *tadāśritya āśritapratyakṣopalabdhilakṣaṇa* (see Mvyut 4406). See Yoshimizu 2010, 144: "the characteristic of the direct cognition [of something] depending on the [imperceptible object to be inferred]." The definition of this term reads, according to Yoshimizu, "The characteristic of the direct cognition [of something] depending on the [imperceptible object to be inferred consists in] such kinds of direct cognition, through which something directly not [cognizable] is inferred."

328. *rang gi rigs kyi dpe nye bar sbyar ba'i mtshan nyid*; *svajātīyadṛṣṭāntopasaṁhāralakṣaṇa* (see Mvyut 4407). The term *upasaṁhāra* means "establishing," in the way of the *sādhana* with respect to the *sādhya*. It is therefore also translated into Tibetan as *nye bar sgrub*, a synonym for *nye ba sbyar ba*, which is used for the Sanskrit *sādhana* too.

329. *lung shin tu rnam par dag pa gtan la phab bar bstan pa'i mtshan nyid*. See Mvyut 4409: *lung shin tu rnam par dag pas gtan la bab par bstan pa'i mtshan nyid* / *lung shin tu rnam par dag pas gtan la dbab par bstan pa'i mtshan nyid*; *suviśuddhāgamopadeśalakṣaṇa*.

"With regard to those five logical proofs:

"The logical proof characterized by (1) the perception that is a direct cognition of the thing to establish consists [for example] in perceiving through a direct cognition that all conditioned phenomena are impermanent, suffering, and without a self as well as anything conforming to this.[330]

"The logical proof characterized by (2) a direct cognition of something existing in dependence on the thing to establish consists in inferring something not directly perceptible by means of something[331] [directly perceptible], as well as in anything conforming to this, [for example]: (a) the perception as a direct cognition of the principle of impermanence that exists in dependence on the things to establish, [namely,] the momentariness of all conditioned phenomena, the existence of a next life, and the consequence of good and bad deeds;[332] (b) the perception as direct cognition of the diversity of beings that exists in dependence on the thing to establish, [namely,] the diversity of karma; or (c) the direct cognition of the happiness and suffering of beings that exists in dependence on the things to establish, [namely,] virtue and nonvirtue.[333]

"You should know that the logical proof characterized by (3) a demonstration through an instance belonging to the same class of phenomena[334] consists in anything conforming to this, [for example] in the demonstration of external and internal conditioned phenomena through (a) the

330. For the sake of readability, I inverted the order of the clauses in the sentences explaining the five points mentioned here. If we translate the Tibetan literally, the pattern would be: [example 1, example 2, etc.] are [the logical proof to be defined].

331. D: *gang gis mngon sum du ma gyur pa la rjes su dpag par bya ba dang / de lta bu dang 'thun pa gang yin pa de ni de la gnas pa mngon sum du dmigs pa'i mtshan nyid yin no*. Yoshimizu's translation of this clause seems incorrect: "The characteristic of the direct cognition [of something] depending on the [imperceptible object to be inferred consists in] such kinds of direct cognition, through which something directly not [cognizable] is inferred, as . . ." followed by sentences (1), (2), and (3).

332. In this explanation of *tadāśritya pratyakṣopalabdhilakṣaṇam*, I do not understand why Yoshimizu takes elements of sentence (1) into sentence (2), in violation of the Tibetan syntax, which is quite clear in the present case. See Yoshimizu 2010, 144.

333. Yoshimizu adds the concept of *vipraṇa* to this sentence, which is not found in the Tibetan. See Yoshimizu 2010, 145.

334. The analogies given as examples seem to be instances of [*para*]*prasiddhānumāṇa* ([*tha snyad du gzhan la*] *grags pa'i rjes dpag*) in that the perception of the analogy must be renowned (*grags pa*) in the world (or established from the perspective of the person to be persuaded), thereby offering a certain level of consensus, which is essential for the validity of this kind of logical proof.

perception of death and rebirth, being born and other forms of suffering,[335] and causal dependence,[336] which are established as facts in all worlds, or (b) the perception of wealth and misery, which are established as facts in all worlds, including those of future lives.[337]

"Thus, you should know that a logical proof characterized by one of the three proofs mentioned above[338] is (4) an actual demonstration because it is conclusive with respect to the thing that must be established.

"Mañjushrī, you should know that the logical proof characterized by (5) a citation from a valid scripture consists in the words taught by quoting the omniscient ones, such as 'Nirvana is peace' and other similar statements.

"Therefore, on account of these five kinds of characteristics, an analysis of cognitive objects founded on the principle of reason based on logical proof is valid.[339] Because such an analysis is valid, you should rely on it."

"Blessed One, how many qualities do those we should consider as having the defining characteristics of the omniscient tathāgatas have?"

"Mañjushrī, they have five qualities: (1) wherever they manifest, they are renowned in this world for their omniscience; (2) they have the thirty-two marks of a great being; (3) by means of their ten powers, they eliminate all qualms affecting beings; (4) the words of the Dharma they teach through the four kinds of assurance cannot be refuted or disputed by any opponent; (5) on the basis of their Dharma and Vinaya, the eightfold noble path as

335. This probably refers to the various kinds of suffering, which include the suffering inherent to the conditioned phenomena as well as to the twelve factors of conditioned existence.

336. *rang dbang med pa*; *asvatantra*.

337. Yoshimizu segments this passage in a different way (see Yoshimizu 2010, 145), as it appears that she did not understand its syntactic structure (or chose not to follow it). The point of these instances in the form of established perceptions for which there is a consensus is to show how one thing (that which must be established) is established from the other (the commonly established perception). The relation here is again of the type *sādhya/sādhana*, this time through an instance belonging to the same class of phenomena. In these sentences, we have the following construction: X *la* Y *dmigs pa nye bar sbyar ba*. In the present case, X (i.e., external and internal conditioned phenomena) is the *sādhya*, and Y is the *sādhana* (i.e., clauses 1–2), which makes the *svajātīyadṛṣṭāntopasaṁhāralakṣaṇam* look like a type of *prasiddhānumāṇa*.

338. These three proofs are (1) a perception that is a direct cognition of the [thing to establish]; (2) a perception that is a direct cognition [of something existing] in dependence on the [thing to establish]; and (3) a demonstration through an instance belonging to the same class.

339. See beginning of 10.7.4 above. Yoshimizu translates *rigs pa brtag pa yongs su dag pa* with "the reasoning to be investigated." See Yoshimizu 2010, 145.

well as the four noble truths manifest for those who have renounced cyclic existence.[340] Thus, you should know that their manifestation, marks, elimination of doubts, freedom from refutations and disputes, and support [for those who have renounced cyclic existence] constitute the defining characteristic of the omniscient tathāgatas.

"Thus, the principle of reason based on logical proof is valid on account of the five characteristics included within these valid cognitions: direct cognitions, inferences, and authoritative scriptures.[341]

"What are the seven logical proofs characterized as invalid? They are the logical proofs characterized by (1) a perception that conforms with something other than the thing to be established,[342] (2) a perception that does not conform with anything other than the thing to establish,[343] (3) a perception that conforms with all things,[344] (4) a perception that does not

340. *dge sbyong bzhi* for *dge sbyong chos bzhi*; see Mvyut 8708: *dge sbyong du byed pa'i chos bzhi ming la*; *catvārah śramaṇakārakadharmāḥ*.

341. This passage is interesting because the five defining characteristics of the principle of reason are reduced to three core ideas. Since *pariniṣpannalakṣaṇa* merely refers to the definition of correct reasoning with regard to the other four defining characteristics, it is understandable that it is not included in this list. However, it is fascinating to see that *svajātīyadṛṣṭāntopasaṁhāralakṣaṇa* is also excluded here, which might confirm that this proof was considered to be a form of *prasiddhānumāṇa* in spite of its seemingly inductive character resulting from the use of instances or examples upon which there is a consensus. However, the "engine" of the proof in the case of this valid cognition is not an induction but the deduction ensuing from facts that are accepted as conventions by virtue of consensus. As a consequence, one could argue that the *svajātīyadṛṣṭāntopasaṁhāralakṣaṇa* has a monotonic aspect explaining why it is not inductive in spite of its empirical aspect. The analogies used in this kind of reasoning are, in a way, carved in marble, in the sense of well-established principles that cannot be refuted by new information drawn from further experience or perception, which is precisely the reason why these reasonings have the capacity to establish the *sādhya*. They are by nature a deduction from a universal law or principle. Hence their possible inclusion in the category of *anumāṇa* as *prasiddhānumāṇa* since they surely do not correspond only to a direct cognition.

342. *de las gzhan dang 'thun par dmigs pa'i mtshan nyid*. See Mvyut 4410: *de las gzhan dang mthun par dmigs pa'i mtshan nyid / de las gzhan dang mthun par mngon sum du dmigs pa'i mtshan nyid*; *tadanyasārūpyopalabdhilakṣaṇa*.

343. *de la gzhan dang mi 'thun par dmigs pa'i mtshan nyid*. See Mvyut 4411: *de las gzhan dang mi mthun pa mngon sum du dmigs pa'i mtshan nyid / de las gzhan dang mi mthun par dmigs pa'i mtshan nyid / de las gzhan dang mi mthun par mngon sum du dmigs pa'i mtshan nyid*; *tadanyavairūpyopalabdhilakṣaṇa*.

344. *thams cad 'thun par dmigs pa'i mtshan nyid*. See Mvyut 4412: *thams cad mthun par dmigs pa'i mtshan nyid*; *sarvasārūpyopalabdhilakṣaṇa*.

conform with anything,[345] (5) a demonstration through an instance belonging to a different class of phenomena,[346] (6) a demonstration that is not actually demonstrating anything, and (7) a citation drawn from an invalid scripture.

"The logical proof characterized by a perception that does not conform with anything[347] is ascertained when the defining characteristics of the proof and the premise do not conform with one another because they are incompatible in terms of reason, essence, karma, quality, or cause and effect.[348]

"Mañjushrī, the logical proof characterized by a perception that does not conform with anything[349] is comprised by the logical proof characterized by a perception that conforms with something other than the thing to be established[350] and similar instances. This proof is therefore inconclusive with respect to the thing to establish.[351] This is called an unestablished logical proof.[352]

"Moreover, the logical proof characterized by a perception that conforms with all things[353] is comprised by the logical proof characterized by a perception that does not conform with anything other than the thing to establish[354] and similar instances. This proof is therefore inconclusive with

345. *thams cad mi 'thun par dmigs pa'i mtshan nyid*. See Mvyut 4413: *thams cad mi mthun par dmigs pa'i mtshan nyid*; *sarvavairūpyopalabdhilakṣaṇa*.

346. *gzhan gyi rigs kyi dpe nye bar sbyar ba'i mtshan nyid*. See Mvyut 4414: *gzhan gyi rigs kyi dpe nye bar sbyar ba'i mtshan nyid*; *anyajātīyadṛṣṭāntopasaṁhāralakṣaṇa*.

347. This refers to point (4) above.

348. For an examination of similarities between Saṁdh. and *Hetuvidyā*, see Yoshimizu 2010.

349. This refers to point (4) above.

350. This refers to point (1) above.

351. This point is not easy to unravel. I understand it in the following way. If the perception [of a logical proof] that does not conform with any[thing] could be used to establish the thesis, it also could be used to establish something that is not the thesis. As a consequence, it would be included in the reasons proving that which is not the thesis and would be therefore inconclusive. In other words, the perception of the proof would be present in both the *sapakṣa* and the *vipakṣa*. The proof of something that does not conform to anything also would be found necessarily in the perception of that which does not conform with that which must be established. As one proceeds to examine the proof, its absence of conformity with the premise is enough to disqualify it, whether it is conforming with something other than the premise or with nothing else.

352. This refers to point (6) above.

353. This refers to point (3) above.

354. This refers to point (2) above.

respect to the thing to establish. This is also called an unestablished logical proof.[355]

"Because these logical proofs are not established, the analysis is invalid according to the principle of reason based on logical proof. Since this analysis is invalid, you should not rely on it. You should know that the logical proof characterized by a citation from an invalid scripture is invalid by nature.

"Whether tathāgatas manifest or not, the constancy of the domain of truth, the nature of phenomena, on account of the constancy of phenomena, constitutes the principle of reason based on the nature of phenomena.[356]

"The condensed and the extensive presentation of cognitive objects consists of first summarizing, then analyzing words and sections of the teaching, and finally concluding the explanation.

"The defining characteristic of the nature of awakening factors consists in the apprehension of a referential object together with its aspects, as I have taught, such as the awakening factors, the four applications of mindfulness, and so on.

"The defining characteristic of their result is the accomplishment of their result, the mundane and supramundane positive qualities, by abandoning the defilements associated with the mundane or the supramundane phenomena.

"The defining characteristic of accounts telling how one experiences them as one proclaims them, explains them, and correctly teaches them to others is the analytical knowledge of the gnosis[357] that liberates within true reality.

"The defining characteristic of the factors disrupting them is the afflicted phenomenon in the form of an obstacle to the practice of these very awakening factors.

355. This point is also not easy to understand. I take it to mean the following: if a perception that conforms with all [things] (i.e., with anything) demonstrates the thesis, it follows that the *dharmin*/*pakṣa* (all phenomena) constitutes the entire *sapakṣa* and there is not even the possibility of having a *vipakṣa*. The demonstration based on such perceptions is therefore inconclusive because it represents a tautology based on a circular argument that nothing could invalidate in the absence of a *sapakṣa* and a *vipakṣa*.

356. "Whether tathāgatas . . ."; see also 4.10 and 7.9. This quote, with minor variations, is found in various other canonical scriptures.

357. F, folio 69.b: *ye shes*.

"The defining characteristic of the factors conducive to them is the phenomenon useful to [enhancing] them.

"The defining characteristic of defects related to them is the fault interrupting them.

"Mañjushrī, you should know that the defining characteristic of their benefit consists in their corresponding positive qualities."

«10.8» Then the bodhisattva Mañjushrī further said to the Blessed One, "Blessed One, please explain the meaning of the formula through which bodhisattvas comply with the underlying intention[358] of the profound Dharma expounded by the tathāgatas, the complete meaning of the sutras, the Vinaya, and the mātṛkās that is not known by those not following you."

"Mañjushrī, listen. I will explain to you the complete meaning of the formula so that bodhisattvas will in this way understand my underlying intention. Mañjushrī, the possessors of qualities resulting from affliction and purification[359] are all without movement and without a person. This is why I taught that all phenomena are in every respect beyond activity. It is not the case that the possessors of qualities resulting from affliction first became afflicted and will then become purified from these afflictions or that the possessors of qualities resulting from purification have become purified from afflictions they previously acquired. Thus, foolish ordinary beings rely on views resulting from their latent dispositions, on account of which they wrongly conceive the body afflicted by corruption as the essence of phenomena and persons. As a consequence, reifying [the ego through concepts such as] 'I' and 'mine,' they mistakenly conceive of the following notions: 'I see,' 'I hear,' 'I smell,' 'I taste,' 'I touch,' 'I am conscious,' 'I eat,' 'I do,' 'I am afflicted,' and 'I am purified.'

"Thus, those who understand this fact as it really is abandon the body afflicted by corruption and instead obtain the body that is not a support for any defilement, being pure, free from mental elaborations, unconditioned, and unproduced by intentional action. Mañjushrī, you should know that this is the complete meaning of the formula."

Then, at that moment, the Blessed One spoke these verses:

358. *ldem por dgongs pa.*

359. I read *kun nas nyon mongs pa'i chos* and *rnam par byang ba'i chos* as *bahuvrīhis*.

"The possessors of qualities resulting from affliction and
purification
Are all without movement[360] and without a person;
Therefore, I declare them to be without activity,
As they are neither purified nor afflicted, be it in the past or the
future.

"Relying on views resulting from their latent dispositions,
On account of which they wrongly conceive the body afflicted by
corruption,
They reify [the ego through concepts such as] 'I' and 'mine.'
As a consequence, notions arise, such as 'I see,' 'I eat,' 'I do,' 'I am
afflicted,' and 'I am purified.'

"Thus, those who understand this fact as it really is
Abandon the body afflicted by corruption
And instead will obtain a body that is not a basis for any
defilement,
Being free from mental elaborations and unconditioned."[361]

«10.9» "Blessed One, how should we know the defining characteristic of the arising of the tathāgatas' mind?"

"Mañjushrī, tathāgatas are not characterized by mind, thought, or cognition.[362] However, you should know that, similar to an emanation,[363] the

360. The verses might have been corrupted. The prose section (D, folio 53.a) reads *'jam dpal kun nas nyon mongs pa'i chos gang dag yin pa dang / rnam par byang ba'i chos gang dag yin pa de dag thams cad ni g.yo ba med pa gang zag med pa yin te / de'i phyir ngas chos rnams rnam pa thams cad du byed pa med par bstan to*, which does not match the variant reading found in the verses (D, folio 53.b): *kun nas nyon mongs chos dang rnam par byang ba'i chos // thams cad byed pa med cing gang zag med pa yin // de phyir de dag byed pa med par ngas bshad do.*
361. 10.8 before the *gāthās*, in which the *dhāraṇī* is given, could be seen as a *mchan 'grel* of these verses (i.e., a "fill-in commentary").
362. See 5.1–6.
363. *sprul pa*; *nirmāṇa*. From the Sanskrit point of view, the juxtaposition of *anabhisaṁskāra* and *nirmāṇa* must have created a cognitive dissonance as it represents a paradox that can only be solved through the notion of nonduality as explained in the next paragraph. The term *anabhisaṁskāra* expresses the notion of something that is uncreated, not brought about, and not the result of any conditioning process—something uncontrived, effortless, spontaneous. In contrast, *nirmāṇa* implies creation, construction, emanation, formation,

tathāgatas' mind arises in the way of something that is not produced by intentional action."

"Blessed One, if the truth body of the tathāgatas is not produced at all by intentional action, how then could their mind arise without being produced by intentional action?"[364]

"Mañjushrī, their mind arises on account of a previous intentional action, namely, the practice of skillful means and wisdom. Mañjushrī, it is like this: although awakening from a state of sleep in which there is no thought ensues [spontaneously] without resulting from intentional action, one will awaken due to previous intentional actions. Although the emergence from the absorption in the state of cessation is not produced by intentional action, one will emerge from it merely due to previous intentional actions. Just as the mind arises from a state of sleep or from the absorption in the state of cessation, you should know that the tathāgatas' mind also arises due to previous intentional actions such as the practice of skillful means and wisdom."

"Blessed One, should we say that the mind emanated by tathāgatas exists or not?"

"Mañjushrī, [their] mind neither exists nor does not exist, because it is causally independent and causally dependent."[365]

"Blessed One, what is the sphere of activity of the tathāgatas? What is the domain[366] of the tathāgatas? Should we consider these two as distinct?"

"Mañjushrī, the sphere of activity of the tathāgatas consists in the pure buddha realms, the arrayed ornaments of inconceivable and boundless positive qualities common to all tathāgatas. The domain of the tathāgatas comprises five domains: the domain of the surrounding universe, the domain of

---

composition, and transformation. A solution to this quandary that would not invoke nonduality is to understand the term *anabhisaṁskāra* as stressing primarily the idea of effortlessness as in the example of the dream given by the Buddha below. Another interpretation could be the apparition in a mirror. A reflection may seem real but is actually neither going nor coming anywhere. It is unproduced and nonexistent, not even "a thing."

364. The question is to determine how the arising of anything is possible on the level of the relative truth in the absence of a causal process.

365. D: *'jam dpal sems yod pa yang ma yin / sems med pa yang ma yin te / sems rang dbang med pa nyid dang / sems kyi dbang nyid yin pa'i phyir ro.*

366. *yul*; *viṣaya.*

beings, the domain of Dharma, the domain of discipline, and the domain of methods of discipline.[367] There is a distinction between the two."

«10.10» "Blessed One, how should we understand the defining characteristic of the tathāgatas' complete and perfect awakening, of their turning of the wheel of Dharma, and of their great parinirvana?"

"Mañjushrī, the tathāgatas are characterized by nonduality.[368] They are neither completely and perfectly awakened nor not completely and perfectly awakened; they neither turn the wheel of Dharma nor do not turn the wheel of Dharma; they neither [attain] the great parinirvana nor do not attain the great parinirvana. This is because the truth body is utterly pure and the emanation body constantly manifests."

"Blessed One, why should we consider that the merit produced by beings on account of seeing, hearing, or serving the tathāgatas' emanation body arises from the tathāgatas?"

"Mañjushrī, it is because these activities consist in taking a superior referential object thanks to the tathāgatas, and also because the emanation body is the tathāgatas' sovereign power."

"Blessed One, since this does not seem to be produced by intentional action, why is it that the great light of gnosis manifests in beings solely

367. See 8.23.

368. *Advayalakṣaṇa* can be read in various ways: (1) as a genitive *tatpuruṣa*: "the defining characteristic of the nondual / of nonduality"; (2) as a *karmadhāraya*: "the nondual defining characteristic"; or (3) as a *bahuvrīhi* (which occurs frequently with *lakṣaṇa* as the second member of the compound): "who has the defining characteristic of nonduality / the nondual defining characteristic" or "who is characterized by nonduality." On the basis of the question and the first part of the answer (D: *bcom ldan 'das de bzhin gshegs pa'i mngon par rdzogs par byang chub pa gang lags pa dang / chos kyi 'khor lo bskor ba gang lags pa dang / yongs su mya ngan las 'das pa chen po gang lags pa de dag gi mtshan nyid ni / ji lta bur rig par bgyi lags / 'jam dpal gnyis su med pa'i mtshan nyid yin te*), I would tend to read the compound as a genitive *tatpuruṣa:* "Mañjushrī, [you should understand it] as the defining characteristic of nonduality." However, the following sentences in the answer are built with the verb *yin*, implying a series of expressions referring to the tathāgatas through the use of nominalized verbal adjectives such as *byang chub pa* (*bodha*) or *bskor ba*; see D, folio 54.a–b: *mngon par rdzogs par byang chub pa yang ma yin / mngon par rdzogs par byang ma chub pa yang ma yin/ chos kyi 'khor lo bskor ba yang ma yin / chos kyi 'khor lo mi bskor ba yang ma yin / yongs su mya ngan las 'das pa chen po yang ma yin / yongs su mya ngan las 'das pa chen po med pa yang ma yin te / chos kyi sku shin tu rnam par dag pa nyid kyi phyir dang / sprul pa'i sku kun tu ston pa nyid kyi phyir ro.* Lamotte translated the passage into French according to the structure defined by "il n'y a pas," which would correspond to the verb *yod* in Tibetan, not *yin.* As a consequence, I chose to translate *advayalakṣaṇa* as a *bahuvrīhi* qualifying the tathāgatas.

through the truth body of the tathāgatas and that innumerable emanated reflections also manifest [as the tathāgatas' emanation body], while this light and its reflections do not manifest from the hearers' and solitary realizers' liberation body?"

"Mañjushrī, while this does not seem to be produced by intentional action, on account of the power of very strong beings and the force of beings' karma, a great light manifests to beings from water and fire crystals produced from the disks of the moon and sun. However, it does not manifest from water and fire crystals produced from other sources. From a precious gem that has been well polished through [intentional] action, reflections corresponding to its engraving manifest [when it is placed before a light source]. However, they do not manifest from another unpolished gem. Likewise, because the truth body of the tathāgatas also is established by having been purified through the practice of skillful means and insight focusing on the immeasurable domain of truth, the great light of gnosis manifests in beings, and innumerable emanated reflections arise. However, they do not manifest from the hearers' and solitary realizers' liberation body."

«10.11»"Blessed One, you said that, through the force of the tathāgatas' and bodhisattvas' sovereign power, one can obtain an excellent body in the realm of desire, such as that of a warrior or a brahman, a body that is like a great sāla tree, or the excellent body of a god residing in the realm of desire, the realm of form, or the realm of the formless. Blessed One, what was your underlying intention with regard to this?"

"Mañjushrī, by means of their sovereign power, tathāgatas teach as they are the paths and practices through which one obtains all these excellent bodies. Those accomplishing these paths and practices will always obtain all these perfect bodies, while those who reject or denigrate these paths and practices, as well as those who have animosity or resentment toward them, will always obtain all kinds of miserable bodies upon their death. Mañjushrī, on account of this skillful means, you should know in this way that, because of the sovereign power of the tathāgatas, one will be reborn in a perfect body as well as in a miserable one."

«10.12»"Blessed One, in the universes that are impure and pure, what is abundant? What is rare?"

"Mañjushrī, in the universes that are impure, eight things are abundant and two are rare. Abundant are (1) followers of traditions other than mine;

(2) suffering beings; (3) beings who are different in terms of lineages, families, and communities, or of wealth and poverty; (4) beings engaging in wrongdoing; (5) beings who have lost their discipline; (6) beings in bad destinies; (7) followers of inferior vehicles; and (8) bodhisattvas with inferior intentions and practices. Rare are (1) the actions of bodhisattvas having superior intentions and practices and (2) the manifestation of tathāgatas.

"Mañjushrī, in the universes that are pure, it is the opposite of this. You should know that these eight things are rare and these two things abundant."

Then the bodhisattva Mañjushrī asked the Blessed One, "Blessed One, what is the name of the teaching imparted in this Dharma discourse that elucidates the Tathāgata's intent? How should I keep it in mind?"

The Blessed One answered, "Mañjushrī, this is a teaching of definitive meaning establishing the deeds of the tathāgatas. Keep it in mind as *The Teaching of Definitive Meaning Establishing the Deeds of the Tathāgatas.*" As the Blessed One expounded this teaching, seventy-five thousand bodhisattvas obtained the perfect analytical knowledge of the truth body.

After the Blessed One had spoken these words, the prince Mañjushrī together with the entire retinue of gods, humans, demigods, and gandharvas rejoiced and praised the words of the Blessed One.

The [tenth chapter of the bodhisattva Mañjushrī] called "The Chapter Establishing the Positive Qualities [of the Tathāgatas]" of [the sutra of] the Great Vehicle called "Elucidating the Intent" is concluded.

Glossary

English-Tibetan-Sanskrit Glossary

ENGLISH	TIBETAN	SANSKRIT
abiding in phenomena	chos gnas pa nyid	dharmasthititā
absorption	snyoms par 'jug pa	samāpatti
absorption in the state of cessation	'gog pa la snyoms par zhugs pa	nirodhasamāpatti
accept	len	ādadante
acceptance that phenomena are non-arisen	mi skye ba'i chos la bzod pa	anutpattidharma-kṣānti
accomplishment of the goal	dgos pa yongs su grub pa	kṛtyānuṣṭhāna
accumulated	kun tu bsags pa	ācita
accused	shag kyis 'chags	codanā
activity of conditioning mental factors	'du byed kyi 'jug pa	saṁskārapravṛtti
actual	yongs su grub pa	pariniṣpanna
actual defining characteristic	yongs su grub pa'i mtshan nyid	pariniṣpannalakṣaṇa
actual essence	yongs su grub pa'i ngo bo nyid, yongs su grub pa'i rang bzhin	pariniṣpannasvabhāva
actualization	mngon du bya ba	ākṣātkāra
actually refer to	mngon par rjod pas rjod pa	abhivadamānā, abhivadanti

English	Tibetan	Sanskrit
affliction	kun nas nyon mongs pa	saṁkleśa
aggregate	phung po	skandha
analysis	brtag pa	parīkṣā
analytical knowledge	so sor yang dag par	pratisaṁvid
analytical knowledge of designations	chos so sor yang dag par rig pa	dharmapratisaṁvid
analytical knowledge of the objects of designation	don so sor yang dag par rig pa	ārthapratisaṁvid
analyze	so sor rtog par byed, so sor rtog pa	pratyavekṣaṇa, pratyavekṣa
appearance	snang ba	pratibhāsa
absence of manifest characteristic	mtshan ma med pa	animitta
applications of mindfulness	dran pa nye bar gzhag pa	smṛtyupasthāna
appropriating cognition	len pa'i rnam par shes pa	ādānavijñāna
argumentative disputation	rtsod pa	vivāda
aspiration	smon lam	praṇidhāna
assumption	mngon par zhen pa	abhiniviśanti
attaining the powers	stobs bskyed pa	balādhāna
attending	rjes su dpyod pa	anucaranti
authoritative scripture	yid ches pa'i lung gi tshad ma	āptāgamapramāṇa
Avalokiteshvara, noble	spyan ras gzigs, 'phags pa	avalokiteśvara, āryāvalokiteśvara
Avalokiteshvara	spyan ras gzigs dbang phyug	avalokiteśvara
awakening	byang chub	bodhi

English	Tibetan	Sanskrit
awakening factors	byang chub kyi phyogs dang 'thun pa'i chos	bodhipakṣyadharma
awakening mind	byang chub kyi sems	bodhicitta
awareness	shes bzhin	samprajāna
bases of supernatural power	rdzu 'phrul gyi rkang pa	ṛddhipādaḥ
belief in a perduring self	'jig tshogs la lta ba	satkāyadṛṣṭi
beryl	bai dUr+ya	vaidūrya
bichiliocosm	stong gnyis pa bar ma'i 'jig rten gyi khams	dvitīyamadhyama sāhasralokadhātu
binding	'ching ba	bandhana
blessed one	bcom ldan 'das	bhagavān, bhagavat
body afflicted by corruption	gnas ngan len gyi lus	dauṣṭhulyakāya
branches of awakening	byang chub kyi yan lag	bodhyaṅgāni
bring together	kun 'byung ba	samudaya
buddha field, buddha realm	sangs rgyas kyi zhing	buddhakṣetra
buddha stage	sangs rgyas kyi sa	buddhabhūmi
can [only] be known by intelligent scholars well versed in the subtle	zhib mo brtags pa'i mkhas pa dang 'dzangs pas rig pa	sūkṣmaṁ nipuṇapaṇḍita-vijñavedanīyaḥ
causal dependence	rang dbang med pa	asvatantra
cause and effect	rgyu dang 'bras bu	hetuphala
changing opinions	blo gros tha dad pa	matibheda
characterized by	rab tu phye ba	prabhāvita
clarified butter	mar gyi snying khu	sarpirmaṇḍa
clear mindfulness	gsal ba	paṭu
Cloud of Dharma	chos kyi sprin	dharmameghā

English	Tibetan	Sanskrit
cognition that is personal and intuitive	so sor rang rig pa	pratyātmavedya, pratyātmavedanīya, pratyātmajñāna, prātyatmam
collection of teachings on the bodhisattva [path]	byang chub sems dpa'i sde snod	bodhisattvapiṭaka
communication	ming du bya ba	saṁjñāpya
complete equanimity	lhag par btang snyoms	adhyupekṣya
completely	thams cad kyi thams cad	sarveṇa sarvam
comprehension	yongs su shes pa	parijñā
concentrated	mnyam par bzhag pa	samāhita
concentration	ting nge 'dzin	samādhi
conception	'du shes	saṁjñā
conception	rtog pa	kalpanā
conceptualization	rnam rtog, rnam par rtog pa	vikalpa
conceptualize	gdags pa	prajñapti
conclusive	gcig tu nges pa	aikāntikaḥ
conditioned	du 'byas	saṁskṛta
conditioned phenomena	du 'byed	saṁskāra
conditioning mental factors	du 'byed	saṁskāra
conditioning process of the mental factors	du byed mngon par 'du bya ba	saṁskārābhisaṁskaraṇa
conducive	grogs	sahāya
confined	rjes su 'brel ba	anubandha
confusion	'khrul pa	bhrānta
consequence	chud mi za ba	avipraṇa
consideration	yongs su rtog pa	paritarka

English	Tibetan	Sanskrit
consisting in	rab tu phye ba	prabhāvita
constancy of phenomena	chos gnas pa nyid	dharmasthititā
constant	rnam par gnas pa	vyavasthita
constituent	khams	dhātu
constituted	rab tu phye ba	prabhāvita
contemplation	bsams pa	cintā
convention	rjes su tha snyad	anuvyavahāra
conventionally	brda	saṁketa
correct concentration	yang dag pa'i ting nge 'dzin	samyaksamādhi
correct self-restraint	yang dag par spong ba	samyakprahāṇa
corruption	gnas ngan len	dauṣṭhulya
decide	gdags pa	prajñapti
dedication of merit	yongs su bsngo ba	pariṇāmanā, pariṇata
Deer Park	ri dags kyi nags	mṛgadāva
defilement	nyon mongs pa	kleśa
defining characteristic	mtshan nyid	svabhāvalakṣaṇa, lakṣaṇa
delusion	gti mug	moha
delusion	kun tu rmongs pa, rnam par rmongs pa	saṁmoha
demonstration	bshad pa	deśana
description	rnam par bsnyad pa	vyākhyā
designation	btags pa	prajñapti
determination	rnam par bzhag pa	vyavasthā
dharani (see formula)	gzungs	dhāraṇī
Dharma discourse	chos kyi rnam grangs	dharmaparyāya
Dharma of the nonexistence of defining characteristics	mtshan nyid med pa'i chos	alakṣaṇadharma

English	Tibetan	Sanskrit
Dharmodgata	chos 'phags	dharmodgata
differentiating	rnam par 'byed pa	vibhājanā
diligence	brtson 'grus	vīrya
direct cognition	mngon sum gyi tshad ma	pratyakṣapramāṇa
direct [their] attention	yid la byed	manasikāra
discerning	rab tu rnam par 'byed pa	pravicaya
discerning	nges par rtog pa, nges par rtogs pa	nirūpaṇā
discipline	tshul khrims	śīla
discourses teaching the Dharma	chos gdags pa rnam par gzhag pa	dharmaprajñapti-vyavasthā(pa)na
discriminating	bye brag 'byed pa	nitīraṇa
discrimination of dharmas	chos rab tu rnam par 'byed pa	dharmapravicaya
distinct	tha dad pa	bheda
distinctive characteristic	bye brag	viśeṣa
distinctive characteristic	bye brag gi mtshan nyid	viṣeśalakṣaṇa
distinctly perceive	rab tu shes	prajānāti
distinguishing	bye brag 'byed pa	nitīraṇa
diversity of things	ji snyed yod pa nyid	yāvadbhāvikatā
domain of truth	chos kyi dbyings	dharmadhātu
domain(s) of mastery	zil gyis gnon pa'i skye mched	abhibhāvāyatana
domain(s)of totality	zad par gyi skye mched	kṛtsnāyatana
effortless	lhun gyis grub pa	anābhoga
elaboration of conventional expressions	tha snyad 'dogs pa'i spros pa	vyavahāraprapañca
eloquence	spobs pa	pratibhāna
emanation	sprul pa	nirmāṇa

ENGLISH	TIBETAN	SANSKRIT
emanation body	sprul sku	nirmāṇakāya
emancipation	nges par 'byung ba	niḥsaraṇa, niryāṇa
emptiness	stong pa nyid	śūnyatā
emptiness devoid of rejection	dor ba med pa stong pa nyid	anavakāraśūnyatā
emptiness of the limitless	mtha' las stong pa nyid	atyantaśūnyatā
emptiness of the substanceless	dngos po stong pa nyid	a(sva)bhāvaśūnyatā
equanimity	btang snyoms	upekṣā
erroneous conception	mngon par zhen pa	abhiniveśa
essence	ngo bo nyid	svabhāva
essencelessness	ngo bo nyid med pa nyid	niḥsvabhāvatā
essencelessness regarding arising	skye ba ngo bo nyid med pa nyid	utpattiniḥsvabhāvatā
essencelessness regarding defining characteristics	mtshan nyid ngo bo nyid med pa nyid	lakṣaṇaniḥsvabhāvatā
essencelessness regarding the ultimate	don dam pa ngo bo nyid med pa nyid	paramārtha-niḥsvabhāvatā
essential characteristic	ngo bo nyid kyi mtshan nyid	svabhāvalakṣaṇa
established	rnam par bzhag pa	vyavasthā
examine	brtag	
examine	rnam par dpyad	vicārita, vicāraṇa
examine	'jal ba	
examining	yongs su dpyod pa	parimīmāṁsā, paricāra
excellence of [their] peaceful conduct	bzod pa dang des pa chen po dang ldan pa	mahākṣāntisauratya-samanvāgataḥ
Excellent Intelligence	legs pa'i blo gros	sādhumatī
excited	bzlums	uddhata

English	Tibetan	Sanskrit
expedient	rnam grangs	paryāya
express [themselves through] conventions	tha snyad 'dogs	vyavaharanti
extent	mthar thug pa	paryanta
fabrication	yongs su rtog pa	parikalpa
factors of conditioned existence	srid pa'i yan lag	bhavāṅga
faculties	bdang po	indriya
faith	dad pa	śraddhā
falsity	skyon chags pa	duṣṭatā
Far Reaching	ring du song ba	dūraṅgamā
faultless state of truth	yang dag pa nyid skyon med pa	samyaktvanyāma
five faculties	dbang po lnga	pañcendriyāṇi
five forces	stobs lnga	pañcabalāni
five great fears	'jig pa chen po lnga	pañcamahābhaya
five sciences	rigs pa'i gnas lnga po	pañcavidyā
flexibility	shin tu sbyangs pa	praśrabdhi
focus [their] minds within	sems nang du 'jog	cittasthāpana
foolish being	byis pa	bāla
force(s)	stobs	bala
formula (mnemonic)	gzungs	dhāraṇī
foundations of training	bslab pa'i gzhi	śikṣāpada
four correct self-restraints	yang dag par spong ba bzhi	catvāri prahāṇāni
four kinds of assurance	mi 'jigs pa bzhi	catvāri vaiśāradyāni
four kinds of sustenance	zas bzhi	catvārāhārāḥ

ENGLISH	TIBETAN	SANSKRIT
four methods of conversion	bsdu ba'i dngos po bzhi'i ming	catvāri saṁgrahavastūni
four noble truths	'phags pa'i bden pa bzhi	catvāri āryasatyāni
four seals of the Dharma	phyag rgya bzhi	caturmudrā
free from covetousness	zang zing med pa	nirāmiṣa
free of any wrongdoing	kha na ma tho ba med pa	anavadya
Gambhīrārtha-saṁdhinirmochana	don zab dgongs pa nges par 'grel	gambhīrārtha-saṁdhinirmocana
gandharva	dri za	gandharva
garuḍa	khyung	garuḍa
gates / doors of liberation	rnam par thar pa'i sgo	vimokṣamukha
gāthā	tshigs su bcad pa	gāthā
generosity	sbyin pa	dāna
gnosis	ye shes	jñāna
gnosis and vision	shes pa dang mthong ba	jñānadarśana
gone forth	nges par 'byung ba	niryātaka, parivrājaka
great emptiness	chen po stong pa nyid	mahāśūnyatā
Guṇākara	yon tan 'byung gnas	guṇākara
had realized the sameness [of all phenomena], the state of a buddha in which there is neither a center nor a periphery	mtha' dang dbus med pa'i sangs rgyas kyi sa mnyam pa nyid bu thugs su chud pa	anantamadhyabuddha-bhūmisamatādhi-gataḥ
Hard to Conquer	shin tu sbyang dka'	sudurjayā
hearer	nyan thos	śrāvaka
hell being	dmyal ba pa	nāraka
how	ji tsam du	tāvatā, tāvat, yāvat

English	Tibetan	Sanskrit
hungry ghost	yi dags	preta
Illuminating	'od byed pa	prabhākarī
image	gzugs brnyan	pratibimba
imaginary	kun brtags pa	parikalpita
imaginary defining characteristic	kun brtags pa'i mtshan nyid	parikalpitalakṣaṇa
imaginary essence	kun brtags pa'i ngo bo nyid, kun brtags pa'i rang bzhin	parikalpitasvabhāva
imagination	kun tu rtog pa	saṁkalpa, parikalpa
Immovable	mi g.yo ba	acalā
in accord with the truth	yang dag pa ji lta ba bzhin du	yathābhūtam
in their own experience	nang gi so sor rang rig pa	adhyātmam, prātyatmam
inconclusive	gcig tu ma nges pa	anaikāntikaḥ
inexhaustible	mi zad pa, ma 'tshal ba	akṣaya
inexpressible	brjod du med	anabhilāpya
inference	rjes su dpag pa'i tshad ma	anumānapramāṇa
innate	lhan cig skyes	sahaja
inner absorption	nang du yang dag bzhag	pratisaṁlāna
innermost	snying po	hṛdaya
inquiry	yongs su tshol ba	paryeṣaṇā
insight	lhag mthong	vipaśyanā
intelligence	blo gros	mati
intention	bsam pa	āśaya
investigating	rtog pa	vitarka
investigation	dpyod pa	vicāra
Jambudvīpa	'dzam bu gling	jambudvīpa
joy	dga' ba	prīti

English	Tibetan	Sanskrit
keep it in mind	gzung bar bgyi	dhārayāmi
keep it in mind	zung shig	dhāraya
keeping it in mind	gzungs	dhāraṇī
kinnara	mi'am ci	kinnara
Kīrtimat	grags pa can	kīrtimat
label	ming du btags, 'jig rten gyi ming du btags pa, 'jig rten gyi tha snyad, 'jig rten gyi tha snyad du btags pa, 'jig rten gyi tha snyad du btags pa'am 'jig rten gyi tha snyad, 'jig rten tha snyad, btags pa'i tshig	lokasaṁjñā
lacked certainty	yid gnyis can	vimati
latent disposition	bag la nyal	anuśaya
liberation	rnam par thar pa	mokṣa
lies hidden	rab tu sbyor bar byed pa	pralayanata
literal	sgra ji bzhin	yathāruta
magical illusion	sgyu ma'i las, sgyu ma byas pa	
mahoraga	lto 'phye chen po	mahoraga
Maitreya	byams pa	maitreya
Manifest	mngon du gyur pa	abhimukhī
manifest characteristic	mtshan ma	nimitta
manifest characteristic of conditioned phenomena		saṁskāranimitta
Mañjushrī	'jam dpal	mañjuśrī
mātṛkā	ma mo	mātṛkā
meaning of true reality	de kho na'i don	tattvārtha

English	Tibetan	Sanskrit
meditative absorption	bsam gtan	dhyāna
mental manifest appearance	sems kyi mtshan ma	cittanimitta
mental elaboration	spros pa	prapañca
mental engagement	rtog pa	vitarka
mental imprint	bag chags	vāsanā
mental inspection	so sor brtag pa	pratisaṁkhyā
mental state	sems las byung ba	caitasika
mental stillness	zhi gnas	śamatha
mere representation	rnam par rig pa tsam	vijñaptimātra
mind	sems	citta
mind containing all the seeds	sa bon thams cad pa'i sems	sarvabījaṁ cittam
mindfulness	dran pa	smṛti
nāga	klu	nāga
naturally present	rang bzhin du gnas pa	svabhāvasthita, nisargabhāva
nature of phenomena	chos nyid	dharmatā
nature of things	ji lta ba bzhin du yod pa nyid	yathāvadbhāvikatā
negate	skur pa 'debs	apavāda
negation	skur pa 'debs pa	apavāda
next life	'jig rten pha rol	paraloka
prologue	gleng gzhi	nidāna
nirvana	mya ngan las 'das pa	nirvāṇa
noble being	'phags pa	ārya
noble truth	'phags pa'i bden pa	āryasatya
non-Buddhist	mu stegs pa	tīrthika
nonduality	gnyis su med pa	advaya

English	Tibetan	Sanskrit
object	dngos po, yul	vastu
object conducive to purification	rnam par dag pa'i dmigs pa	*viśuddhyālambana
object of experience	spyod yul	gocara
obscuration	kun tu rmongs pa	saṁmoha
obscuration of cognitive objects	shes bya'i sgrib pa	jñeyāvaraṇa
obstacle	gegs	vibandha
obstruction	sgrib pa	āvaraṇa
of a single nature	ro gcig pa	ekarasa
one-pointedness of mind	sems rtse gcig pa nyid	cittaikāgratā
ordinary being	so so'i skye bo	pṛthagjana
other-dependent	gzhan gyi dbang	paratantra
other-dependent defining characteristic	gzhan gyi dbang gi mtshan nyid	paratantralakṣaṇa
other-dependent essence	gzhan gyi dbang gi ngo bo nyid, gzhan gyi dbang gi rang bzhin	paratantrasvabhāva
Paramārthasamudgata	don dam yang dag 'phags	paramārthasamudgata
parinirvana	yongs su mya ngan las 'das pa	parinirvāṇa
pathway	nges par 'byung ba	niḥsaraṇa, niryāṇa
patience	bzod pa	kṣānti
paying attention	yang dag par rjes su mthong ba	samanupaśyati
perfection	pha rol tu phyin pa	pāramitā
perfection of wisdom	shes rab kyi pha rol tu phyin pa	prajñāpāramitā
perfectly pure cognition	blo shin tu rnam par dag pa	suviśuddhabuddhiḥ

English	Tibetan	Sanskrit
perfectly skilled in the sameness of the three times	dus gsum mnyam pa nyid tshar phyin pa	tryadhvasamatā-niryātaḥ
point where phenomena end	dngos po'i mtha'	vastvanta
point where the sphere of space ends	nam mkha'i khams kyi mthas gtugs pa	ākāśadhātu-paryavasānaḥ
posited	rnam par bzhag pa	vyavasthā
possessed the gnosis bodhisattvas vow to accomplish	ye shes byang chub sems dpa' thams cad kyis yang dag par mnos pa	sarvabodhisattva-sampratīcchīta-jñanaḥ
inference through what is commonly known or recognized	grags pa'i rjes dpag	prasiddhānumāṇa
prātimokṣha	so sor thar pa	prātimokṣa
predisposition	bag la nyal	anuśaya
primordially in the state of peace	gzod ma nas zhib	ādiśānta
prince	gzhon nur gyur pa	kumārabhūta
principle of reason	rigs pa	yukti
principle of reason based on cause and effect	bya ba byed pa'i rigs pa	kāryakāraṇayukti
principle of reason based on dependence	de la ltos pa'i rigs pa	apekṣāyukti
principle of reason based upon logical proof	'thad pas sgrub pa'i rigs pa	upapattisādhanayukti
principle of reason based upon the nature of phenomena itself	chos nyid kyi rigs pa	dharmatāyukti
producing/bringing about a (new) existence	lus mngon par 'grub cing 'byung bar 'gyur ba	ātmabhāvam abhinirvartayanti
purification	rnam par dag pa	viśuddhi

English	Tibetan	Sanskrit
purity of [their] merit	yon yongs su sbyong ba chen po	mahādakṣiṇā-pariṣodhakaḥ
quality	chos	dharma
Radiant	'od 'phro ba can	arciṣmatī
reason	rtags	hetu
recluse	dge sbyong	śrāmaṇa
recollect what [they] have heard	thos pa'i gzungs	śrutidhāraṇī
referential object	dmigs pa	ālambana
reflection	gzugs brnyan	pratibimba
results produced by the maturation [of their karma]	rnam par smin pa'i 'bras bu	vipākaphala
room	gnas	sthāna
Ṛṣhivadana	drang srong smra ba	ṛṣivadana
sapakṣha		sapakṣa
scrutinizing	lta ba	prekṣate
secondary defilement	nye ba'i nyon mongs	upakleśa
sense domain	skye mched	āyatana
sentient being	sems can	sattva
setting	rab tu 'dzin pa	pradhāraṇa
seven precious substances	rin po che sna bdun	saptaratna
sharing a common destiny	bde ba gcig pa'i don gyis	ekayogakṣemārthena
shift in one's basis of existence	gnas gyur pa	āśrayaparivṛtti
single vehicle	theg pa gcig pa	ekayāna
six destinies	'gro ba drug	sadgati
slow-witted	blo gros ngan pa	kumati

English	Tibetan	Sanskrit
solitary realizer	rang sangs rgyas	pratyekabuddha
sovereign power	byin gyi rlabs	adhiṣṭhāna, adhiṣṭhita
space	nam mkha'	ākāśa
specific defining characteristic	rang gi mtshan nyid	svalakṣaṇa
sphere of activity	spyod yul	gocara
spontaneously accomplished	lhun gyis grub pa	anābhoga
stage	sa	bhūmi
stage of engagement through aspiration	mos pa spyod pa'i sa	adhimukticaryā-bhūmiḥ
stainless	sbyangs pa	uttapta, viśuddha
Stainless	dri ma med pa	vimala
Subhūti	rab 'byor	subhūti
sublime perfection, the supreme indivisible gnosis of the Tathāgata's liberation	de bzhin gshegs pa ma 'dres pa'i rnam par thar par mdzad pa'i ye shes kyi mthar phyin pa	asaṁbhinnatathāgata-vimokṣajñāna-niṣṭhāgataḥ
subliminal	kun gzhi	ālaya
subliminal cognition	kun gzhi rnam par shes pa	ālayavijñāna
subtle transgression	ltung ba phra mo	sūkṣmāpatti
superficial	lpags shun	
superimpose	sgro btags	samāropa
superimposition	sgro 'dogs pa	samāropa
superior knowledge	mngon par shes pa	abhijñā
superior mind	lhag pa'i sems	adhicitta
sustenances	zas	āhāra
Suvishuddhamati	blo gros shin tu rnam dag	suviśuddhamati
tathāgata	de bzhin gshegs pa	tathāgata

English	Tibetan	Sanskrit
teachings on the basis of serious downfalls	pham pa'i gnas lta bu'i chos, pham pa'i gnas lta bu	pārājayikasthānīya-dharmāḥ, pārājayikasthānīya
teachings on the basis of transgressions	ltung ba'i gnas lta bu'i chos	mananāpatti-sthānīya[dharmāḥ]
teachings on the ceremony of taking [the vows of the bodhisattva discipline]	[byang chub sems dpa'i tshul khrims kyi sdom pa] yang dag par blang ba	[bodhisattvaśīla-saṁvara] samādāna
ten powers	stobs bcu	daśabala
that which must be established	grub par bya ba	sādhya
thesis	so so'i shes pa, dam bcas	pratijñā
thing	dngos po, ngo bo	bhāva
think	bye brag phyed pa	mata
those not following you	slad rol pa	tīrthika
thought	yid	manas
three forms of knowledge	rigs pa gsum	trividyā
three worlds	khams gsum	tridhātu, traidhātuka
timira	rab rib pa	timira
to be comprehended	yongs su shes par bya ba'i dngos po	parijñeyavastu
trichiliocosm	stong gsum gyi stong chen po'i 'jig rten gyi khams	trisāhasra mahāsāhasraloka-dhātu
true nature	'di ltar don	yathārtha
true reality	de bzhin nyid, de kho na, de nyid	tathatā, tattva
truly	ji tsam du	yāvat, tāvatā, tāvat
truth	bden pa	satya

English	Tibetan	Sanskrit
truth body	chos kyi sku	dharmakāya
two truths	bden pa gnyis	satyadvaya
ultimate	don dam pa, don dam	paramārtha
ultimate limit of existence	yang dag pa'i mtha'	bhūtakoṭi
ultimate reality	de bzhin nyid don dam pa	
ultimate within the domain of truth	chos kyi dbyings kyis klas pa	dharmadhātuparamaḥ
unborn	ma skyes pa	anutpanna
unconditioned	'du ma byas	asaṁskṛta
underlying condition	gnas pa	sthāna
understood all practices	spyod pa thams cad dang ldan pa'i blo	sarvacaryā-samanvāgata-buddhiḥ
unite them evenly	zung du 'jug pa	yuganaddha
universe of a thousand worlds	stong gi 'jig rten gyi khams	sāhasracūḍikaloka-dhātu
unproduced by intentional action	mngon par 'du bya ba med pa	anabhisaṁskāraṇa, anabhisaṁskāra
unreal	yongs su ma grub pa	apariniṣpanna
unsurpassable good	grub pa dang bde ba	yogakṣema
useful	gces spras byed pa	bahukara
Utmost Joy	rab tu dga' ba	pramuditā
Uttarakuru	byang gi sgra mi snyan pa	uttarakuru
valid	yongs su dag pa	pariśuddha
valid cognition	tshad ma	pramāṇa
Vārāṇasī	bA rA Na sI	vārāṇasī
Vidhivatparipṛcchaka	tshul bzhin kun 'dri	vidhivatparipṛcchaka
vigor	brtson 'grus	vīrya

English	Tibetan	Sanskrit
vipakṣha		vipakṣa
Vishālakīrti		viśālakīrti
Vishālamati	blo gros yangs pa	viśālamati
vow	sdom pa	saṁvara
wander like beggars	spongs zhing rgyu	caraṁti bhikṣāṁ
wavering	rgyu ba med pa	apracāra
whose defining characteristic is beyond all speculation	rtog ge thams cad las yang dag par 'das pa	sarvatarkasamatikrānta
whose defining characteristic is of a single nature everywhere	thams cad du ro gcig pa'i mtshan nyid	*sarvatraikarasalakṣaṇa
wisdom	shes rab	prajñā
wishlessness	smon pa med pa	apraṇihita
with outflows	zag pa dang bcas pa	sāsrava
without a person	zag med	anāsrava
without support	mi gnas pa	apratiṣṭhita
wrongly conceive	mngon par zhen	abhiniviśanti
yakṣha	gnod sbyin	yakṣa
yoga	sbyor ba	yoga

Appendixes

Appendix I: *The Translation Choice for* Nimitta

Introduction

The *Saṁdhinirmocana Sūtra* stands as a foundational text for the Yogāchāra tradition, offering sophisticated analyses of consciousness, perception, and the nature of reality. Within this framework, the concept of *nimitta* (*mtshan ma*) plays a pivotal role in describing both the objects of consciousness and the cognitive processes through which these objects are apprehended. Furthermore, the meditative state of *animittā* (absence of manifest characteristics) represents one of the three doors to liberation.

The translation of Buddhist technical terminology presents unique challenges for scholars and practitioners alike. Among the most nuanced and consequential translation decisions in my rendering of the *Saṁdhinirmocana Sūtra* has been the choice of an appropriate English equivalent for the Sanskrit term *nimitta*. After extensive textual analysis, consideration of the term's usage across various contexts within the sutra, and consultation with both classical commentaries and contemporary scholarship, I have opted to translate *nimitta* as "manifest characteristics." Here, due to the importance of this term across a range of Buddhist literature, I explain why I have chosen to do so in this context.

Etymology and Semantic Range of *Nimitta*

The Sanskrit term *nimitta* derives from the verbal root √*mi* with the prefix *ni-*, originally indicating "that which is measured out" or "established." In classical Sanskrit usage, the term carries multiple meanings, including "sign," "mark," "cause," "reason," "indication," and "characteristic." The Tibetan translation *mtshan ma* for *nimitta* similarly encompasses a broad semantic field, denoting any distinguishing feature or characteristic that allows for identification or recognition.

In early Buddhist texts, *nimitta* often refers to the mental image or representational aspect of meditation objects. In the Abhidharma literature, it can denote both the perceptual features of an object and the conceptual constructs associated with those features. The term thus spans both perceptual and conceptual domains from its earliest usages in Buddhist literature.

As Buddhist thought evolves, especially within the Mahayana traditions, the semantic range of *nimitta* expands significantly. However, it is important to emphasize that the sense of *nimitta* as "sign," particularly in the context of logical inference (e.g., "there is fire because there is smoke"), remains a valid and influential meaning, notably within the Pramāṇa tradition of Buddhist epistemology. In Prajñāpāramitā literature, *nimitta* takes on additional significance as that which is to be transcended in the realization of emptiness (*śūnyatā*). Here, *nimitta* encompasses all phenomenal appearances or manifest characteristics that the mind grasps as signs of inherent existence.

In Yogāchāra texts, the term's usage becomes even more sophisticated. In this context, abandoning all *nimitta*s refers to relinquishing all conceptual overlays, signs, mental images, as well as any putative "objective referent" of those, not to mention the very distinction between any sign and its related object of reference. This is probably why Schmithausen understands *nimitta* in the *Yogācārabhūmi-Śāstra* as meaning a "phenomenon" arising from designations and conceptions, which are not necessarily mental images for those who are opposed to Yogāchāra ideas, but are ultimately essenceless.[369] In his view, *nimitta* includes sense objects.[370] He therefore understands *animitta* as "transphenomenal" while he uses "transconceptual" for *nirvikalpa*.[371] Referring to the "Mahāyāna way of transcending entities themselves," he mentions that their essencelessness is reached through transphenomenal and transconceptual experience, distinguishing between these two kinds of experiences.

If we follow Schmithausen here, a better term for *nimitta* would probably be "phenomenal experience." Waldron understands *nimitta* as "phe-

369. Schmithausen 1987, 297.
370. Schmithausen 1987, 404.
371. Schmithausen 1987, 202.

nomenon,"[372] and he refers to Schmithausen's work on elucidating the meaning of *nimitta* in the context of early Yogāchāra thought:

> Schmithausen gives an excellent and succinct definition of *nimitta* here in relation to the rest of this formidable formulation: "In this context: [*nimitta* means][373] objective phenomena as they are experienced or imagined, admitting of being associated with names, and being (co-)conditioned by subjective conceptual activity (*vikalpa*), which has become habitual so that it permeates all (ordinary) perceptions and cognitions."[374]

This distinction between *animitta* as "transphenomenal" and *nirvikalpa* as "transconceptual" suggests that transcending *nimitta* involves moving beyond phenomenal experience itself, not merely beyond conceptualization based on symbols, indicators, or signs. Rather, *nimitta*s as the very phenomena appearing to consciousness through both sensory perception and conceptual cognition are themselves whatever characteristics manifest as projections of consciousness rather than features, attributes, or signs of an external, objective world.

Terminological Continuity and Evolution: From Abhidharma to Mahāyāna

A critical aspect of understanding *nimitta* is recognizing the continuity between Abhidharma and Mahayana traditions in terms of terminology, alongside the reinterpretation and redirection of meaning that occurs on a semantic level. This process of terminological evolution is evidenced in the *Saṁdhinirmocana Sūtra* itself, where the first four chapters present a Mahayana critique of Abhidharma traditions and doctrines before moving into distinctly Mahayana philosophical territory in the later chapters.

In the Abhidharma context, *nimitta* primarily functions as a characteristic or distinguishing mark of a phenomenon, often tied to directly perceptible qualities. The Abhidharma literature is concerned with analyzing

372. See Waldron 2003, 166 passim.
373. Words in brackets are mine.
374. Schmithausen 1987, 357n511.

phenomena into their constituent factors (*dharmas*), each with its own specific characteristic (*svalakṣaṇa*). Within this framework, *nimitta* operates as an identifiable feature that helps categorize phenomena according to their appearance in a broad sense.

The *Saṁdhinirmocana Sūtra* preserves this terminology but subtly shifts its semantic content and philosophical significance. Rather than accepting characteristics as indicators of inherently existing phenomena, the text reframes them as manifestations or conventional appearances that lack inherent existence. This semantic evolution reflects the text's broader project of providing a middle way between Abhidharma realism and the radical cataphatic approach of the Prajñāpāramitā literature. The text doesn't simply reject Abhidharma terminology, but rather repurposes it within a new philosophical framework.

Nimitta in the *Saṁdhinirmocana Sūtra*

Within the *Saṁdhinirmocana Sūtra* specifically, *nimitta* is used in several distinct but interrelated contexts:

1. As the phenomenal appearance of objects to consciousness, whether perceptual or conceptual
2. As the basis for mental proliferation (i.e., conceptual elaboration)
3. As that which is to be transcended in advanced meditative states
4. As a key element in the explanation of the three natures (*trisvabhāva*)

In chapter 2 of the sutra, the Buddha describes ultimate reality as "the domain in which there is no *nimitta*," while the conventional realm is characterized as "the domain of *nimitta*." This indicates that *nimitta* encompasses all aspects of phenomenal experience within the conditioned realm, not merely conceptual signs or labels:

> I have explained that the ultimate is what is cognized by noble beings in a personal and intuitive way, whereas ordinary beings' knowledge [resulting from interacting] with one another belongs to the domain of speculation. Therefore, Dharmodgata,

> you should know in this way through this approach that the ultimate is what is characterized as transcending all speculation. Moreover, Dharmodgata, I have explained that the ultimate represents the domain in which there is no *nimitta*, whereas speculation is the domain of *nimitta*.

Similarly, in chapter 2, the text states:

> Those who have indulged in desire and have been burnt by the torment of desire for a long time cannot imagine, infer, or appreciate the inner happiness of the recluse, which is independent from all *nimitta* related to form, sound, smell, taste, and contact.

This passage confirms that *nimitta* encompasses all sensory objects and their characteristics, not merely conceptual signs or indicators.

In chapter 8, on meditation, the text discusses how practitioners must progress beyond attachment to all *nimitta*, including both conceptual and perceptual aspects of experience (§8.26):

> "[Bodhisattvas] discard the manifest characteristics of designations and objects of designation by directing their attention on true reality. They discard names by not taking the essence of names as a referential object and by not paying attention to the manifest characteristics that constitute their basis."

This usage demonstrates that *nimitta* includes both the conceptual overlay (designation) and the object to which that overlay is applied. In these contexts, *nimitta* clearly refers to the totality of phenomenal appearances as they manifest to consciousness.

Nimitta in Relation to the Three Defining Characteristics and Meditation Practice

The translation of *nimitta* as "manifest characteristics" gains further justification when we examine its function within the framework of the three defining characteristics (*trilakṣaṇa*) presented in chapter 6 and the meditative instructions in chapter 8.

In chapter 6, the Buddha outlines three defining characteristics (*lakṣaṇa*) of phenomena:

1. The imaginary defining characteristic (*parikalpitalakṣaṇa*): The superimposition onto phenomena of an essence or a defining characteristic existing from its own side by means of designations or conventional expressions.
2. The other-dependent defining characteristic (*paratantra-lakṣaṇa*): The dependent arising of phenomena, referring to manifest characteristics upon which an imaginary defining characteristic is superimposed.
3. The actual defining characteristic (*pariniṣpannalakṣaṇa*): The permanent and immutable reality of phenomena, the ultimate unerring object that is manifest once the selflessness of phenomena is realized.

Within this framework, *nimitta* operates primarily in relation to the other-dependent defining characteristic, representing the manifest characteristics in the sense of phenomenal appearances that arise in dependence upon causes and conditions. These are the very appearances that serve as the basis for superimposing imaginary characteristics.

As explained in chapter 7:

> The manifest characteristic (*nimitta*) of conditioned phenomena, namely, the basis of the imaginary defining characteristic, the object of conceptualization, is the other-dependent defining characteristic.

In chapter 8 on meditation practices of mental stillness (*śamatha*) and insight (*vipaśyanā*), *nimitta* plays a central role in the practitioner's progression from conceptual to nonconceptual awareness. The text explains:

> "Blessed One, when do the bodhisattvas practice only insight?" "Whenever they direct their attention toward mental manifest characteristics (*cittanimitta*) without interruption." "When do the bodhisattvas practice only mental stillness?" "Whenever they direct their attention toward the unimpeded mind without

> interruption." "When do they combine both insight and mental stillness and unite them evenly?" "Whenever they direct their attention toward the one-pointedness of mind."

Here, *nimitta* functions as the object of meditative attention in the practice of insight, representing the phenomenal appearances to which the practitioner directs attention. As the practitioner progresses, they learn to recognize these manifest characteristics as mere projections of consciousness, ultimately leading to liberation from attachment to them.

Later in chapter 8, we find:

> "Blessed One, as bodhisattvas practice mental stillness and insight, which kinds of manifest characteristics do they discard? How do they direct their attention to achieve this?"

The Buddha replies that they let go of the nimitta of designations and their objects by attending to true reality, and that they set aside names by not taking any essential feature as an object and by not attending to the nimitta that underlies them (8.26), thus clarifying the practice.

This passage clearly shows that *nimitta* encompasses both the conceptual designations and the phenomenal appearances that serve as their basis. The practitioner's goal is to transcend attachment to both.

Soteriological Implications: *Nimitta* in Bondage and Liberation

The soteriological significance of *nimitta* is particularly evident in the *Saṁdhinirmocana Sūtra*'s treatment of bondage and liberation. In chapter 3, the text explicitly identifies attachment to *nimitta* as a form of bondage from which the practitioner must be liberated:

> If the defining characteristic of conditioned phenomena and the defining characteristic of the ultimate were distinct, even those who realize the truth would, as a consequence, not be detached from the manifest characteristics (*nimitta*) of conditioned phenomena. Since they would not be detached from the manifest

> characteristics of conditioned phenomena, they would also not be liberated from the bondage of manifest characteristics. If they were not liberated from the bondage of manifest characteristics, they would not be liberated from the bondage of corruption.

This passage reveals that *nimitta* is not merely a cognitive or perceptual phenomenon but is intimately connected to the very bondage that keeps beings trapped in samsara. Liberation entails freedom from attachment to *nimitta*.

Further, the text connects liberation explicitly to the transcendence of *nimitta* through meditative practice, as evidenced in the concluding verses of chapter 3:

> As beings practice mental stillness and insight,
> They will be liberated from the bonds of corruption
> And the bonds of manifest characteristics.

Chapter 7 elaborates on this soteriological dimension by connecting *nimitta* to the three kinds of essencelessness (*niḥsvabhāvatā*):

1. Essencelessness regarding defining characteristics (*lakṣaṇaniḥsvabhāvatā*): The essencelessness of the imaginary defining characteristic, like a sky flower.
2. Essencelessness regarding arising (*utpattiniḥsvabhāvatā*): The essencelessness of the other-dependent defining characteristic, like a magical illusion.
3. Essencelessness regarding the ultimate (*paramārthaniḥsvabhāvatā*) in its two aspects:

The first aspect relates to "phenomena arising in dependence upon causes, which lack an essence on account of lacking an essence in terms of arising and also lack an essence on account of lacking an ultimate essence."

The second aspect is indeed the "actual defining characteristic of phenomena" which is referred to as "selflessness of phenomena" and is "the ultimate."

Within this framework, liberation involves recognizing that all *nimitta*s lack inherent existence in all three senses. This recognition leads to freedom from attachment to manifest characteristics, which is essential for attaining awakening.

Evaluating Translations of *Nimitta*: A Few Methodological Considerations

The translation of *nimitta* as "sign" presents several practical problems when applied to the *Saṁdhinirmocana Sūtra*. First and foremost, "sign" is semantically underpervasive relative to the original conceptual field of *nimitta*. In modern English usage, a "sign" is primarily understood as an indicator or symbol that points to something beyond itself—a semiotic relationship between signifier and signified. However, as my analysis demonstrates, *nimitta* encompasses not only symbolic representations but also direct perceptual content and the phenomena themselves as they appear to consciousness.

The translation of Sanskrit *nimitta* as "sign" carries philosophical implications that can inadvertently import a Sautrāntika epistemological framework incompatible with the orientation of the *Saṁdhinirmocana Sūtra*. While some pre-Mahayana Buddhist traditions, particularly the Sautrāntika school with its representational theory of perception, explicitly conceived of *nimitta* as perceptual marks or mental representations mediating between consciousness and external objects, the *Saṁdhinirmocana Sūtra* explicitly rejects such external realism.

Even within the Theravāda tradition, where *nimitta* features prominently in meditation practices such as *kasiṇa* exercises described in the *Visuddhimagga*, we find a representationalist framework that would be incompatible with the *Saṁdhinirmocana Sūtra*'s approach. In these practices, the meditator cultivates progressively refined mental images (*nimitta*) of an external object, moving from initial perception (*parikamma-nimitta*) to acquired mental image (*uggaha-nimitta*) to conceptualized counterpart (*paṭibhāga-nimitta*). This entire structure presupposes a fundamental distinction between the external object and its mental representation as a "sign," maintaining precisely the kind of subject-object dichotomy and representationalist epistemology that the *Saṁdhinirmocana Sūtra* systematically undermines.

However, the *Saṁdhinirmocana Sūtra*'s presentation of "representation-only" (*vijñaptimātra*) explicitly rejects such externalism, asserting in chapter 8, for example, that "this image is merely a representation." From this perspective, *nimitta* encompasses not merely a representing sign but the entire phenomenologically manifesting characteristic of experience itself, without positing a distinct substrate "behind" the appearance. Translating *nimitta* as "sign" thus risks importing a subject-object dualism and representationalist epistemology at odds with the sūtra's nondualistic phenomenological orientation.

The modern understanding of "sign" among English readers tends to evoke a relatively simplistic indicator function, wherein a sign (or symbol) points to something beyond itself in a straightforward manner. This concept differs significantly from Ferdinand de Saussure's sophisticated linguistic model, where the sign (*signe*) constitutes an inseparable unity of signifier (*signifiant*) and signified (*signifié*), bound together arbitrarily yet conventionally within a linguistic system (referred to as *nāma* in the *Saṁdhinirmocana Sūtra*). When translating *nimitta* as "sign," readers may mistakenly assume a mere indicator relationship rather than grasping the complex phenomenological unity that *nimitta* represents in texts at the inception of Yogāchāra thought. While Saussure's model might initially seem more compatible with Buddhist representational theories, even this comparison proves inadequate, as Saussurean semiotics still operates within a convention-based linguistic framework that presupposes stable referential structures—exactly what the *Saṁdhinirmocana Sūtra* challenges through its analysis of the imaginary defining characteristic. The sutra presents *nimitta* not as a representational bridge between consciousness and an external world, but as the very manifestation of experiential reality within consciousness itself, encompassing both the appearing aspect and what appears, without recourse to external referents.

To sum up, from a semiotic perspective, translating *nimitta* as "sign" therefore creates a problematic implication that what is being referenced is merely the signifier, while excluding the signified. In the *Saṁdhinirmocana Sūtra*, however, *nimitta* clearly includes both the signifier and the signified—both the conceptual designation and the object being designated. When the text refers to *nimitta* in relation to the five aggregates, it includes both their conceptual designations and their direct manifest characteristics.

When examining passages that discuss liberation as freedom from the "bondage of *nimitta*," the translation "bondage of signs" suggests merely a freedom from symbolic thinking or conceptual labels. However, the text clearly indicates a more profound liberation from attachment to all manifest characteristics, both conceptual and perceptual. Similarly, when the text discusses the appropriation of "mental imprints producing the elaboration of conventional expressions with regard to *nimitta*, names, and conceptualizations," translating *nimitta* as "signs" creates redundancy and confusion with "names," which already function as signs or linguistic symbols in the conventional sense.

Other potential translations also present important limitations. "Appearance" or "phenomenal appearance," while capturing the experiential aspect of *nimitta*, may overemphasize the visual or perceptual dimension at the expense of conceptual content. "Feature" or "attribute" tend to suggest properties that belong to a "property-bearer" as an independently existing object, thereby potentially reinforcing substantialist assumptions that the philosophical framework of the *Saṁdhinirmocana Sūtra* explicitly rejects.

In developing my translation, I have relied on a methodologically rigorous approach that combined traditional textual analysis with computational methods. Using key-word-in-context (KWIC) tables to analyze every occurrence of *mtshan ma* in the Tibetan text, I have identified patterns of usage and contextual nuances. These KWIC tables were invaluable for determining how various potential translations would function across the different contexts in which *nimitta* appears in the text. By systematically examining each occurrence and its contextual relationships, I have been able to evaluate whether a proposed translation would maintain consistency and accuracy throughout the text.

Additionally, I have utilized reasoning language models trained on Mahayana Buddhist texts to evaluate the semantic scope of *nimitta* in the original text against potential English equivalents. This approach aimed to ensure the closest possible match in terms of logical pervasion between *definiens* and *definiendum* across source and target languages.

From this methodological perspective, "manifest characteristics" and "phenomenal appearance" emerged as the English terms with the highest degree of semantic overlap with *nimitta* as used in the *Saṁdhinirmocana Sūtra*. This computational analysis confirmed what close textual reading had suggested: "manifest characteristics" achieves a significantly higher degree of semantic coverage than alternatives such as "sign," "mark," or "appearance."

Alternative Translation Considerations

In earlier versions of this translation, I had rendered *nimitta* as "phenomenal appearance," which remains a valid and defensible option. This translation choice effectively captures the experiential dimension of *nimitta* as that which appears to consciousness, and it accurately conveys the sense of phenomena as they manifest in experience rather than as independently existing entities. However, upon further reflection, I determined that "phenomenal appearance," while conceptually appropriate, presents certain limitations, as mentioned above. First, the term is somewhat abstract and technical, potentially creating distance for readers without philosophical training.

More significantly, this translation option obscures an important terminological parallelism in the Tibetan language between *mtshan ma* (*nimitta*) and *mtshan nyid* (*lakṣaṇa*). The Tibetan terms share the root *mtshan*, indicating their conceptual relatedness for Tibetans as they translated the Sanskrit original terms. By translating *mtshan ma* as "manifest characteristics" and *mtshan nyid* as "defining characteristics," I preserve this morphological and conceptual connection, making the relationship between these terms more transparent to readers of the English translation. This parallelism is particularly important given how frequently these terms appear in relation to each other throughout the text, especially in discussions of the three natures (*trisvabhāva*) and meditative practice. While "phenomenal appearance" remains philologically sound, "manifest characteristics" better serves the text's internal conceptual coherence while maintaining terminological clarity and consistency.

Justification for "Manifest Characteristics" and Philosophical Implications

My choice of "manifest characteristics" for *nimitta* offers several significant advantages over conventional alternatives. The term "manifest" indicates the appearing aspect of phenomena, while "characteristics" encompasses the distinguishing features that allow for identification and conceptualization. Together, they convey that *nimitta* refers to both how things appear and how they are characterized in experience.

"Manifest characteristics" aligns precisely with the philosophical framework of the *Saṁdhinirmocana Sūtra*, according to which all phenomenal experience is understood as a manifestation of consciousness, a mere representation (*vijñaptimātra*), with apparent distinctions between subject and object arising through the constructive activity of consciousness itself. The term effectively conveys this sense of phenomena as they appear to consciousness, without implying an external, objective reality independent of cognition.

This translation choice has profound implications for understanding the central doctrine of the three natures (*trisvabhāva*) as presented in the *Saṁdhinirmocana Sūtra*. In chapters 6 and 7, the text presents the three defining characteristics (*trilakṣaṇa*) of phenomena:

1. In the imaginary nature (*parikalpitasvabhāva*), manifest characteristics (*nimitta*) appear as inherently existing entities with independent reality. The mind grasps these manifest characteristics as if they were self-existent, attributing to them an intrinsic identity they do not possess.
2. In the dependent nature (*paratantrasvabhāva*), manifest characteristics are understood as dependently arising appearances within consciousness, conditioned by causes and conditions rather than existing independently.
3. In the perfected nature (*pariniṣpannasvabhāva*), there is a complete cessation of attachment to manifest characteristics, revealing the ultimate nature of phenomena as empty of the imaginary nature while encompassing the purified dependent nature.

To conclude on this point, my translation of *nimitta* as "manifest characteristics" maintains terminological consistency with related concepts in the text, particularly *lakṣaṇa*, which I translate as "defining characteristic." While *nimitta* refers to the characteristics that manifests to consciousness, *lakṣaṇa* refers to the characteristics that establish and define a phenomenon's identity. This terminological distinction is crucial for understanding key passages in the text, particularly chapters 6–8, which discuss the "three defining characteristics" of phenomena.

Practical Applications in Translation

My translation choice resolves several interpretive difficulties that arise with conventional translations. For example, the translation of *nimitta* as "sign" creates confusion in passages that list both *nimitta* and conceptual designations, suggesting redundancy or unclear distinction. In the passage describing "the appropriation of mental imprints producing the elaboration of conventional expressions with regard to *nimitta*, names, and conceptualizations," the conventional translation would yield "signs, names, and conceptualizations"—an unclear sequence with apparent overlap between "signs" and "names."

With "manifest characteristics," the sequence becomes clear: phenomenal characteristics manifest to consciousness, names are applied to these characteristics, and conceptualizations elaborate upon these named appearances. This clarity preserves the text's nuanced analysis of the cognitive process without introducing artificial distinctions or redundancies.

As 8.26 states, bodhisattvas relinquish the nimitta of designations and their objects by directing attention to true reality; they also abandon names by refusing any essence as object and by not attending to the underlying nimitta that would ground them, which is the point at issue.

This rendering clarifies that practitioners transcend both conceptual designations and the phenomenal characteristics they designate, a nuance that would be lost with "sign" or similar translations.

The translation of *nimitta* as "manifest characteristics" offers significant benefits for readers' comprehension of the *Saṁdhinirmocana Sūtra*. It provides terminological consistency throughout the text, allowing readers to trace the concept across different contexts and discussions. It facilitates understanding of the text's philosophical subtleties without requiring readers to constantly mentally substitute a more appropriate meaning for an inadequate translation. Finally, it supports readers in connecting the philosophical content with their own experiential practice by clearly identifying *nimitta* as encompassing all aspects of phenomenal experience—perceptual and conceptual, subjective and objective.

Conclusion

My translation of *nimitta* as "manifest characteristics" represents a carefully considered solution to a significant terminological challenge. This choice addresses the limitations of other terminological choices while attempting to accurately reflect the term's usage throughout the *Saṁdhinirmocana Sūtra*. By encompassing both the perceptual and conceptual dimensions of *nimitta*—how phenomena appear to consciousness and how they are characterized—my translation aim is to capture the term's semantic range within the philosophical framework of the sutra.

At the same time, I recognize that no translation can perfectly render all nuances of the original term. The goal of translation of texts with a high degree of "philosophical content" like the *Saṁdhinirmocana Sūtra* is not merely linguistic equivalence but conceptual clarity—enabling readers to understand the philosophical insights of the text as accurately as possible. This is important in order to transfer into the target language the logical network of ideas contained in the source text. By translating *nimitta* as "manifest characteristics," I aim to facilitate this understanding, making the profound philosophical teachings of the *Saṁdhinirmocana Sūtra* more accessible to contemporary readers while remaining faithful to the text's original meaning and intent.

Appendix II: Source Text and Various Versions

The only extant complete versions of the *Saṁdhinirmocana Sūtra* are Chinese and Tibetan translations produced from Sanskrit manuscripts. All the recensions of the sutra in Tibetan include a prologue followed by ten chapters. In addition to the various Kangyur editions, the sutra is also quoted in full in the *Viniścayasaṁgrahaṇī* of the *Yogācārabhūmi*. The list of the available recensions of the text across Sanskrit, Chinese, and Tibetan include:[375]

Sanskrit (including Buddhist Hybrid Sanskrit)

Buescher 2007: 102–104 (quotations in TrBh, 33.25–34.4, drawn from Saṁdh. 5.5 and 5.7; see also Lévi 1925: 33–34)

Matsuda 1995 (complete reconstruction from manuscript of Saṁdh. 9.1–6)

Matsuda 2013 (fragments of Saṁdh. 2.4 and 3.1, fragments of 8.39–40, complete reconstruction from manuscript of 8.41)

Nagao 1964: 43 (gives the list of the seven kinds of tattva mentioned in Saṁdh. 8.20.2 and quoted in the *Madhyāntavibhāgabhāṣya*)

Nagao 1982–1987: I.4, I.7[376]

Tucci 1971: 1 (two verses from Saṁdh. 3.7 quoted in Kamalashīla's *Bhāvanākrama*: (*nimittabandhanāj jantur atho dauṣṭhulabandhanāt / vipaśyanāṁ bhāvayitvā śamathañ ca vimucyata iti*) and ibid., 22 (a sentence

375. In bold are textual resources I used to translate the text into English. On the relationship between the *Saṁdhinirmocana Sūtra* and the *Yogācārabhūmi*, see Delhey 2013 and 2022.

376. See Powers 2015. Unfortunately, I haven't been able to consult this reference work at the time of completing this translation.

drawn from 7.15 also quoted in the *Bhāvanākrama:ekāntasattvārthavimukhasya ekāntasaṁsārābhisaṁskāra-vimukhasya [nā] uttarā samyaksaṁbodhir uktā mayeti*)

Chinese

相續解脫地波羅蜜了義經 (Taishō 678) and 相續解脫如來所作隨順處了義經 (Taishō 679) translated by Guṇabhadra (394–468 CE) between 435 and 443 CE (these two texts include, respectively, chapters 9 and 10)

深密解脫經 (Taishō 675) translated by Bodhiruci (fl. 508–535 CE) in 514 (includes a prologue followed by ten chapters as in the Tibetan versions of the text)

佛說解節經 (Taishō 677) translated by Paramārtha (498–569 CE) in 557 (mentioned in Wonch'uk's commentaries on the sutra; the prologue is different from those translated by Bodhiruci and Xuanzang; only the first four chapters are translated)

解深密經 (Taishō 676) translated by Xuanzang (596–664 CE) in 647 (a complete translation of the prologue and the ten chapters)

Tibetan

Tshalpa group

KB116 mdo sde, ca 1b1–71a1 (vol. 57)[377]

377. Here is a list of the sigla I used to identify the various witnesses of Saṁdh.:

(1) Witnesses of the sutra found in the available Kangyurs and canonical collections (MsK = manuscript Kangyur, PK = xylograph): Kb: Berlin MsK; C: Choné PK; Cz: Chizhi; D: Degé PK; Dd: Dodedrak; Dk: Dongkarla; F: Phukdrag MsK; H: Lhasa PK; Gt: Gangteng; He: Hemis I; J: 'Jang sa tham/Lithang PK; L: London (Shelkar) MsK; Lg: Lang mdo; N: Narthang PK; Ng: Namgyal; Np: Neyphug; O: Tawang; Pj: Phajoding I; Pz: Phajoding II; K0774: Peking 1737 PK; R: Ragya; S: Stok MsK; T: Tokyo MsK; U: Urga PK; V: Ulaanbaatar MsK; X: Basgo MsK; Z: Shey Palace MsK. Other canonical collections: Bd: Bardan (Zanskar), Do: Dolpo, Go: Gondhla (Lahaul). Source: http://www.rkts.org (last accessed on July 20, 2020). I am following the typology of Kangyur groups suggested by rKTs (Vienna University). I would like to warmly thank Professor Helmut Tauscher and Bruno Lainé for making available to me the editions I used for this translation project. For a general discussion of some Tibetan sources, see Skilling 1994, 775.

(2) Xylographs of the *Viniścayasaṁgrahaṇī* of the *Yogācārabhūmi* from the Tengyur: VD Degé, VG Golden, VP Peking. My thanks go to Kojirō Katō for having shared

C747 mdo sde, ca 1b1–71a7 (vol. 29)
D106 mdo sde, ca 1b1–55b7 (vol. 49)
J51 mdo sde, ca 1b1–59b8 (vol. 44)
K0774 mdo sna tshogs, ngu 1b1–60b7 (vol. 29, 1)
R106 mdo sde, ca 1b1–55b7 (vol. 49)
U106 mdo sde, ca 1b1–55b7 (vol. 49)
VD D4038 mdo 'grel (sems tsam), zi 44a–97b
VG GT3542 mdo 'grel (sems tsam), 'i 59b–136a
VP Ko̧5539 mdo 'grel (sems tsam), 'i 47b–109a
Thempangma group
L82 mdo sde, na 1b1–80b1 (vol. 42)
S106 mdo sde, na 1b1–80b1 (vol. 63)
T107 mdo sde, na 1b1–70b1 (vol. 68)
V156 mdo sde, na 1b1–69b6 (vol. 65)
Z137 mdo, na 1b1–93a6 (vol. 59)
Mustang group
X mdo sde, wa 66a–132a
He64.6 mdo, wa 62b5–125b8
Bhutan group
Cz082-001 mdo, na 1b1–82a5
Dd031-001 mdo, ca 1b1–69b2
Dk034-001 mdo, na 1b1–87b1
Gt028-001 mdo, na 1b1–72b3
Np012-001 mdo, na 1b1–87a7
Pj043-001 mdo, ca 1b1–62b4
Pz045-001 mdo ca 1b1–61a5
Mixed/Independent editions
F156 mdo sde, ba (tsha) 1b1–72a7 (vol. 68)
H109 mdo sde, ca 1b1–87b7 (vol. 51)
Lg11.8 mdo, da-L74 224b5–276a2
N94 mdo sde, ca 1–81a7 (vol. 51)
Ng13.07 mdo pa dgongs 111b3–162a8
O23 mdo sde, cha

with me the bibliographical detail of these witnesses. The *Viniścayasaṃgrahaṇī* is also available in Chinese under the following title: 瑜伽師地論卷第七十六攝決擇分.

Other canonical collections
Ablaikit collection IOM, RAS Tib.979/117
G019,01 ka 1b–36a6 (vol. 19)
Bd3.7 vol. 3 (ta) pha 1b1–84a6
Do mdo sde, da 196a–246b

Dunhuang manuscripts

SaṁdhDh: Stein Tib. n°194 (49 folios); Stein Tib. n°683 (1 folio) (these folios cover ca. 40 percent of the sutra; see Hakayama 1984–1987)[378]

In addition, five commentaries have been composed on the *Saṁdhinirmocana Sūtra*:

Asaṅga's *Āryasaṁdhinirmocanabhāṣya* (*dgongs pa nges par 'grel pa'i rnam par bshad pa*) D3981 mdo 'grel (mdo), ngi 1b–11b

Wonch'uk's **Āryagambhīrasaṁdhinirmocanasūtraṭīkā* (*dgongs pa zab mo nges par 'grel pa'i mdo rgya cher 'grel pa*) D4016 mdo 'grel (mdo), ti 1b– di 175a[379]

Jñāṇagarbha's *Āryasaṁdhinirmocanasūtre āryamaitreyakevala-parivartabhāṣya* (*dgongs pa nges par 'grel pa'i mdo las 'phags pa byams pa'i le'u nyi tshe bshad pa*) D4033 mdo 'grel (sems tsam), bi 318b–345a

**Āryasaṁdhinirmocana-sūtravyākhyāna* (*mdo sde dgongs pa nges par 'grel pa'i 'grel chen*), D4358 mdo 'grel, co 1b–jo 183b, a text sometimes ascribed to Asaṅga or Klu'i rgyal mtshan (see Almogi 2022)

Trisong Detsen (khri srong lde brtsan)'s **Samyagvākpramāṇoddhṛta-sūtra* (*bka' yang dag pa'i tshad ma las mdo btus* pa) D4352 mdo 'grel (bstan bcos sna tshogs), co 173a–205b

378. For the reference of possible additional folios, see Chayet 2005, 67 (n°615—1 folio, n°590—6 folios).

379. 解深密經疏 (ZZ369) is a text originally composed in Chinese that has been translated into Tibetan. On Wonch'uk's life and works, see Powers 1992a.

Bibliographies

Primary Sources

Kangyur (Canonical Scriptures)

Buddhabhūmisūtra (*sangs rgyas kyi sa'i mdo*). Tōh 275, Degé Kangyur vol. 68 (mdo sde, ya), folios 36.a–44.b.

Māyājāla (*mdo chen sgyu ma'i dra ba*). Tōh 288, Degé Kangyur vol. 71 (mdo sde, sha), folios 230.a–244.a.

'phags pa dgongs pa nges par 'grel pa zhes bya ba theg pa chen po'i mdo (*Āryasaṁdhinirmocananāmamahāyānasūtra*). Tōh 106, Degé Kangyur vol. 49 (mdo sde, ca), folios 1.b–55.b.

'phags pa dgongs pa nges par 'grel pa zhes bya ba theg pa chen po'i mdo. bka' 'gyur (dpe bsdur ma) [Comparative Edition of the Kangyur], krung go'i bod rig pa zhib 'jug ste gnas kyi bka' bstan dpe sdur khang [The Tibetan Tripitaka Collation Bureau of the China Tibetology Research Center]. 108 volumes. Beijing: krung go'i bod rig pa dpe skrun khang (China Tibetology Publishing House), 2006–09, vol. 49, 3–131.

Tathāgataguṇajñānācintyaviṣayāvatāranirdeśasūtra (https://read.84000.co/translation/toh185.html) (*de bzhin gshegs pa'i yon tan dang ye shes bsam gyis mi khyab pa'i yul la 'jug pa bstan pa'i mdo*). Tōh 185, Degé Kangyur vol. 61 (mdo sde, tsa), folios 106.a–143.b.

Other Canonical Sources for Saṁdh.

Bd3.7 vol. 3 (ta) pha, folios 1.b–84.a
C747 vol. 29 (mdo sde, ca), folios 1.b–71.a
Dd031-001 (mdo ca), folios 1.b–69.b
Dk034-001 (mdo na), folios 1.b–87.b
Do (mdo sde, da), folios 196.a–246.b
F156 vol. 68 (mdo sde, tsha), folios 1.b–72.a
G019,01 vol. 19 (ka), folios 1.b–36.a

Gt028-001 (mdo na), folios 1.b–72.b
H109 vol. 51 (mdo sde, ca), folios 1.b–87.b
He64.6 (mdo, wa), folios 62.b–125.b
J51 vol. 44 (mdo sde, ca), folios 1.b–59.b
K0774 vol. 29 (mdo sna tshogs, ngu), folios 1.b–60.b
L82 vol. 42 (mdo sde, na), folios 1.b–80.b
N94 vol. 51 (mdo sde, ca) folios 1.a–81.a.
Np012-001 (mdo na), folios 1.b–87.a
Pj043-001 (mdo ca), folios 1.b–62.b
Pz045-001 (mdo ca), folios 1.b–61.a
R106 vol. 49 (mdo sde, ca), folios 1.b–55.b
S106 vol. 63 (mdo sde, na), folios 1.b–80.b
U106 vol. 49 (mdo sde, ca), folios 1.b–55.b
X (mdo sde, wa), folios 66.a–132.a
Z137 vol. 59 (mdo, na), folios 1.b–93.a

Tengyur (Canonical Treatises)

Asaṅga. *rnal 'byor spyod pa'i sa* (*Yogācārabhūmi*). Tōh 4035, Degé Tengyur vol. 127 (sems tsam, tshi), folios 1.b–283.a.

Asaṅga. *rnal 'byor spyod pa'i sa rnam par gtan la dbab pa bsdu ba* (*Yogācārabhūmiviniścayasaṁgraha*). Tōh 4038, Degé Tengyur vol. 130 (sems tsam, zhi), folios 1.b–289.a; vol. 131 (sems tsam, zi), folios 1.b–127.a.

Kamalaśila. *bsgom pa'i rim pa* (*Bhāvanākrama*). Tōh 3915, Degé Tengyur vol. 110 (dbu ma, ki), folios 22.a–41.b; Tōh 3916, Degé Tengyur vol. 110 (dbu ma, ki), folios 42.a–55.b; and Tōh 3917, Degé Tengyur vol. 110 (dbu ma, ki), folios 55.b–68.b.

Mahāvyutpatti (*bye brag tu rtogs par byed pa chen po*). Tōh 4346, Degé Tengyur vol. 204 (sna tshogs, co), folios 1.b–131.a.

Trisong Detsen (*khri srong lde brtsan*). *bka' yang dag pa'i tshad ma las mdo btus pa* (*Samyagvākpramāṇoddhṛtasūtra*). Tōh 4352, Degé Tengyur vol. 204 (sna tshogs, co), folios 173.b–203.a.

Vasubandhu. *dbus dang mtha' rnam par 'byed pa'i 'grel pa* (*Madhyāntavibhāgabhāṣya*). Tōh 4027, Degé Tengyur vol. 124 (sems tsam, bi), folios 1.b–27.a.

Wonch'uk. *dgongs pa zab mo nges par 'grel pa'i mdo rgya cher 'grel pa* (**Āryagambhīrasaṁdhinirmocanasūtraṭīkā*). Tōh 4016, Degé Tengyur vol. 118 (mdo 'grel, ti), folios 1.b–291.a; vol. 119 (mdo 'grel, thi), folios 1.b–175.a.

Other Tibetan and Sanskrit works

IOL Tib J 194 (http://idp.bl.uk/database/oo_loader.a4d?pm=IOL Tib J 194;img=1). British Library, London. Accessed through the International Dunhuang Project: The Silk Road Online.

Modern Sources

Almogi, Orna (ed.). 2022. *Evolution of Scriptures, Formation of Canons: The Buddhist Case*. Indian and Tibetan Studies Series 13. Hamburg: Department of Indian and Tibetan Studies, Universität Hamburg.

Bhattacharya, Ramkrishna. 2000. "Uttarakuru: The (E)utopia of Ancient India." *Annals of the Bhandarkar Oriental Research Institute* 81, no. 1/4: 191–201.

Billeter, Jean-François. 2014. *Trois essais sur la traduction*. Paris: Allia.

Braarvig, Jens. 1985. "Dhāraṇī and Pratibhāna: Memory and Eloquence of the Bodhisattvas." *Journal of the International Association of Buddhist Studies* 8, no. 1: 17–30.

Brunnhölzl, Karl. 2018. *A Compendium of the Mahāyāna: Asaṅga's "Mahāyānasaṃgraha" and Its Indian and Tibetan Commentaries*. 3 vols. Boulder: Shambhala.

Buescher, Hartmut. 2007. *Sthiramati's Triṃśikāvijñaptibhāṣya: Critical Editions of the Sanskrit Text and its Tibetan Translation*. Vienna: Verlag der Österreichischen Akademie der Wissenschaften.

———. 2008. *The Inception of Yogācāra-Vijñānavāda*. Vienna: Verlag der Österreichischen Akademie der Wissenschaften.

Buswell, Robert E., Donald S. Lopez, and Juhn Ahn, eds. 2014. *The Princeton Dictionary of Buddhism*. Princeton University Press.

Chayet, Anne. 2005. "Pour servir à la numérisation des manuscrits tibétains de Dunhuang conservés à la Bibliothèque Nationale : un fichier de Jacques Bacot et autres documents." *Revue d'Études Tibétaines* 9: 4–107.

Cleary, Thomas F. 1999. *Buddhist Yoga: A Comprehensive Course*. Boston: Shambhala.

Conze, Edward. 1975. *The Large Sutra on Perfect Wisdom: with the Divisions of the Abhisamayālaṅkāra*. Berkeley: University of California Press.

Cornu, Philippe. 2005. *Soûtra du dévoilement du sens profond*. Paris: Fayard.

Cousins, Lance S. 1992. "VITAKKA/VITARKA and VICĀRA: Stages of Samādhi in Buddhism and Yoga," *Indo-Iranian Journal* 35: 2–3, 137–57.

Dayal, Har. 2004. *The Bodhisattva Doctrine in Buddhist Sanskrit Literature*. Delhi: Motilal Banarsidass.

Delhey, Martin. 2013. "The Yogācārabhūmi Corpus: Sources, Editions, Translations, and Reference Works." In *The Foundation for Yoga Practitioners. The Buddhist Yogācārabhūmi Treatise and Its Adaptation in India, East Asia, and Tibet*, edited by Ulrich Timme Kragh, 498–561. Harvard Oriental Series 75. Cambridge, MA: Harvard University Press.

———. 2022. "On the Authoritativeness of the *Yogācārabhūmi* as an Abhidharma Work." In *Evolution of Scriptures, Formation of Canons: The Buddhist Case*, edited by Orna Almogi, 43–62. Indian and Tibetan Studies Series 13. Hamburg: Department of Indian and Tibetan Studies, Universität Hamburg.

Eckel, Malcolm David. 1994. *To See the Buddha: A Philosopher's Quest for the Meaning of Emptiness*. Princeton, NJ: Princeton University Press.

Edgerton, Franklin. 1937. "Buddhist Sanskrit saṃdha, saṃdhi(-nirmocana)." *Journal of the American Oriental Society* 5, vol. 2: 185–88.

———. 1953. *Buddhist Hybrid Sanskrit Grammar and Dictionary*. Vol. 2, Dictionary. New Haven: Yale University Press.

Fiordalis, David V. 2012. "The Wondrous Display of Superhuman Power in the *Vimalakīrtinirdeśa*: Miracle or Marvel?" In *Yoga Powers: Extraordinary Capacities Attained Through Meditation and Concentration*, edited by Knut Axel Jacobsen, 96–125. Leiden: Brill.

Forgues, Gregory. 2024. *Radical Nonduality: Ju Mipham Namgyal Gyatso's Discourse on Reality*. Wiener Studien zur Tibetologie und Buddhismuskunde No. 106. Vienna: Arbeitskreis für Tibetische und Buddhistische Studien Universität Wien.

———. n.d. "From the Network to the Text: Selecting Key Witnesses across Tibetan Collections of Canonical Texts." [Article in the Proceedings of the Vienna Kanjur Symposium (October 24–25, 2022) in Honour of Helmut Tauscher]. Vienna: Arbeitskreis für Tibetische und Buddhistische Studien Universität Wien.

Frauwallner, Erich. 1969. *Die Philosophie des Buddhismus*. Berlin: Akademie-Verlag.

Gómez, Luis O. 2011. "On Buddhist wonders and wonder-working." *Journal of the International Association of Buddhist Studies* 33, no. 1–2: 513–54.

Hall, Bruce Cameron. 1986. "The Meaning of Vijñapti in Vasubandhu's Concept of Mind." *Journal of the International Association of Buddhist Studies* 9, no. 1: 7–23.

Hakayama, Noriaki. 1984. "The Old and New Tibetan Translations of the Saṃdhinirmocana-sūtra: Some Notes on the History of Early Tibetan Translation." In *Komazawa daigaku bukkyōgakubu kenkyū kiyō* 42, 192–76.

———. 1986. "A Comparative Edition of the Old and New Tibetan Translations of the Saṃdhinirmocanasūtra (I)." In *Komazawa daigaku bukkyōgakubu ronshū* 17, 616(1)–600(17).

———. 1987a. "A Comparative Edition of the Old and New Tibetan Translations of the Saṃdhinirmocana-sūtra (II)." In *Komazawa daigaku bukkyōgakubu kenkyū kiyō* 45, 354(1)–320(35).

———. 1987b. "A Comparative Edition of the Old and New Tibetan Translations of the Saṃdhinirmocana-sūtra (III)." In *Komazawa daigaku bukkyōgakubu ronshū* 18, 606(1)–572(35).

Hopkins, Jeffrey. 1999. *Emptiness in the Mind-Only School of Buddhism*. Berkeley: University of California Press.

———. 2002. *Reflections on Reality: The Three Natures and Non-Natures in the Mind-Only School. Dynamic Responses to Dzong-ka-bā's "The Essence of Eloquence"* 2. London: University of California Press.

———. 2006. *Absorption in No External World: 170 Issues in Mind Only Buddhism. Dynamic Responses to Dzong-ka-bā's "The Essence of Eloquence"* 3. Ithaca: Snow Lion.

Kapstein, Matthew. 1988. "Mi-pham's Theory of Interpretation." In *Buddhist Hermeneutics*, edited by Donald Lopez, 149–74. Honolulu: University of Hawai'i Press.

———. 2001. *Reason's Traces: Identity and Interpretation in Indian and Tibetan Buddhist Thought*. Boston: Wisdom Publications.

Katō, Kojirō. 2002. 唯識」という文脈で語られる影像：『解深密経』「分別瑜伽品」と「声聞地」の比較検討を通して. ("Pratibimba in the Context of Vijñaptimātra Theory: A Comparative Study of the *Śrāvakabhūmi* and the *Sandhinirmocanasūtra* [Chap. VI])." In インド哲学仏教学研究= インド テツガク ブッキョウガク ケンキュウ (=*Studies in Indian Philosophy and Buddhism, Tokyo University*, 53–65. Tokyo: Tokyo University).

———. 2004. "On the Terms vijñaptimatratā and vijñaptitathatā as Found in the Sandhinirmocanasūtra." *Journal of Indian and Buddhist Studies* (=*Indobukkyogaku Kenkyu*) 52, no. 2: 38–40.

———. 2006. "On the Tibetan Text of the *Saṃdhinirmocanasūtra*: Towards a Comparative Study of Manuscripts and Editions which belong to the East and West Recensions." *Journal of Indian and Buddhist Studies* (=*Indobukkyogaku Kenkyu*) 54, no. 3: 1205–11.

———. 2011. における二種類の勝義無自性解釈について. ("On the Two Different Interpretations of *paramārthaniḥsvabhāva* in the *Saṃdhinirmocanasūtra* 7.6.") *Journal of Indian and Buddhist Studies* (=*Indobukkyogaku Kenkyu*) 59, no. 2: 976–81.

———(forthcoming). "Critical edition of the *Sandhinirmocanasūtra*." PhD diss., University of Tokyo.

Kawasaki, Shinjo. 1976. "Analysis of yoga in the *Sandhinirmocanasūtra*." *Buzan Gakuho* 21: 170–156.

Keenan, John Peter. 1980. "A Study of the *Buddhabhūmyupadeśa*: The Doctrinal Development of the Notion of Wisdom in Yogācāra Thought." PhD diss., University of Wisconsin-Madison.

———. 2000. *The Scripture on the Explication of Underlying Meaning*: Translated from the Chinese of Hsüan-tsang. BDK English Tripiṭaka 25-4. Berkeley: Numata Center for Buddhist Translation and Research.

Kritzer, Robert. 2000. "Rūpa and the Antarābhava." *Journal of Indian Philosophy* 29: 235–72.

Lamotte, Étienne. 1935. *Saṃdhinirmocana sūtra: l'explication des mystères*. Louvain: Bureaux du recueil, Bibliothèque de l'Université.

———. 1944–49. *Le traité de la grande vertu de sagesse de Nāgārjuna, Mahāprajñāpāramitāśāstra*. Louvain: Université de Louvain, Institut orientaliste.

———. 1973. *La somme du grand véhicule d'Asaṅga: Mahāyānasaṃgraha*. Louvain: Université de Louvain, Institut orientaliste.

La Vallée Poussin, Louis de. 1925. *L'Abhidharmakośa de Vasubandhu*. Paris: P. Geuthner.

———. 1934–35. "Notes Bouddhiques: XX. Les Trois 'Caractères' et les trois 'Absences de Nature Propre' dans le *Samdhinirmocana*, Chapitres VI et VII." *Bulletin de la Classe des Lettres et des Sciences Morales et Politiques*, Académie Royale de Belgique: 284–303.

Lévi, Sylvain. 1925. *Vijñaptimātratāsiddhi: deux traités de Vasubandhu: Viṁśatikā (La vingtaine) accompagnée d'une explication en prose, et Triṁśikā (La trentaine) avec le commentaire de Sthiramati*. Paris: H. Champion.

Lin, Chen Kuo. 1991. "The *Saṃdhinirmocana Sūtra*: A Liberating Hermeneutic." PhD diss., Temple University.

———. 2010. "Truth and method in the *Saṃdhinirmocana Sūtra*." *Journal of Chinese Philosophy* 37: 261–75.

Lusthaus, Dan. 2002. *Buddhist Phenomenology: A Philosophical Investigation of Yogācāra Buddhism and the* Ch'eng Wei-shih lun. London: RoutledgeCurzon.

Mathes, Klaus-Dieter. 2007. "The Ontological Status of the Dependent (*paratantra*) in the *Saṃdhinirmocanasūtra* and the *Vyākhyāyukti*." In *Indica et Tibetica: Festschrift für Michael Hahn*, edited by Konrad Klaus and Jens-Uwe Hartmann, 323–39. Vienna: Arbeitskreis für Tibetische und Buddhistische Studien Universität Wien.

Matsuda, Kazunobu. 1995. "Sanskrit Text of the Bodhisattva's Ten Stages in the *Saṃdhinirmocanasūtra*: Based on the Kathmandu Fragment of the *Yogācārabhūmi*." *Bulletin of the Research Institute of Bukkyō University* 2: 59–77.

———. 2013. "Sanskrit Fragments of the *Saṃdhinirmocanasūtra*." In *The Foundation for Yoga Practitioners: The Buddhist Yogācārabhūmi Treatise and Its Adaptation in India, East Asia, and Tibet*, edited by Ulrich Timme Krag, 772–90. Harvard Oriental Series 75. Cambridge, MA: Harvard University Press.

Muller, Charles A. 2011. "Woncheuk 圓測 on Bimba 本質 and Pratibimba 影像 in His Commentary on the *Saṃdhinirmocana-sūtra*." *Journal of Indian and Buddhist Studies* 59, no. 3: 1272–80.

Nagao, Gadjin. 1964. *Madhyāntavibhāga-bhāṣya: A Buddhist Philosophical Treatise Edited for the First Time from a Sanskrit Manuscript*. Tokyo: Suzuki Research Foundation.

———. 1982, 87. Shōdai jōron. Wayaku to chūkai. 2 vols. Tokyo: Kodansha. Nance, Richard F. 2012. *Speaking for Buddhas: Scriptural Commentary in Indian Buddhism*. New York: Columbia University Press.

Obermiller, Eugène. 1933. *Analysis of the Abhisamayālaṃkāra*. London: Luzac.

Powers, John. 1991a. "The Term '*Saṃdhinirmocana*' in the Title of the *Saṃdhinirmocana-sūtra*." *Studies in Central and East Asian Religions* 4: 52–62.

———. 1991b. "The Concept of the Ultimate (*don dam pa, paramārtha*) in the *Sandhinirmocanasūtra*." *Indian Journal of Buddhist Studies* 3, no. 1: 1–24.

———. 1991c. "The Concept of the Ultimate (*don dam pa, paramārtha*) in the *Sandhinirmocana-Sūtra*: Analysis, translation, and notes." PhD diss., University of Virginia.

———. 1992a. "Lost in China, Found in Tibet: How Wonch'uk Became the Author of the Great Chinese Commentary." In *Journal of the International Association of Buddhist Studies* 15, no. 1: 95–103.

———. 1992b. *Two Commentaries on the Samdhinirmocana-Sutra by Asanga and Jnanagarbha*. Studies in Asian Thought and Religion 13. Lewiston: Edwin Mellen Press.

———. 1993a. "The Tibetan Translations of the *Saṃdhinirmocanasūtra* and Bka' 'gyur Research." *Central Asiatic Journal* 37, no. 3/4 (1993): 198–224.

———. 1993b. *Hermeneutics and Tradition in the Sandhinirmocana-sūtra*. Leiden: Brill.

———. 1995. *Wisdom of Buddha: The Saṁdhinirmocana Sūtra*. Tibetan Translation Series 16. Berkeley: Dharma Publishing.

———. 1998. *Jñānagarbha's Commentary on Just the Maitreya Chapter from the Saṃdhinirmocana-Sūtra: Study, Translation and Tibetan Text*. New Delhi: Indian Council of Philosophical Research.

———. 2015. "*Saṃdhinirmocanasūtra*." In Brill's *Encyclopedia of Buddhism*, edited by Jonathan Silk et al., vol. 1, Literature and Languages, 240–48. Leiden: Brill.

Punnaji, Hingulwala. 2017. "A Study of the Practice of Recollections (Anussati) in Buddhist Meditation." PhD diss., Huafan University.

Radich, Michael. 2007. "The Somatics of Liberation: Ideas about Embodiment in Buddhism from Its Origins to the Fifth Century C.E." PhD diss., Harvard University.

Rahula, Walpola. 2001. *Abhidharmasamuccaya: The Compendium of Higher Teaching (Philosophy) by Asanga*. Fremont: Asian Humanities Press.

Rhys Davids, T. W., and William Stede. 1921. *The Pali Text Society's Pali-English Dictionary*. Chipstead: The Pali Text Society.

Sakuma, Hidenori S. 1990. *Die āśrayaparivṛtti-Theorie in der Yogācārabhūmi*. 2 vols. Stuttgart: Steiner.

Schmithausen, Lambert. 1984. "On the Vijñaptimātra Passage in Saṁdhinirmocanasūtra VIII.7." *Acta Indologica* 6: 433–55.

———. 1987. *Ālayavijñāna: On the Origin and the Early Development of a Central Concept of Yogācāra Philosophy*. Tokyo: International Institute for Buddhist Studies.

———. 2005. *On the Problem of the External World in the* "Ch'eng wei shih lun." Studia Philologica Buddhica. Tokyo: The International Institute for Buddhist Studies.

———. 2014. *The Genesis of Yogācāra-Vijñānavāda: Responses and Reflections*. Kasuga Lectures Series 1. Tokyo: The International Institute for Buddhist Studies.

Skilling, Peter. 1994. "Kanjur Titles and Colophons." In *Tibetan Studies: Proceedings of the 6th Seminar of the International Association for Tibetan Studies*, Fagernes 1992, edited by Per Kvaerne, 2:768–80. Oslo: The Institute for Comparative Research in Human Culture.

———. 2013. "Nets of Intertextuality: Embedded Scriptural Citations in the Yogācārabhūmi." In *The Foundation for Yoga Practitioners: The Buddhist "Yogācārabhūmi" Treatise and Its Adaptation in India, East Asia, and Tibet*, edited by Ulrich Timme Kragh, 772–90. Cambridge, MA: Harvard University Press.

Steinkellner, Ernst. 1989. "Who is *Byaṅ chub rdzu 'phrul*? Tibetan and non-Tibetan Commentaries on the *Saṃdhinirmocanasūtra* – A Survey of the Literature." *Berliner Indologische Studien* 4/5: 229–52.

Takahashi, Kōichi. 2006. "A Premise of the trilakṣaṇa theory in the *Sandhinirmocanasūtra*." In *Journal of Indian and Buddhist Studies* (*=Indobukkyogaku Kenkyu*) 54, no. 3: 85–92.

Takasaki, Jikido. 1966. *A Study on the Ratnagotravibhāga (Uttaratantra): Being a Treatise on the Tathāgatagarbha Theory of Mahāyāna Buddhism*. Serie Orientale Roma 32. Roma: Istituto italiano per il Medio ed Estremo Oriente.

Thurman, Robert A.F. 1984. *Tsong Khapa's Speech of Gold in the Essence of True Eloquence: Reason and Enlightenment in the Central Philosophy of Tibet*. Princeton, NJ: Princeton University Press.

Tillemans, Tom J. F. 1997. "On a recent translation of the *Saṃdhinirmocanasūtra*." In *Journal of the International Association of Buddhist Studies* 20, no. 1: 153–64.

Tubb, Gary A., and Emery R. Boose. 2007. *Scholastic Sanskrit: A Manual for Students*. New York: American Institute of Buddhist Studies.

Tucci, Giuseppe. 1971. *Minor Buddhist Texts Part III: Third Bhāvanākrama*. Serie Orientale Roma 43. Roma: Istituto italiano per il Medio ed Estremo Oriente.

Vinay, Jean-Paul, and Jean Darbelnet. 1958. *Comparative Stylistics of French and English: A Methodology for Translation*. Amsterdam: John Benjamins.

Waldron, William S. 2003. *The Buddhist Unconscious: The ālaya-vijñāna in the context of Indian Buddhist Thought*. London: RoutledgeCurzon.

———. 2023. *Making Sense of Mind Only: Why Yogācāra Buddhism Matters*. Boston: Wisdom Publications.

Ware, James. 1937. "Review of *Saṃdhinirmocanasūtra*, l'explication des mystères, by Étienne Lamotte." *Journal of the American Oriental Society* 57, no. 1: 122–24.

Wayman, Alex. 1974. "The Mirror as a Pan-Buddhist Metaphor-Simile." *History of Religions* 13, no. 4: 251–69.

Wedemeyer, Christian K. 2003. "Review of Jñānagarbha's Commentary on Just the Maitreya Chapter from the Saṃdhinirmocanasūtra: Study, Translation and Tibetan Text, by John Powers." *Journal of the American Oriental Society* 123, no. 3: 681–84.

Xing, Guang. 2005. *The Concept of the Buddha: Its Evolution from Early Buddhism to the* Trikāya *Theory*. RoutledgeCurzon Critical Studies in Buddhism. London: RoutledgeCurzon.

Yokoyama, Kōitsu, and Hirosawa Takayuki, eds. 1996. *Index to the Yogācārabhūmi, Chinese-Sanskrit-Tibetan*. Tokyo: Sankibō Busshorin. http://www.buddhism-dict.net/cgi-bin/xpr-ddb.pl? q=%E8%AB%AB%E8%AA%A8

Yoshimizu, Chizuko. 1996. "On the Four Kinds of yukti in the Tenth Chapter of the *Saṃdhinirmocanasūtra*." *Journal of Naritasan Institute for Buddhist Studies* 19: 123–68.

———. 2010. "The Logic of the *Sandhinirmocanasūtra*: Establishing Right Reasoning Based on Similarity (*sārūpya*) and Dissimilarity (*vairūpya*)." In *Logic in Earliest Classical India*, edited by Brendan S. Gillon, 139–66. Delhi: Motilal Banarsidass.

———. 2022. "Revisiting the Tenth Chapter of the *Saṃdhinirmocanasūtra*: A Scripture on Rational Reflection." In *Evolution of Scriptures, Formation of Canons: The Buddhist Case* edited by Orna Almogi, 63–94. Indian and Tibetan Studies Series 13. Hamburg: Department of Indian and Tibetan Studies, Universität Hamburg.

Index

Abhidharma, 5, 13, 194, 195–96
abodes, 3, 36, 37, 107–8, 109
absorption in cessation, 164
accumulations of merit and gnosis, 84, 86, 87, 88, 89, 136
actual defining characteristic (*parinispannalakṣaṇa*), 7, 12
  basis of, 76
  defining, 73, 74
  emptiness and, 116
  essencelessness regarding ultimate and, 81
  and imaginary (*parikalpita*), opposition between, 41n53, 73n124
  purification and, 61n94
afflicted domain, 5–6, 7–8
afflictions, 11, 82, 152–53
  defining characteristic, 55, 56
  manifest characteristics, 114
  object conducive to, 108, 109
  of others, repelling, 136
  phenomena characterized by, 76, 77
  possessors of qualities from, 162, 163
  trilakṣaṇa and, 12
aggregates, 49, 59, 61, 62, 79, 85, 108, 202
agitation, 106, 107, 117, 145
ālayavijñāna. *See* subliminal cognition
analytical knowledge
  of designations, 11, 107, 114
  of gnosis that liberates within true reality, 161
  of objects of designation, 107–14
  of truth body, 119, 131, 167
anger, 56, 110
animitta/animittā (absence of manifest characteristics), 193, 194, 195
applications of mindfulness, 60, 61, 62, 79, 92, 110, 161
appropriating cognition (*ādānavijñāna*), 6–7, 12, 66–68, 69, 122
argumentative disputation, 49, 50
Asaṅga, 212
aspiration, 97, 149
  perfection of, 137–38, 140, 146
  stage of engagement through, 51
  three types, 136
attachment
  on bodhisattva levels, 118, 130, 133
  on Buddha Stage, 133, 134
  to *nimitta*, 197, 199–200, 202–3, 205
  perfections and, 140, 141n290, 144
  to self, 49
attention, directing (*manasikāra*), 22
  in analytical knowledge, 107
  on bodhisattva levels, 130–31, 132, 134
  distraction and, 118
  in mental stillness, 10–11, 98–99
  in mental stillness and insight, 100–101, 104–6, 112–13
  on path of practice, 122
  in perfections, 138
  in setting the mind, 106
  spontaneous, 107
  toward emptiness, 115
  toward true reality, 11, 101, 120
Avalokiteshvara, 3, 4, 39, 129–49
aversion, 84, 130
awakening, 101, 106, 108. *See also* perfect awakening
awakening factors, 13, 130, 132, 154, 161–62

awakening mind (*bodhicitta*), 24, 96, 126, 137
awareness, 148, 198–99

basis (*āśraya*), 4–6
basis of existence (*āśrayaparivṛtti*), 11, 13, 103–4, 132n275, 151
Bhāvanākrama, 57n88, 86n154, 209–10
birth
  affliction of, 84, 85, 118
  of bodhisattvas, 135–36
  four kinds, 66
  purification of, 135
bodhicitta. *See* awakening mind
bodhisattvas, 3, 11–12, 85, 94, 117, 127
  attaining acceptance of phenomena, 96
  birth of, 135–36
  concentration of, 116
  faculties of, 102
  hearers belonging to, 86–87
  perceptions of, 7, 75–77
  powers of, 12, 122–24
  skilled in defining characteristics of phenomena, 77
  skilled in the ultimate, 68–69
  twofold appropriation of, 65–66
body afflicted by corruption, 14, 15, 103n190, 118, 132, 162, 163
bondage, 53–54, 57, 117, 199–200, 202–3
buddha fields/buddha realms, 38, 122, 152, 164
Buddha Shākyamuni
  qualities of, 37–38
  teaching style of, 5, 9, 57, 61, 87
Buddha Stage, 129, 132n275, 133, 134, 135, 144, 147
Buddhabhūmisūtra, 17
buddhas, 5, 12, 37, 90, 125, 135, 149. *See also* tathāgatas

capacity of beings, 85–89
causal dependence, 158
cognitions
  conditioned, 7, 8, 9
  conceptual, 195
  mere representation and, 12, 99
  personal and intuitive, 48, 121, 196
  six kinds, 67–69
  See also appropriating cognition (*ādānavijñāna*); direct cognition (*pratyakṣa*); subliminal cognition (*ālayavijñāna*); valid cognition (*pramāṇa*)
cognitive objects, 13, 112, 161
  analysis of, 154–55, 158
  on Buddha Stage, 134
  liberation from, 86, 131
  types, 110
cognitive obstructions, 119, 133, 147
compassion, 65, 71, 80, 136
  for beings, 77, 90
  of hearers, 86
  immeasurable, 102
  perfections and, 140, 145
  purification of, 135
comprehension, three kinds, 153
conceit, 59, 60, 63, 118
concentration, correct, 92–93
conception through expedients, 43, 44
conceptual images, 10–11, 99, 101, 106n199
conceptualization, 9, 44, 118, 144
conditioned phenomena, 6, 77, 84, 85, 105
  arising of, 155
  causality and, 62
  defining characteristics, 51–57
  emptiness of, 114
  esencelessness of, 55, 56
  impermanence of, 56, 63n99, 84
  logical proofs and, 157–58
  manifest characteristics of, 90–93
  as mere representations, 11, 113n216
conditioning mental factors, 72, 86, 116, 133
conditions, 67–68
confidence, 84, 86–89, 96, 139n286
confusion, 8–9, 117, 118, 130, 133
consciousness, 193, 196, 199, 204, 205, 206
conventional expressions, 5–6, 7, 8–9, 41, 42, 43–45, 155, 198. *See also* elaboration of conventional expressions

conventional truth, 14, 103–4n190, 139, 143
corruptions, 90, 124, 147
on bodhisattva levels, 133–34
bondage of, 53, 54, 57, 117, 123, 200
destroying, 105
distraction from, 118
eliminating, 11, 103n190, 122
eliminating, time in, 147–48
See also body afflicted by corruption
craving, 117, 118

defilements, 86, 123
affliction of, 84, 85, 109
on bodhisattva levels, 132, 146, 147–48
on Buddha Stage, 134
distraction and, 118
perfections and, 137–38, 139, 142, 146
release from, 90, 161
secondary, 107
defining characteristics (*lakṣaṇa*), 79, 111, 204, 205
of conditioned phenomena and ultimate, distinctions between, 51–57
topics of, 154
universal, 55
See also under individual topics
definitive meaning, 10, 27, 93–94, 96
delusion, 56, 110, 133–34, 149
dependent arising, 8, 59, 61, 62, 72, 79
designations, 85, 112–13, 125. *See also* objects of designation
desire, 49, 56, 84, 85, 110, 118, 133. *See also* objects of desire
devotion, 87, 95, 129, 136
Dharma, ten practices related to, 87–88, 95, 129, 137
Dharma discourses, 87, 97–98, 103. *See also* twelve collections
Dharma eye, 96, 127
Dharmodgata, 3, 4, 39, 47–50, 196–97
diligence, 76, 136, 137, 138, 139, 140, 142–43
direct cognition (*pratyakṣa*), 13, 156, 157, 158n338, 159
discipline, 111, 145, 165, 167
perfection of, 136, 137, 138, 139, 142
pure, 38, 116
on second level, 131
superior, 129, 136
domain of infinite cognition, 102, 123
domain of infinity of space, 102, 123
domain of neither conception nor lack of conception, 102, 123
domain of nothingness, 102, 123
doubt, 37, 60, 117, 141, 142, 159
drowsiness, 106, 107

ego, 14, 162, 163
eighteen constituents, 60, 79
eightfold path, 60, 61, 62, 79, 158–59
elaboration of conventional expressions, 66, 203, 260
eloquence, 105, 134
emanation bodies (*nirmāṇakāya*), 13, 14, 152, 163–64, 165
emptiness, 87
defining characteristic of, 116
manifest characteristics eliminated by, 11–12, 114–16
purpose of teaching, 12
in second Dharma wheel, 95
equanimity, 107, 120–21, 131
essencelessness
apprehension of, 145–46
regarding arising, 8, 76n133, 80–81, 143, 200
regarding defining characteristics, 8, 76n132, 80–81, 143, 200
regarding the ultimate, 8, 9–10, 82, 143, 200
See also threefold essencelessness
essential characteristic, 11, 91, 92–93

faith, 86–87, 144–45
fear, 39, 86, 89, 142
five sciences, 143
flexibility, physical and mental, 98. 99
four immeasurable kinds of mental stillness, 102
four kinds of sustenance, 59–60, 62, 79
four noble truths, 60, 61, 92, 94–95, 110, 159

defining characteristics, 79
manifest characteristics, 121
selflessness of, 62
true reality of, 108
four seals of Dharma, 102n188

Gambhīrārthasaṁdhinirmochana, 3, 4, 39, 41–45
generosity, 136, 137, 139, 142, 145, 146
gnosis (*jñāna*), 3, 11, 121
analytical knowledge of, 161
domain of, 10
gradual attainment of, 139n286
light of, 165–66
and mind, opposition between, 48n68
nondual, 5, 6, 7, 62
See also accumulations of merit and gnosis
gnosis and vision utterly free from attachment and hindrance, 12, 119, 131
Great Vehicle, 3
and Abhidharma, continuity of, 195–96
deviating from, 116
second Dharma wheel in, 95
single principle in, 12, 148
sutras, multiformity and intertextuality of, 27
Guṇākara, 3, 4, 39, 71–77

hearers (*śrāvakas*), 3, 94, 110, 117, 127
basis of existence, shift in, 151
concentration of, 116
liberation of, 96, 108, 166
lineage, 85–86
single principle in, 12, 148
heavenly realms, 138
hungry ghosts, 145

idealism, 30
ignorance, 45, 72, 76n133, 116
images (*pratibimba*), 10–11. *See also* conceptual images
imaginary defining characteristic (*parikalpitalakṣaṇa*), 7, 12
basis of, 75–76, 90–93
defining, 71–72, 74, 76n132
emptiness and, 116
essencelessness regarding defining characteristics and, 80–81
See also under actual defining characteristic (*pariniṣpannalakṣaṇa*)
impermanence, 56, 63n99, 84, 102
inference (*anumāna*), 13, 159, 194
inquiry, 101, 106
insight (*vipaśyanā*), 31, 36, 57, 100, 101, 166
as antidote, 118–19
aspiring to, 99
causes and results, 116–17
as established or not established in Dharma, 102
instructions, 98
mental distractions, 117–18
mental engagement and investigation in, 105–6
and mental stillness, unified, 11, 97, 99, 100–101
nimitta's role in, 198–99, 200
obstacles and obstructions, 12, 117
referential object, specific, 102–3
referential objects, 10, 97, 101
intentional action, 151, 162, 164, 165–66
investigation (*vicāra*), 11, 105–6, 153

Jambudvīpa, 109
Jamgön Mipham Gyatso, 18
Jñānagarbha, 212
joy, 36, 39, 102, 105, 106, 123, 126, 140

karma, 145, 160, 166
affliction of, 7, 84, 85, 109, 118
diversity of, 157
maturation of, 133, 142, 144
karmic obscuration of rejecting truth, 89
Kīrtimat world, 47
Kīṭāgiri sutta, 139n286

latent dispositions, 7, 14, 147, 162, 163
laziness, 117, 118, 145
lethargy, 117, 118
letters, 111, 113
liberation, 52, 53–54, 84–85n150, 85, 110, 200
liberation body, 151, 166

logic, pre-Dignāgean, 22
logical proofs, 156–61

Madhyāntavvibhāgabhāṣya, 209
Mahāvyutpatti, 20
Maitreya, 3, 4, 10, 12, 21–22, 39, 97–127
manifest characteristics (*nimitta*), 105
conditioned, 11–12, 52, 53
discerning one's own, analogies, 113
domain of, 5
eliminating, 112–13, 122
equanimity toward, 120–21
insight arising from, 100, 101
manifest and coarse, 106
meditative objects in agreement with, 102
mental distractions produced by, 118
of space, free from, 63
subtle, 106
on ten levels, 130–31, 133–34
in ultimate and speculation domains, 48–49
See also *nimitta* (*mtshan ma*)
Mañjushrī, 3, 4, 12–13, 39, 151–67
Māra, 89
mātṛkās, 13, 154, 162
Māyājāla, 18n11
meditation
nimitta in, 197
terms related to, translating, 21–22
meditative absorption(s)
attachment to, 133
four of form realm, 102, 123
perfection of, 136, 137, 138, 139, 143
mental appropriation, 11, 66, 68, 111, 203, 206
mental distractions, 118, 126, 145
mental elaborations, 6, 13, 15, 45, 126, 140, 143, 151, 162, 163
mental engagement (*vitarka*), 11, 105–6
mental imprints, 7, 66, 75, 203, 206
mental inspection, 113, 136
mental stillness (*śamatha*), 36, 57, 100, 101–2, 106
as antidote, 118–19
aspiring to, 98
causes and results, 116–17
as established or not established in Dharma, 102
and insight, unified, 11, 97, 99, 100–101
mental distractions, 117–18
mental engagement and investigation in, 105–6
nimitta's role in, 198–99, 200
obstacles and obstructions, 12, 117
referential object, specific, 102–3
referential objects, 10, 97, 101
mere representation, 10–11, 12, 30, 99, 100, 101, 114, 205
merit, 95–96, 137, 140, 144, 165. *See also* accumulations of merit and gnosis
metaphors
butter, clarified, 94
conch, 56
cow hoofprints, 87, 96
crystal, 74–75
dirt in fingernail, 96
excrements, 141
gem, well-polished, 166
ginger, dried, 93
gold, 56, 122
magical illusions, 8, 10, 43, 44, 81, 200
mirrors, 67, 68, 100
nightmares, 9
painting's canvas, 94
sky flower, 8, 81, 200
sleep, 164
sound, 56
space, 8, 81, 94
taste, 49
timira visual disorder, 74
virtual reality, 9, 10
water and waves, 67, 68
mind, 123–24
appropriating, 9, 66
investigating itself, 99–100
purification of, 135
as referential object, 98, 99
sixteen ways of arising, 122–23
superior, training in, 136
unimpeded, 101, 106n198
See also awakening mind (*bodhicitta*)

mind containing all seeds (*sarvabījaṁ cittam*), 6–7, 66. *See also* appropriating cognition (*ādānavijñāna*)
mindfulness, 36, 153. *See also* applications of mindfulness

names, collections of, 111
nimitta (*mtshan ma*), 203
  in Abhidharma, 195–96
  in early Buddhist texts, 194
  etymology and semantic range, 193–95
  and *lakṣana* (*mtshan nyid*), in Tibetan, 204
  as manifest characteristics, 204–5, 206, 207
  as phenomenal appearance, 204
  in *Saṁdhinirmocana*, 196–99, 202, 203
  as "sign," translating, 201–3, 206
  soteriology and, 199–200
nirvana, 8, 102, 133, 136
  with aggregates remaining, 124–25
  all phenomena in, 80, 82
  attaining, 52, 53, 90
  of hearers', 85
  with no aggregates remaining, 49, 124, 125
  and samsara, equanimity toward, 130
noble beings, 42, 45, 48, 121

objects of concentration, 10–12, 99–100, 101, 106n199, 112, 115, 118
objects of conceptualization, 90–93
objects of designation, 11, 197, 199
  comprehension and communication, five items, 110–11
  manifest characteristics of, discarding, 112–13
  ten points, 107–10
  three wisdoms and, 111–12
objects of desire, 118, 126, 140, 152
objects of enjoyment, 109, 114–15, 117
objects of experience, 37
obscuration of cognitive objects, 86. *See also* cognitive obstructions
obscuration of defilements, 86, 119
one-pointedness of mind, 11, 101, 199
ordinary beings, 44, 48, 52, 53, 162, 196–97
other-dependent defining characteristic (*paratantralakṣaṇa*), 7, 12, 61n94
  appropriating mind and, 9
  basis of, 76
  defining, 72, 74, 75, 76n133
  emptiness and, 116
  essencelessness regarding arising and, 81
  nimitta and, 198
outflows, 56, 96, 127

Paramārthasamudgata, 3, 4, 8, 9–10, 39, 76nn132–33, 79–80, 90–94
parinirvana, 14, 165
path (*mārga*), 4–5, 6–7, 11
path of practice, 122
path of seeing, 121
patience, 38, 129, 136, 137, 138, 139, 140, 142
perception, 11, 157, 159–61, 195, 201
perfect awakening, 3, 42, 108, 134, 145, 165
  aspiration for, 97
  attaining, 48, 52, 144, 145
  bondage and, 53, 54
  as defining characteristic of phenomena, 73
  of emanation body, 152
  state of peace and, 86
  through mental stillness and insight, 120–22
perfections, 12
  and afflicted phenomena, four practices involving, 140–41
  divisions of each, 139
  factors adverse to, 140
  functions, 144
  meaning of name, 139–40
  order of teaching, 138
  powers and benefits, 145
  purification, 135, 141
  purifications, specific to each, 141–43
  results, 140
  training in, 136–37
  two classifications, 137–38
  vastness, 144

permanence, 63, 75, 82
phenomena
  as beyond activity, 162, 163
  conditioned and unconditioned, relationship of, 5, 6, 41–45
  defining characteristics, 47, 76, 77
  ending point, 97, 121
  equality of, 108
  essencelessness of, 80–82
  illusory, 14
  nature of, 6, 44, 61–63, 82
  See also conditioned phenomena
Prajñāpāramitā sutras, 5, 27, 194, 196
Pramāṇa tradition, 13, 159, 194
prātimokṣa (bodhisattva), 13, 154
predispositions. *See* latent dispositions
provisional meaning, 9, 10, 86, 93–94
pure domain of the ultimate, 5, 7
pure realms, 6, 14
purification, 14–15, 105, 114
  of mental stillness and insight, 117
  objects conducive to, 108, 109–10
  phenomena characterized by, 76, 77
  possessors of qualities from, 162, 163
  referential objects and, 61–62, 81, 91, 92, 93
  single path, 9, 85, 90
  stage of, 11
  sutra topics on, 153
  three defining characteristics and, 12
purity, defining characteristic of, 55, 56

realm of desire, 123, 166
realm of form, 66, 123, 166
realm of formlessness, 66, 166
reason, four principles of, 13, 155–56
rebirth, 45, 65–66, 84, 140, 166
referential objects
  mental distraction from, 118
  of mental stillness and insight, 97, 98, 101, 102
  purification and, 61–62, 81, 91, 92, 93
  specific and universal teachings as, 102–5, 106, 112
  superior, 165
  on ten stages, 121–22
  universal teachings as, 143
  to unrealized beings, 59–61
representation-only (*vijñaptimātra*), 18, 201–2
result (*phala*), 5, 110
  defining characteristic of, 161
  overview, 12–15
roots of virtue, 84, 86, 135
Ṛṣhivadana, 94

Saṁdhinirmocana Sūtra (*Elucidating the Intent*)
  chapter 10 formula, 13–15, 162
  commentaries, 18, 212
  content, narrative and doctrinal, 28–29
  epistemology and, 201
  intertextuality, 17–18
  nidāna, 3, 25, 35–39
  nīthārthanirdeśa in, 27
  overview, 5–15
  philosophy of, 205, 207
  semantic evolution of, 195–96
  sources, 15–16, 19–20, 209–12
  structure, 3–5, 27–28
  as systemized teaching, 29–30
  title, 19
  translation, current, 20–27, 30–31
  translations, 16–17
sameness, 37n45, 38
samsara, 22, 45, 65, 84, 119, 130, 133
**Samyagvāk-pramāṇoddhṛta-sūtra*, 20, 212
Sautrāntika school, 201
scriptures, authoritative, 13, 158, 159
self, 49, 114
selflessness, 6, 55, 56, 82
selflessness of persons, 114, 121
selflessness of phenomena, 56
  as actual defining characteristic, 7, 91, 92, 93, 200
  as essencelessness regarding ultimate, 81
  manifest characteristic, 114, 121
  as referential object of meditation, 102
  in second Dharma wheel, 9–10
  as unconditioned, 62–63
sense domains, 59, 61, 62, 79, 108, 109

sense facilities, 66
sense objects, 194, 197
sentient beings, 65n101, 152
setting the mind, 106
single nature, 4, 60–63
Single Vehicle, 3, 4, 9, 12, 30, 85, 90, 148–49
skillful means, 12, 13, 124, 144, 166
  on bodhisattva levels, 130, 134
  of emanation body, 152
  perfection of, 137
  wisdom and, 164
solitary realizers, 85, 94, 108, 148, 151, 166
soteriology, 10, 199–200
sovereign power (*adhiṣṭhāna*), 13, 36, 152, 165, 166
space, 8, 38, 63, 81, 94
speculation, domain of, 48–49, 87, 196–97
stage of engagement through aspiration, 51
stages (*bhūmi*), ten, 12, 105, 121
  delusion and corruption on, 133–34
  descriptions, 129–31
  names, 129, 131–32
  obstacles and antidotes on, 118–19
  perfection on, three types, 146
  purifications, 129, 135
  See also Buddha Stage
Subhūti, 59–63
subliminal cognition (*ālayavijñāna*), 6–7, 11, 66, 68, 83n147, 103n190. *See also* appropriating cognition (*ādānavijñāna*)
suffering, 14, 56, 141, 145, 158
  arising of, 72
  hearers' fear of, 86
  as meditation object, 102
  for others' sake, 136
  release from, 90
superior knowledge, 134
sutras, 13, 152–53, 162. *See also* Dharma discourses
Suvishuddhamati, 3, 4, 39, 51–57

Tathāgataguṇajñānācintyaviṣayāvatāra-nirdeśa-sūtra, 17
tathāgatas, 13, 63, 86, 105, 110, 117
  characterized by nonduality, 14, 165
  concentration of, 116
  defining characteristics of, 158–59
  domains of, 164–65
  lineage of, 85, 121
  minds of, 163–64
  superiority of, 151
tathatā (true reality), 5, 29, 62n96, 73–74nn124–125, 103n190
Teaching of Definitive Meaning Establishing the Deeds of the Tathāgatas, 167
Teaching of Definitive Meaning on the Stages and Perfections, 149
Teaching of Definitive Meaning on the Ultimate, 96
Teaching of Definitive Meaning on Yoga, 126
Theravāda tradition, 201
thirty-seven branches of awakening, 60, 61, 62, 79, 110
three defining characteristics (*trilakṣaṇa*), 4, 7–9, 71–74
  accepting, 85
  meditation and, 12
  negating, 88
  nimitta and, 197–99, 205
  perfection of wisdom and, 143
  relationship between each, 74–75
  three Dharma wheels and, 10
  wrongly conceiving, 83–84
three Dharma wheels, 3, 9–10, 94–95, 165
three gates of liberation, 3, 36, 143
three trainings, 136
threefold essencelessness, 90, 143
  metaphors for, 81
  nimitta and, 200
  provisional meaning in, 86
  purpose of teaching, 82–85
  three defining characteristics and, 8, 80–81, 90–93
  in three Dharma wheels, 9–10
  wrongly conceiving, 88
translation process, 193
  direct, 23–24

oblique, 24–26
stages of, 20–23, 26–27
Trisong Detsen, 20, 212
true reality, seven aspects, 108, 120, 121, 154
truth, domain of (*dharmadhātu*), 3, 14
truth body (*dharmakāya*), 11, 103n190, 164
analytical knowledge of, 119, 131, 167
attaining, 14, 105
defining characteristic, 12–13, 151
and emanation body, relationship of, 152, 166
utter purity of, 165
Tsongkhapa, 18
twelve collections, 97–98, 104
two truths, 5–6, 14, 30, 44n63

ultimate, 4, 5
defining characteristic, 52, 60–63
inexpressible and nondual, 4, 41
manifest characteristic, 114
transcending speculation, 196–97
ultimate beyond distinction or indistinction, 4
ultimate beyond speculation, 4, 47–50
ultimate truth, 14, 139, 143
universes, impure and pure, 166–67
unskillful means, 140, 141
Uttarakuru, 49

valid cognition (*pramāṇa*), 13, 159
Vārāṇasī, 94
Vidhivatparipṛcchaka, 3, 4, 39, 41–42
views
considering one's own as supreme, 88, 89
correct, 109
from latent dispositions, 14, 163
pure, 116
See also wrong view
Vinaya, 13, 86, 89, 153, 154, 158–59, 162
Viniścayasaṁgrahaṇī, 16, 17–18, 19, 209, 210n377
virtue, 84, 137, 141
virtuous qualities, 88, 117, 146
Vishālakīrti, 47
Vishālamati, 3, 4, 39, 65–69
Visuddhimagga, 201

wisdom, 85, 108, 134
from hearing, contemplating, meditation, 111–12, 113, 137
perfection of, 136, 137, 138, 139, 143, 146
skillful means and, 164
straying from, 88
superior, training in, 136
transcendent, 44
Wonch'uk, 35n36, 132n276, 210, 212
words, literal meaning and underlying intent, 112
wrong view, 108, 109, 145
wrongdoing, 84, 109, 114–15, 117, 144

Xuanzang, 15, 16, 17, 72n121, 72n123, 100n184, 210

Yogācārabhūmi-Śāstra, 18n11, 194. See also *Viniścayasaṁgrahaṇī*
Yogāchāra tradition, 27, 193, 194, 195, 202